The Western Junior League Cookbook

THE PARTICIPATING JUNIOR LEAGUES INCLUDE:

The Junior League of Albuquerque, New Mexico
The Junior League of Bakersfield, California
The Junior League of Billings, Montana
The Junior League of Boise, Idaho
The Junior League of Butte, Montana
The Junior League of Calgary, Alberta
The Junior League of Denver, Colorado
The Junior League of Edmonton, Alberta
The Junior League of Eugene, Oregon
The Junior League of Great Falls, Montana
The Junior League of Long Beach, California
The Junior League of Los Angeles, California
The Junior League of Mexico City, Mexico
The Junior League of Newport Harbor, California
The Junior League of Oakland-East Bay, California
The Junior League of Ogden, Utah
The Junior League of Palo Alto, California
The Junior League of Pasadena, California
The Junior League of Phoenix, Arizona
The Junior League of Portland, Oregon
The Junior League of Pueblo, Colorado
The Junior League of Riverside, California
The Junior League of Sacramento, California
The Junior League of Salt Lake City, Utah
The Junior League of San Diego, California
The Junior League of San Francisco, California
The Junior League of San Jose, California
The Junior League of Santa Barbara, California
The Junior League of Seattle, Washington
The Junior League of Spokane, Washington
The Junior League of Tacoma, Washington
The Junior League of Tucson, Arizona
The Junior League of Vancouver, British Columbia

• • • • • • • • • • • • • • • • • • • •

Illustrations by Lauren Jarrett

• • • • • • • • • • • • • • • • • • •

The Western Junior League Cookbook

Edited by Ann Seranne

David McKay Company, Inc.
New York

THE WESTERN JUNIOR LEAGUE COOKBOOK

Library of Congress Cataloging in Publication Data

Main entry under title:
The Western Junior League cookbook.

Includes index.
1. Cookery, American—Western style.
I. Seranne, Ann, 1914–
TX715.W53168   1984   641.5978   84-21756
ISBN: 0-517-464268

Manufactured in the United States of America

2   3   4   5   6   7   8   9

Preface

The purpose of the Junior League is exclusively educational and charitable and is to promote voluntarism; to develop the potential of its members for voluntary participation in community affairs; and to demonstrate the effectiveness of trained volunteers.

Proceeds from the sale of Junior League cookbooks go into the Community Trust Funds, which finance the Leagues' community programs.

To find out how to obtain a particular Junior League's own book of recipes, turn to pages 515–519.

Contents

Metric Equivalent Chart

LENGTH

1 inch (in)	=	2.5 centimeters (cm)
1 foot (ft)	=	30 centimeters (cm)
1 millimeter (mm)	=	.04 inches (in)
1 centimeter (cm)	=	.4 inches (in)
1 meter (m)	=	3.3 feet (ft)

MASS WEIGHT

1 ounce (oz)	=	28 grams (g)
1 pound (lb)	=	450 grams (g)
1 gram (g)	=	.035 ounces (oz)
1 kilogram (kg) or 1000 g	=	2.2 pounds (lbs)

LIQUID VOLUME

1 fluid ounce (fl. oz)	=	30 milliliters (ml)
1 fluid cup (c)	=	240 milliliters (ml)
1 pint (pt)	=	470 milliliters (ml)
1 quart (qt)	=	950 milliliters (ml)
1 gallon (gal)	=	3.8 liters (l)
1 milliliter (ml)	=	.03 fluid ounces (fl. oz)
1 liter (l) or 1000 ml	=	2.1 fluid pints or 1.06 fluid quarts
1 liter (l)	=	.26 gallons (gal)

Dips, Spreads, and Finger Food

Pickadillo Almond Dip

½ pound ground beef
½ pound ground pork
1 teaspoon salt
¼ teaspoon pepper
4 medium tomatoes, peeled and chopped
2½ cloves garlic, minced
3 green onions, minced
1 6-ounce can tomato paste
2 jalapeño peppers, rinsed, seeded, and chopped
Dash oregano
¾ cup chopped pimento
¾ cup seedless raisins
¾ cup whole blanched almonds

In a saucepan crumble beef and pork and cook until brown. Add salt, pepper, and enough water to cover meat. Bring to a boil, reduce heat, and simmer for 30 minutes. Drain off fat and excess liquid and add remaining ingredients. Bring to a boil and simmer for 45 minutes, or until mixture is very thick.

Serve hot with tortilla chips.

YIELD: 6 CUPS

Colorado Cache
THE JUNIOR LEAGUE OF DENVER, COLORADO

· · · · · · · · · · · · · · · · · · · ·

Avocado and Bacon Salad or Dip

1 large ripe avocado, mashed
½ pound bacon, crisply cooked and crumbled
1–2 green onions, chopped
3 tablespoons sour cream
1 teaspoon lemon juice
Salt and pepper to taste
½ tomato, seeded and chopped

Mix above ingredients and serve in lettuce cups for salad or with corn chips as a dip.

Refrigerate with avocado pit to prevent discoloration.

YIELD: ABOUT 1 PINT

THE JUNIOR LEAGUE OF BILLINGS, MONTANA

. . . .

Mexican Bean Dip

2 1-pound cans refried beans
1 cup butter or margarine
1 pound sharp Tillamook cheese, shredded
1 bunch green onions, including green tops, chopped
Dash each garlic salt, Tabasco, Worcestershire sauce

Put all ingredients in a saucepan. Cook, stirring, over low heat until cheese is melted and ingredients are blended. The mixture will be rather smooth when it is ready. It can be prepared ahead of time and reheated. Keep hot while serving.

Especially good served with tortilla chips, and leftovers can be used on tostadas.

YIELD: 10 SERVINGS

Epicure
THE JUNIOR LEAGUE OF NEWPORT HARBOR, CALIFORNIA

. . . .

Mrs. Louis' Crabmeat Dip

2 pounds crabmeat
2 8-ounce packages cream cheese
8 tablespoons mayonnaise
3 tablespoons grated onion
3–4 small tomatoes, peeled and chopped
2 tablespoons Worcestershire sauce
Salt to taste
2 teaspoons lemon juice

Pick over crabmeat thoroughly. Soften cream cheese with mayonnaise. Add grated onion, chopped tomatoes, and seasonings. Whip with electric mixer for about 1 minute. Fold in crabmeat.

Serve as hot or cold dip with appetizer crackers.

YIELD: 16 SERVINGS

THE JUNIOR LEAGUE OF TUCSON, ARIZONA

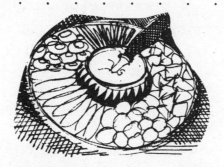

Vegetables with Curry Dip

1 head cauliflower, cleaned
2 medium green peppers
2 bunches radishes
½ pound fresh mushrooms, washed

Separate cauliflower into flowerettes; clean and cut green peppers into thin strips. Clean radishes and slice mushrooms. Arrange on a serving platter with bowl of dip in the center.

CURRY DIP:
2 cups mayonnaise or mayonnaise-type salad dressing
¼ cup chili sauce
2 tablespoons white vinegar
1½ teaspoons curry powder
½ teaspoon salt
1 teaspoon paprika
¼ teaspoon ground pepper

Combine all ingredients, blend well, and place in a medium-size bowl. Cover and refrigerate for 3 hours.

YIELD: 2 CUPS DIP

THE JUNIOR LEAGUE OF VANCOUVER, BRITISH COLUMBIA

Swiss Fondue

1 pound Swiss cheese, cut into ¼-inch cubes
1½ cups dry white wine
2 tablespoons flour
3 tablespoons cognac
French bread cut into ¼-inch cubes

Stir cheese and wine over low flame on stove until soupy-smooth; combine flour and cognac and stir into the melted cheese. Still stirring, set over chafing dish flame and encourage guests to continue the stirring by spearing a bread cube on a fondue fork and dipping it into the wine-cheese mixture.

YIELD: 8 SERVINGS

THE JUNIOR LEAGUE OF LONG BEACH, CALIFORNIA

Mexican Fondue

6 slices bacon
8–10 ounces cheddar cheese, shredded
1 onion, finely chopped
1 4-ounce can chopped green chilies

Fry bacon, drain well, and crumble.

Place remaining ingredients in a fondue pot. Heat until cheese is melted, stirring frequently. Add bacon. Keep warm over low heat.

Serve with tortilla chips.

YIELD: 6 SERVINGS

THE JUNIOR LEAGUE OF SACRAMENTO, CALIFORNIA

• • • • • • • • • • • • • • • • • •

Gazpacho Dip

1 pound tomatoes, peeled, seeded, and finely chopped
¼ pound mushrooms, finely chopped
1 bunch green onions, green part only, finely chopped
1 4-ounce can chopped green chilies
1 4-ounce can chopped ripe olives
1 8-ounce can tomato sauce
½ teaspoon garlic salt
3 tablespoons oil
2 tablespoons vinegar

Mix all ingredients and chill several hours or overnight. Drain off excess liquid before serving with tortilla chips.

YIELD: 6–8 SERVINGS

THE JUNIOR LEAGUE OF LOS ANGELES, CALIFORNIA

• • • • • • • • • • • • • • • • • •

Fiesta Guacamole

2 ripe avocados, peeled and quartered
4 tablespoons sour cream
2 tablespoons mayonnaise
2 tablespoons lemon juice
1 clove garlic, minced
1 tablespoon chopped onion
1½ teaspoons salt
¼ teaspoon pepper
2–4 tablespoons chopped green chilies

Combine all ingredients in blender and blend until smooth. Empty mixture into a bowl and press wax paper against surface to prevent discoloration. Chill until ready to serve.

Serve with corn or tortilla chips.

YIELD: 2 CUPS

Something New Under the Sun
THE JUNIOR LEAGUE OF PHOENIX, ARIZONA

. . . .

Liptauer Cheese Spread

8 ounces cream cheese, softened
1 cup softened butter
1 tablespoon capers
1 tablespoon chopped chives
1 tablespoon chopped green onion
1 clove garlic, minced
1 teaspoon caraway seeds
1 teaspoon paprika
¼ teaspoon prepared mustard
⅛ teaspoon salt
⅛ teaspoon pepper

Recipe continues . . .

Beat cream cheese and butter until mixture is smooth. Stir in remaining ingredients. Refrigerate 2 hours or more. Bring to room temperature before serving with unsalted crackers or fresh vegetables.

YIELD: 8–10 SERVINGS

Heritage Cookbook
THE JUNIOR LEAGUE OF SALT LAKE CITY, UTAH

. . . .

Potted Crab

8 ounces cooked crabmeat, finely shredded
6 tablespoons butter or margarine
3 egg yolks, carefully separated from whites
2 tablespoons heavy cream
1 tablespoon sherry
1 tablespoon lemon juice
Salt and pepper to taste
Cayenne to taste
1 tablespoon grated Parmesan cheese

In saucepan combine the first six ingredients and cook over low heat, stirring constantly, until smooth and thick. Add salt, pepper, cayenne, and cheese. Stir well until smooth and well blended. Add more sherry and lemon juice, if the taste buds say so!

Pack tightly into a nonmetallic cocktail dish or other serving dish. Chill until serving time.

Serve with crusty French bread torn into bite-size pieces or with wheat crackers or squares of crisp toast. May be frozen.

YIELD: 8–10 SERVINGS

From an Adobe Oven . . . to a Microwave Range
THE JUNIOR LEAGUE OF PUEBLO, COLORADO

. . . .

Rumaki Pâté

½ pound chicken livers
¼ cup butter
2 tablespoons lemon juice
1 tablespoon soy sauce
2 teaspoons brown sugar
1 teaspoon chopped green onion
½ teaspoon dry mustard
Dash ground ginger
Dash garlic powder
1 5-ounce can water chestnuts, drained and finely chopped
6 slices bacon, crisply cooked and crumbled
Chopped green onion

Cook chicken livers in butter, stirring occasionally, for 10 minutes, or until pinkness is gone. Cool.

Purée chicken livers and liquid in blender until smooth. Add lemon juice, soy sauce, sugar, onion, mustard, ginger, and garlic powder, blending until smooth. Stir in water chestnuts and bacon. Chill.

Garnish with green onions. Serve with crisp crackers or Melba toast rounds.

YIELD: ABOUT 1 PINT

Epicure
THE JUNIOR LEAGUE OF NEWPORT HARBOR, CALIFORNIA

· · · · · · · · · · · · · · · · · ·

Almond-Bacon-Cheese Spread

2 slices bacon, crisply cooked and crumbled
1 cup shredded mild cheese
1 tablespoon chopped green onion
¼ teaspoon salt
½ cup mayonnaise
¼ cup toasted slivered almonds

Recipe continues . . .

Mix bacon, cheese, onion, salt, and mayonnaise. Refrigerate and sprinkle with almonds before serving.

Serve with crackers or Melba toast.

YIELD: ABOUT 1½ CUPS

THE JUNIOR LEAGUE OF BILLINGS, MONTANA

· · · · · · · · · · · · · · · ·

Sombrero Spread

½ pound ground beef
¼ cup chopped onion
¼ cup extra-hot catsup
1½ teaspoons chili powder
½ teaspoon salt
1 8-ounce can kidney beans
½ cup shredded sharp cheddar cheese
½ cup chopped onion
¼ cup chopped stuffed green olives

Brown meat and the ¼ cup chopped onion in a skillet or chafing dish. Stir in catsup, chili powder, and salt. Add beans, including liquid, and mash to mix thoroughly with other ingredients.

Heat and garnish with shredded cheese, chopped onion, and olives. Serve with corn chips.

YIELD: ABOUT 3 CUPS

A Taste of Oregon
THE JUNIOR LEAGUE OF EUGENE, OREGON

· · · · · · · · · · · · · · · ·

Salmon Ball

2 cups cooked, flaked salmon
8 ounces cream cheese, softened
1 tablespoon lemon juice
2 teaspoons grated onion
1 teaspoon prepared horseradish
¼ teaspoon salt
¼ teaspoon liquid smoke
¼ cup chopped pecans
3 tablespoons snipped parsley

Combine salmon and all other ingredients except pecans and parsley. Chill for 1 hour. Form into a ball and roll in pecans and parsley.
Serve with toast or crackers.

YIELD: 12 SERVINGS

THE JUNIOR LEAGUE OF SEATTLE, WASHINGTON

Liver Pâté Spread

½ pound chicken livers
1 teaspoon salt
½ pound softened butter
¼ teaspoon nutmeg
1 teaspoon dry mustard
⅛ teaspoon ground cloves
2 tablespoons minced onion
Dash cayenne

Recipe continues . . .

Cook livers in simmering water to cover for 15–20 minutes. Drain and put through food chopper. Combine with all other ingredients, beating thoroughly. Turn into 2-cup mold and refrigerate.

YIELD: ABOUT 2 CUPS

THE JUNIOR LEAGUE OF CALGARY, ALBERTA

· · · · · · · · · · · · · · · · · · ·

Artichoke Frittata

2 6-ounce jars marinated artichoke bottoms or hearts
1 medium onion, chopped
2 cloves garlic, minced
4 eggs
¼ cup fine, dry bread crumbs
½ teaspoon salt
¼ teaspoon pepper
¼ teaspoon oregano
⅛ teaspoon cayenne
2 cups shredded sharp cheddar cheese
2 tablespoons minced parsley

Drain marinade from the artichokes into a skillet. Chop the artichokes and set aside. Add onion and garlic to skillet and sauté until onion is limp, about 5 minutes.

In a bowl, beat the eggs with a fork. Add the crumbs, salt, pepper, oregano, and cayenne. Stir in cheese, parsley, artichokes, and onion mixture.

Turn into a buttered 9 x 13-inch baking dish. Bake in a 325° oven for about 30 minutes, or until set. Let cool in pan, then cut into bite-size squares.

Can be reheated in the dish in a 325° oven for 10–12 minutes.

YIELD: 6 DOZEN

THE JUNIOR LEAGUE OF OAKLAND-EAST BAY, CALIFORNIA

· · · · · · · · · · · · · · · · · · ·

Sutter's Gold Crescent Canapés

3 ounces cream cheese
¼ cup shredded sharp cheddar cheese
2 tablespoons chopped olives
2 tablespoons chopped green chilies
1 tablespoon chopped onion
5 drops Tabasco
1 package refrigerated crescent rolls

Mix cream cheese, cheddar cheese, olives, chilies, onion, and Tabasco together. Spread on the crescent rectangles. Roll from wide end of triangle to the point. Cut into 1-inch slices and arrange on a greased cookie sheet.
Bake at 400° for 10–12 minutes.
May be frozen before baking.

YIELD: 24–32 CANAPÉS

THE JUNIOR LEAGUE OF SACRAMENTO, CALIFORNIA

·　·　·　·　·　·　·　·　·　·　·　·　·　·　·　·　·　·

Mini Swiss Tarts

¼ cup grated onion
2 tablespoons butter
½ pound Swiss cheese, shredded
3 eggs, beaten
1½ cups heavy cream
¼ teaspoon dry mustard
1 teaspoon salt
⅛ teaspoon cayenne
48 Cream Cheese Pastry Shells

Sauté onion in butter until transparent. Mix onion with cheese. In a bowl stir together eggs, cream, dry mustard, salt, and cayenne. Combine egg mixture with cheese and onion mixture.

Recipe continues . . .

Fill pastry shells two-thirds full of cheese filling. Bake at 350° for 30 minutes. Serve warm from oven or at room temperature.

YIELD: 48 TARTS

CREAM CHEESE PASTRY SHELLS:
1 cup butter
2 3-ounce packages cream cheese
2 cups unsifted flour

Cream together the butter and cream cheese; work in the flour. Chill if very soft. Roll into 48 balls and press each over bottom and sides (up to top) of small muffin-pan cups, each 1¾ inches across top.

THE JUNIOR LEAGUE OF SAN DIEGO, CALIFORNIA

Curried Crab Crescents

1 8-ounce can crabmeat, drained and rinsed slightly
1 4-ounce can water chestnuts, drained and sliced
½ cup shredded Swiss cheese
⅓ cup mayonnaise
1 green onion, sliced, or 1 tablespoon chopped onion
1 tablespoon lemon juice
1 tablespoon chopped pimento
1 teaspoon Worcestershire sauce
¼ teaspoon salt
¼–½ teaspoon curry powder
1 can refrigerated quick crescent dinner rolls

Mix together gently all ingredients except the dinner rolls.

On an ungreased pan, separate the rolls. Spoon 2 tablespoons of the crab mixture on each triangle. Roll up tightly and arrange on the pan. Bake in a preheated 375° oven for 15–18 minutes, or until golden brown. Serve hot.

YIELD: 8 ROLLS

THE JUNIOR LEAGUE OF TACOMA, WASHINGTON

Hot Clam Rolls

2 6½-ounce cans minced clams, drained
8 ounces cream cheese, softened
1-pound loaf thinly sliced white sandwich bread, trimmed
¼ pound butter, melted
Grated Parmesan cheese

Mix clams with cream cheese. Spread thinly on bread slices. Roll like tiny jelly rolls, then cut each into four pieces. Dip pieces into melted butter, roll in Parmesan cheese to coat, and place seam side down on baking sheet. Bake 15 minutes at 400°, or until browned lightly.

YIELD: 20 SERVINGS

THE JUNIOR LEAGUE OF SAN JOSE, CALIFORNIA

Marinated Mushrooms and Artichoke Hearts

2 10-ounce packages artichoke hearts
2 pounds small mushrooms, halved
1½ cups water
1 cup cider vinegar
½ cup salad oil
1 clove garlic, halved
1½ teaspoons salt
½ teaspoon peppercorns
½ teaspoon dried thyme
½ teaspoon oregano

Cook artichoke hearts according to directions on package. Combine all the ingredients and marinate for 8 hours in a crockery or glass bowl.

Discard garlic and serve the mushrooms and artichoke hearts as an hors d'oeuvre with wooden picks. Do not put in a metal bowl.

YIELD: 20 SERVINGS

THE JUNIOR LEAGUE OF TUCSON, ARIZONA

· ·

Mushroom Roll-Ups

½ pound mushrooms, cleaned and chopped
½ cup butter
3 tablespoons flour
¾ teaspoon salt
1 cup cream
1 loaf decrusted bread

Sauté mushrooms in butter for 5 minutes. Add flour, salt, and cream. Cook, stirring, until mixture comes to a boil and thickens. Roll slices of bread under wax paper on a board. Spread mixture on each slice. Roll jelly-roll fashion. Freeze.

When ready to use, defrost, cut in thirds, and bake in 400° oven for about 12 minutes, or until light brown.

YIELD: 12 SERVINGS

THE JUNIOR LEAGUE OF SPOKANE, WASHINGTON

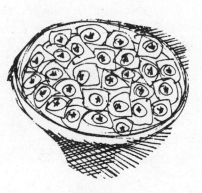

Nachos

1 8-ounce bag tortilla or corn chips
1 8-ounce can jalapeño bean dip
1 4-ounce can chopped green chilies
½ pound cheddar cheese, diced

Place tortilla or corn chips on cookie sheet. Top each chip with a dab of bean dip, followed by a dab of green chili. Finish each with a small square of cheese. Bake nachos in 350° oven for 15–20 minutes, or until cheese is melted. Serve hot.

YIELD: 8 SERVINGS

Gourmet Olé
THE JUNIOR LEAGUE OF ALBUQUERQUE, NEW MEXICO

Shrimp Dijon

2 pounds medium shrimp, shelled and deveined
2 tablespoons pickling spice
½ cup wine vinegar
¼ cup salad oil
1½ teaspoons salt
2 tablespoons minced chives
2 tablespoons chopped dill pickle
2 tablespoons prepared mustard with horseradish

Simmer shrimp in water to cover with the pickling spice for 2–3 minutes. Drain. Mix remaining ingredients and pour over warm shrimp. Cover and chill overnight or for several hours. Drain before serving.

Serve on lettuce as a first course or in a bowl with picks as an appetizer.

YIELD: 10–12 SERVINGS

Gourmet Olé
THE JUNIOR LEAGUE OF ALBUQUERQUE, NEW MEXICO

· · · · · · · · · · · · · · · · · · · ·

Seafood Canapés

1 cup cooked, chopped shrimp or crabmeat
1 cup shredded Swiss cheese
2 tablespoons thinly sliced green onion
Mayonnaise to bind
½ teaspoon garlic powder
½ teaspoon curry powder (optional)
½ cup thinly sliced water chestnuts
Chopped parsley for topping
1 package refrigerator butterflake dinner rolls

Combine the seafood, cheese, green onion, mayonnaise, and seasonings. Separate the rolls into thin rounds and place on a cookie sheet. Top

with the shrimp mixture and water chestnuts. Sprinkle with p
at 375° for 10 minutes.

May be made ahead and refrigerated, covered.

YIELD: 3 DOZEN CANAPÉS

No Regrets
THE JUNIOR LEAGUE OF PORTLAND, OREGON

. . . .

Stuffed Snow Peas

½ pound fresh snow peas
1 3¾-ounce can smoked salmon
8 ounces cream cheese, softened

Boil snow peas in a small amount of salted water until barely tender, about
1–2 minutes. Drain and chill.

Mash salmon and mix into cream cheese. Carefully slit open one side
of pea pods and stuff each with a teaspoon of cheese mixture. Refrigerate
until ready to serve.

A very attractive summer hors d'oeuvre.

YIELD: 48 STUFFED PODS

Private Collection:
Recipes from The Junior League of Palo Alto
THE JUNIOR LEAGUE OF PALO ALTO, CALIFORNIA

. . . .

Deviled Shrimp

2 pounds medium to large raw shrimp
1 lemon, thinly sliced
1 medium red onion, thinly sliced
1 cup well-drained pitted black olives
2 tablespoons chopped pimento
¼ cup vegetable oil
2 cloves garlic, minced
1 tablespoon dry mustard
1 tablespoon salt
½ cup lemon juice
1 tablespoon red wine vinegar
1 bay leaf, crumbled
Dash cayenne
Chopped parsley

Shell and devein shrimp. Bring 1 quart salted water to a boil, add the shrimp, and cook for a scant 3 minutes. Drain at once, rinse in cold water, drain, and set aside.

In a bowl, combine lemon slices, onion, black olives, and pimento; toss well. Combine oil, garlic, mustard, salt, lemon juice, wine vinegar, bay leaf, cayenne, and parsley, and add to the bowl with the lemon mixture. Arrange shrimp on a serving dish and pour marinade over them. Cover and chill no longer than 3 hours. Serve with wooden picks.

YIELD: 8–10 SERVINGS

San Francisco à la Carte
THE JUNIOR LEAGUE OF SAN FRANCISCO, CALIFORNIA

Teriyaki Treats

¼ cup sherry
¼ cup honey
¼ cup soy sauce
2 teaspoons lemon juice
1 pound beef steak 1 inch thick, cut in 1-inch cubes

Combine sherry, honey, soy sauce, and lemon juice. Add meat and stir to coat well. Marinate meat in the sherry sauce for at least 2 hours. Arrange meat pieces in an 8 x 12-inch pan. Bake in 475° oven for 6–8 minutes.
   Serve with wooden picks

YIELD: 6–8 SERVINGS

THE JUNIOR LEAGUE OF EDMONTON, ALBERTA

. . . .

Teriyaki Meat Balls

2 pounds ground chuck or lean ground beef
½ cup fine dry bread crumbs
½ cup milk
2 eggs
1½ teaspoons salt (or part garlic or seasoned salt)

Combine all ingredients in a bowl. Mix lightly to blend. Shape into balls about the size of large marbles and arrange in shallow baking pans. Bake in a 500° oven for 4–5 minutes, or until lightly browned. Remove and add to the prepared Teriyaki Sauce, along with pan juices. Cool, then refrigerate until time to serve.
   Reheat in chafing dish or over candle warmer and serve with wooden picks for spearing.

YIELD: 100 MEAT BALLS

Recipe continues . . .

TERIYAKI SAUCE:
2 tablespoons cornstarch
⅓ cup soy sauce
¼ cup sugar
1 clove garlic, minced
2 teaspoons minced fresh ginger or ½ teaspoon ground ginger
2¼ cups beef broth

In a pan, blend cornstarch, soy sauce, sugar, garlic, and fresh or ground ginger. Stir in beef broth. Cook, stirring until thickened.

From an Adobe Oven . . . to a Microwave Range
THE JUNIOR LEAGUE OF PUEBLO, COLORADO

· ·

Chestnut Meat Balls

2 cups bread cubes
½ cup milk
1 pound ground beef
½ teaspoon onion powder
1 teaspoon garlic salt
1 tablespoon soy sauce
½ teaspoon hot pepper sauce
½ teaspoon monosodium glutamate
1 5-ounce can Chinese water chestnuts
Oil for browning

Soak bread cubes in milk; squeeze out as much milk as possible. Add meat and seasonings. Drain chestnuts, chop, add to meat, and mix everything

thoroughly. Shape into about 4 dozen small balls. Brown in hot sho̶̶̶̶ ̶̶̶̶̶̶̶̶
or salad oil a few at a time, using ¼ cup in all.

Serve warm from a chafing dish.

YIELD: 4 DOZEN BALLS

What's Cooking
THE JUNIOR LEAGUE OF OGDEN, UTAH

·   ·   ·   ·   ·   ·   ·   ·   ·   ·   ·   ·   ·   ·   ·   ·   ·   ·   ·

Tiropete
(Greek Triangles)

1 1-pound package phyllo sheets
2 eggs
¾ pound feta cheese, crumbled
8 ounces cottage cheese
8 ounces cream cheese
Nutmeg
White pepper
½ pound butter, melted

Remove pastry sheets from freezer at least 2 hours before making the pastries.

Beat eggs until thick. Add feta cheese, cottage cheese, cream cheese, a little nutmeg and pepper, and 1 tablespoon of the melted butter. Beat until fluffy. Chill.

Using two sheets of pastry at a time, cut pastry into 2 2½-inch strips. Place strips on wax paper and brush with melted butter. Place 1 teaspoon of the cheese mixture on one end of the pastry strip and fold end over into a triangle. Continue folding from side to side to the end of the strip, keeping each little package in a triangular shape. Proceed until all pastry and filling are used. Keep phyllo sheets covered with wax paper and a damp towel over the wax paper. (If allowed to dry out they cannot be used.)

Recipe continues . . .

Transfer triangles to a baking sheet, brush with remaining butter, and bake at 350° for about 10 minutes, or until nicely browned. Serve hot.

YIELD: 48 TRIANGLES

THE JUNIOR LEAGUE OF SPOKANE, WASHINGTON

· ·

Green Chili Won Tons

½ pound Monterey Jack cheese, shredded
1 4-ounce can chopped green chilies
1 package won ton skins
Oil for browning

Mix cheese and green chilies. Place 1 teaspoon mixture on a won ton skin and fold like an envelope. Fry in 2 inches of hot oil until brown, turning so that both sides will be brown. Drain.

Serve hot with Guacamole sauce.

YIELD: 30 WON TONS

GUACAMOLE SAUCE:
2 large, ripe avocados
3 tablespoons fresh lime juice
½ teaspoon salt
½ teaspoon ground coriander
2 teaspoons minced green onion
3 tablespoons mayonnaise

Mash pulp of avocado and blend in lime juice. Add remaining ingredients and blend until smooth. Cover and refrigerate until used.

Colorado Cache
THE JUNIOR LEAGUE OF DENVER, COLORADO

· ·

Pork Won Tons

½ pound ground pork
¼ teaspoon salt
½ teaspoon sugar
½ teaspoon cornstarch
1½ teaspoons butter
⅛ teaspoon monosodium glutamate
1 teaspoon soy sauce
1 tablespoon sherry
2 green onions, chopped
½ pound won ton skins
1 egg white
2 cups peanut oil

Cook ground pork over medium heat until color turns from pink to gray, approximately 5 minutes. Pour off fat. Add salt, sugar, cornstarch, butter, monosodium glutamate, soy sauce, sherry, and green onions. Mix and refrigerate until cool.

Dab each won ton skin with ½ teaspoon filling. Moisten edges with egg white. Fold each won ton skin into a triangle and seal edges well. Fill all won ton skins before cooking. Place on wax paper and cover with plastic wrap to prevent skins from drying out. Do not stack or let skins touch before cooking.

Heat wok; add oil. When hot, cook 6–8 won tons at a time; drain on paper toweling, then serve immediately.

Won tons may be frozen on trays. Wrap with plastic wrap when frozen. If frozen, remove from freezer early in the day and reheat in a 350° oven for 10 minutes.

Dip in Won Ton Sauce at serving time.

YIELD: 50 WON TONS

Recipe continues . . .

WON TON SAUCE:

2 tablespoons cornstarch
1 cup chicken broth
½ cup pineapple juice
3 tablespoons catsup
3 tablespoons wine vinegar
4 tablespoons sugar
½ tablespoon soy sauce
⅛ teaspoon monosodium glutamate

Beat all ingredients together in small saucepan. Cook, stirring constantly, until sauce thickens.

THE JUNIOR LEAGUE OF OAKLAND-EAST BAY, CALIFORNIA

· · · · · · · · · · · · · · · · · ·

Crab Won Tons

8 ounces cream cheese
1 3½-ounce can flaked crabmeat
2 tablespoons finely chopped green onion
2 tablespoons finely chopped celery
2 tablespoons soft bread crumbs
¼ teaspoon salt
2–3 drops Tabasco
1 8-ounce package frozen egg roll wrappers, defrosted
Vegetable oil

Beat cream cheese until light. Add the crabmeat, onion, celery, crumbs, salt, and Tabasco. Mix well.

Fill the wrappers with a generous teaspoon of the cheese mixture. Moisten the edges of the wrappers and pinch to seal. Heat 2–3 minutes, or until golden brown.

Serve with Sweet and Sour Sauce.

YIELD: 50 WON TONS

SWEET AND SOUR SAUCE:
1 cup chili sauce
1 8-ounce can crushed pineapple, drained
1 tablespoon sweet pickle relish
1 tablespoon chopped onion
1 tablespoon molasses
2 teaspoons dry mustard

Mix all ingredients.

THE JUNIOR LEAGUE OF TACOMA, WASHINGTON

Appetizers
and Sandwiches

Chicken Liver Pâté

8 ounces fresh chicken livers
1 small white onion, chopped
1 clove garlic
4 ounces sweet butter (1 stick)
1 tablespoon good brandy
Pinch thyme
Clarified butter*

Gently sauté chicken livers, onion, and garlic in 1 tablespoon of the butter. Cook until onion is soft and livers are just cooked. Put in blender.

Melt remaining butter and add to the blender mixture. Add the brandy and thyme. Blend on high speed until all ingredients are puréed, stopping to stir down if necessary.

Pour liver mixture into a small bowl or crock in which it can be served. Pour a little clarified butter over the top. Refrigerate. This is best served just at room temperature with toast triangles or Melba rounds.

May also be served as a first course by pouring it, while warm, into a small spring-form loaf pan, slicing it when cold, and serving it on lettuce leaves with a wedge of lemon.

YIELD: 12 APPETIZERS; 8 FIRST-COURSE SERVINGS

*TO CLARIFY BUTTER:

Melt 1 pound butter over low heat. Skim foam off surface and pour the clear oil carefully from the milky sediment which will settle to the bottom of the saucepan. Pour into a crock or bowl. Cover and refrigerate to use as needed or freeze.

THE JUNIOR LEAGUE OF SANTA BARBARA, CALIFORNIA

Mousse de Foies de Volaille

8 ounces fresh chicken livers, halved
¼ cup finely chopped shallots or green onions
¼ cup finely chopped celery
4 tablespoons butter
¾ cup chicken broth
¼ teaspoon salt
¼ teaspoon pepper
Big pinch allspice
¼ teaspoon thyme
¼ cup cognac, port, or Madeira
1½ teaspoons unflavored gelatin
Sour cream or mayonnaise

Cook liver, onions, and celery in butter until liver is cooked and vegetables are tender. Stir in ¼ cup of the chicken broth, and the seasonings. Remove from heat. Stir in cognac or wine. Cool.

Soften gelatin in remaining broth and heat until dissolved. Set aside. Purée liver mixture in blender and stir in gelatin. Turn into mold and chill until set.

Unmold on chilled platter and decorate with sour cream or mayonnaise. Slice and serve with French bread.

YIELD: 12 SERVINGS

THE JUNIOR LEAGUE OF LONG BEACH, CALIFORNIA

California Jalapeño Mold

1 envelope unflavored gelatin
1 cup cold water
1 cup sour cream
½ cup mayonnaise
¼ teaspoon salt
8 ounces cheddar cheese, shredded
2 tablespoons finely chopped green pepper
2 tablespoons finely chopped pimento
1–2 tablespoons minced onion
4 ounces green chilies, finely chopped
1 teaspoon Worcestershire sauce
Parsley sprigs
1 red pepper, seeded and cut in thin rings

Sprinkle gelatin over cold water in a small saucepan. Stir constantly over low heat until dissolved, about 3–4 minutes. In a mixing bowl combine sour cream and mayonnaise and gradually add gelatin. Mix until well blended. Stir in the salt, cheese, green pepper, pimento, onion, chilies, and Worcestershire, mixing well. Chill until slightly thickened, about 20–30 minutes, then stir and refrigerate for 4 hours, or until firm.

Unmold onto a serving platter and garnish with parsley and red pepper rings. Serve with crackers or toast rounds.

This tastes better if it stands overnight.

YIELD: 6–8 SERVINGS

The California Heritage Cookbook
THE JUNIOR LEAGUE OF PASADENA, CALIFORNIA

Easy Escargot

1 stick butter, softened
2 small cloves garlic, minced
2 teaspoons chopped green onion, including tops
1 tablespoon minced parsley
18 snail shells (real or ceramic)
18 extra-large canned snails, washed and drained thoroughly
8 tablespoons grated Parmesan cheese
18 slices French bread or
2 French bread rolls sliced ¼ inch thick, lightly toasted

Combine butter, garlic, onion, and parsley and mix until well blended. Put a small portion of butter mixture in each snail shell then put in snail. Add another small amount of butter mixture and sprinkle with cheese.

Place each shell, openings up, on snail pans or shallow baking dish. Bake at 500° for 5 minutes, or until browned and bubbling. To serve, remove snail from shell and place on top of toast; pour butter mixture on the toast. May also be served in the snail plates with toast to dip in the pungent butter.

YIELD: 3–4 FIRST-COURSE SERVINGS; 18 APPETIZERS

THE JUNIOR LEAGUE OF BOISE, IDAHO

· · · · · · · · · · · · · · · · · ·

Escargot and Mushrooms

12 large button mushrooms
12 escargot, rinsed in cold water
1 tablespoon minced parsley
1 clove garlic, minced
½ cup melted butter

Recipe continues . . .

Remove stems from mushrooms and place escargot in the caps. Mix parsley and garlic with melted butter and pour over mushrooms. Place under broiler until brown and warm.

YIELD: 12 SERVINGS

From an Adobe Oven . . . to a Microwave Range
THE JUNIOR LEAGUE OF PUEBLO, COLORADO

• • • • • • • • • • • • • • • • • • •

Acapulco Ceviche

3 pounds red snapper or mackerel filets
1 cup lemon or lime juice
½ cup salad oil
1½ cups tomato juice
½ cup orange juice
1 teaspoon salt
1 teaspoon pepper
1 cup finely chopped onion
1 tablespoon chopped parsley
1 cup diced tomatoes
½ cup chopped green olives
Tabasco

Cut fish in small pieces. Pour lemon juice over fish to cover and leave in refrigerator, turning a few times, for 3 hours. Pour off any leftover juice. Fish is now "cooked" by acid from lemon.

Add oil, juices, and spices; stir. Add onion, parsley, tomatoes, and olives; stir. Add Tabasco to taste. Store overnight in refrigerator so flavors will blend.

Serve on lettuce leaves or avocado halves.

YIELD: 12 SERVINGS

Que Sabroso!
THE JUNIOR LEAGUE OF MEXICO CITY, MEXICO

• • • • • • • • • • • • • • • • • • •

Ceviche Sacramento

1½ pounds mild white fish (scallops, turbot, halibut, or sole)
1 cup fresh lime juice
3–4 canned California green chilies, chopped
1 cup minced onion (green, red, white, or yellow)
1 teaspoon salt
½ teaspoon crumbled oregano leaves (more if desired)
Dash white pepper
¼ cup olive oil
2–3 large tomatoes, peeled, seeded, and chopped
Lettuce leaves
8 large avocado halves
Chopped parsley or coriander
Sour cream
Chopped green onion

Cut fish into ½-inch cubes. Place in a stainless steel bowl. Stir in lime juice. Place in refrigerator for 3 hours, or overnight. Just before serving, stir in chilies, onion, seasoning, oil, and tomatoes.

To serve, place lettuce leaves on salad plates. Place avocado halves in center of each plate. With a slotted spoon, fill each avocado half with fish mixture. Garnish with chopped parsley or coriander leaves or sour cream and chopped green onion.

YIELD: 8 SERVINGS

THE JUNIOR LEAGUE OF SACRAMENTO, CALIFORNIA

Stuffed Mushrooms

4 ounces butter (1 stick)
½ medium onion, minced
10 medium mushrooms, chopped
2 green onions, minced
¼ teaspoon salt
Dash pepper
½ cup white vermouth
2 tablespoons Worcestershire sauce
3 heaping tablespoons chopped, fresh parsley
1 cup sour cream
1 cup seasoned bread crumbs
4 ounces Monterey Jack cheese, shredded
8 giant mushrooms (3 inches in diameter),
hollowed out and brushed with melted butter

In a sauté pan, melt the butter over medium heat and in it sauté the onion, mushrooms, and green onions until limp. Reduce heat to low and add the remaining ingredients, except the giant mushrooms, in order given. Correct seasoning. The mixture should be the consistency of cooked oatmeal. Correct consistency by adding sour cream or bread crumbs as needed. Remove from heat. Pack the filling into the giant mushrooms, mounding it slightly.

Arrange mushrooms on buttered baking sheet. Bake at 350° for 20–25 minutes.

Stuffed mushrooms may be covered and refrigerated until baking time. They make an excellent first course or luncheon dish.

YIELD: 8 GIANT MUSHROOMS

THE JUNIOR LEAGUE OF SAN JOSE, CALIFORNIA

Greek Appetizer

1 jar or can grape leaves (about 3 dozen)
1 medium onion, finely chopped
1 tablespoon finely chopped parsley
1 clove garlic, minced
¾ cup olive oil
1 tablespoon fresh chopped dill or dry dill weed
¾ cup raw rice
¼ cup pine nuts
¼ cup seedless currants, soaked in white wine to cover
Salt and pepper to taste
¼ cup lemon juice
1 10½-ounce can beef consommé
½ cup red wine plus ½ cup water
Lemon wedges

Remove grape leaves from the jar, scald with hot water, and drain. Cut off stems from the leaves carefully, pat each leaf dry, and place on paper towels with shiny surface down.

In a skillet, sauté onion, parsley, and garlic in 2 tablespoons of hot olive oil; add dill, rice, pine nuts, the currants with wine, and salt and pepper. Cover and simmer for 15 minutes; set aside to cool.

When cool, place 1 teaspoon of the mixture in the center of each grape leaf and roll up with sides folded in. Arrange in a pot in layers; sprinkle each layer with lemon juice and 2 tablespoons olive oil. Pour consommé, red wine plus water, and the remaining olive oil over all. Place a plate on top to hold them down and simmer over low heat for 40–50 minutes.

Remove from heat, drain, and cool before serving.

To serve, arrange on a platter garnished with lemon wedges. Accompany with a bowl of chilled plain yogurt.

YIELD: ABOUT 3 DOZEN

THE JUNIOR LEAGUE OF EDMONTON, ALBERTA

Lamb-Filled Pastries

1 onion, chopped
2 cloves garlic, minced
2 pounds lean ground lamb
3 tablespoons olive oil
1 cup dry white wine
1 teaspoon each coriander, rosemary, ginger, and salt
¼ cup tomato paste
1 tablespoon grated lemon rind

Cook the onion, garlic, and lamb in oil until onion is transparent. Add wine and remaining ingredients. Cover and simmer for 10 minutes. Transfer mixture to a bowl. Cover and chill until needed.

Make pastry and line about 3 dozen small tart shells with it. Fill tart shells with meat mixture, cover with a pastry lid, and bake for 15 minutes at 375°, or until pastry is golden.

Freeze if desired.

DILL-FLAVORED PASTRY:
1 cup butter
6 ounces cream cheese
3 cups flour
Salt, parsley, and dill to taste

Make cream cheese pastry by working butter, cream cheese, flour, salt, parsley, and dill into a smooth dough.

YIELD: 36 SMALL APPETIZERS

THE JUNIOR LEAGUE OF EDMONTON, ALBERTA

Western Quiche

1 11-ounce package pie crust mix
1 teaspoon chili powder
2 tablespoons cold water
1 cup shredded cheddar cheese
1 cup shredded Monterey Jack cheese
3 large eggs
1 teaspoon salt
¼ teaspoon white pepper
1½ cups half and half
1 4-ounce can chopped green chilies
1 2¼-ounce can sliced ripe black olives
2 tablespoons finely chopped green onion

Preheat oven to 350°. In a medium bowl blend pie crust mix and chili powder. Add the water. Mix with a fork until the dough holds together. With your hands, form the dough into a smooth ball. Roll the dough out on a floured surface until it is larger than a 9-inch pie pan. Ease the dough into the pan and flute the edges.

Mix the cheeses together and spread on the bottom of the pastry. In another bowl mix the eggs, salt, pepper, cream, chilies, olives, and green onion. Pour egg mixture over the cheese-covered pastry. Bake in 350° oven for 45 minutes, or until a knife inserted comes out clean.

If desired, top each piece with a little guacamole and sour cream.

YIELD: 4–6 SERVINGS

THE JUNIOR LEAGUE OF TACOMA, WASHINGTON

Tomato Quiche

1 8–10 inch pastry-lined pie plate
2 large tomatoes
¼ cup flour
½ teaspoon salt
¼ teaspoon pepper
3 tablespoons oil
½ cup sliced ripe olives
1 cup minced green onion
3 slices Provolone cheese
2 eggs, slightly beaten
1 cup shredded cheddar cheese
1 cup heavy cream

Bake pie shell 8 minutes at 425°, then cool.

Cut tomatoes into slices ½ inch thick. Dip into flour mixed with salt and pepper. Sauté quickly in oil until lightly browned on both sides. Arrange olives and all but 2 teaspoons onion in bottom of pie shell. Add Provolone cheese and tomatoes.

Stir eggs and cheddar cheese into heavy cream. Pour into pie shell. Bake at 375°–400° for 45 minutes, or until filling is set. Sprinkle onions on top. Cool 5 minutes before cutting.

YIELD: 6 SERVINGS

THE JUNIOR LEAGUE OF SPOKANE, WASHINGTON

Bacon and Vegetable Quiche

6 slices bacon
1 onion, chopped
1 clove garlic, finely minced
4 cups cooked broccoli and cauliflower pieces
4–6 eggs, beaten
2 cups medium or sharp shredded cheese
½ teaspoon salt
½ teaspoon each cumin and marjoram or crushed basil
1 9-inch pastry-lined pie plate

Fry bacon in skillet until brown and crisp. Drain half the drippings out of the skillet. Add onion, garlic, and vegetables and sauté lightly. Cover and braise vegetables in their own juices for 2 minutes. Stir in eggs, cheese, salt, and herbs.

Pour into prepared pie plate and bake for 30–40 minutes at 325°, or until set.

YIELD: 6–8 SERVINGS

THE JUNIOR LEAGUE OF SPOKANE, WASHINGTON

· ·

Italian Sausage Quiche

2 eggs
2 egg yolks
1 cup light cream
1½ cups shredded Monterey Jack cheese
½ pound mild Italian sausage, cooked, crumbled, and drained
2 tablespoons canned chopped green chilies
½ teaspoon salt
¼ teaspoon pepper

Recipe continues . . .

Beat eggs and cream together. Stir in cheese, sausage, chilies, salt, and pepper. Pour into partially baked pastry shell. Bake in 350° oven for 30–35 minutes, until center is no longer soft.

Top with sliced avocado and tomatoes if desired.

RICH PASTRY:
1 cup flour
½ teaspoon salt
½ cup chilled butter (1 stick)
3 tablespoons ice water

Mix flour and salt. Cut in butter until mixture resembles corn meal. Stir in ice water and form dough into a ball. Chill for at least 2 hours. Roll out dough and fit it loosely into a 9-inch quiche pan or pie plate. Flute edge. Bake in 450° oven for 5 minutes. Watch dough carefully and remove from oven before it starts to buckle. Cool shell before filling.

YIELD: 6 SERVINGS

THE JUNIOR LEAGUE OF SANTA BARBARA, CALIFORNIA

· · · · · · · · · · · · · · · · · · ·

Spinach Mushroom Squares

1 10-ounce package frozen chopped spinach, thawed
1 cup sliced mushrooms
⅔ cup chopped green onion
4 eggs
1½ cups milk
2 tablespoons flour
1 teaspoon salt
1 large clove garlic, minced
½ teaspoon oregano
⅛ teaspoon pepper

Press all liquid out of spinach. Reserve half the mushrooms; combine other half with remaining ingredients. Turn into greased shallow 7 x 11-inch baking dish. Decorate top with reserved mushrooms. Bake at 350° for 50 minutes, or until set.

Serve hot or warm.

YIELD: 8 SERVINGS

THE JUNIOR LEAGUE OF LOS ANGELES, CALIFORNIA

· ·

Spanakopeta

2 10-ounce packages frozen chopped spinach, thawed, or
2 pounds fresh spinach, steamed and finely chopped
2 tablespoons olive oil
1 small onion, peeled and minced
15–20 sprigs parsley, minced
½ pound feta cheese, crumbled
6 eggs, lightly beaten
Salt and pepper to taste
12 sheets phyllo pastry (½ pound)
½ pound butter, melted

Drain liquid from spinach and squeeze dry with hands. Set aside.

Heat olive oil in heavy skillet. Add onion and stir until golden. Mix with parsley, cheese, eggs, salt, and pepper. Add spinach and mix thoroughly.

Brush a 9 x 13-inch baking pan with melted butter. Cover pan with one layer of phyllo pastry; let edges hang over sides. Brush generously with butter. Repeat layering and buttering with phyllo dough, until there are five layers. Spoon in spinach mixture and smooth it over the pastry. Cover with another layer of phyllo, brush with butter, and continue adding five more layers, brushing each with butter. Melt more butter if needed.

Recipe continues . . .

Using sharp knife, cut off any surplus pastry around edge of pan. Bake in preheated 375° oven for 45 minutes, or until puffed and golden brown. Remove from oven; cool slightly and cut into 24 squares. Serve warm.

Spanakopeta can be baked ahead of time, then reheated in a hot oven.

YIELD: 24 SQUARES

THE JUNIOR LEAGUE OF LOS ANGELES, CALIFORNIA

. . . .

Spinach Roll with Mushrooms

3 10-ounce packages frozen spinach
¼ cup bread crumbs
2 teaspoons salt
¾ teaspoon pepper
Dash ground nutmeg
6 tablespoons melted butter
4 eggs, separated
4 tablespoons grated Parmesan cheese
1½ pounds mushrooms, sliced
¼ cup butter
1½ tablespoons flour
1 cup Hollandaise sauce

Thaw spinach; squeeze out all excess moisture. Chop. Butter a 10 x 15-inch jelly-roll pan; line with wax paper. Butter wax paper and sprinkle with bread crumbs.

Place spinach in bowl, add 1 teaspoon salt, ¼ teaspoon pepper, nutmeg, and melted butter. Beat in egg yolks one at a time. Beat egg whites in a small bowl until they hold soft peaks—if not using a copper bowl, add ⅛ teaspoon cream of tartar when egg whites reach foamy stage. Fold into spinach mixture. Spoon mixture onto prepared pan and smooth the top evenly with a spatula. Sprinkle with Parmesan cheese. Bake at 350° for 15 minutes, or until the center feels barely firm when touched.

While the spinach roll is baking, sauté mushrooms quickly in ¼ cup butter. Sprinkle mushrooms with 1½ tablespoons flour, remaining 1 teaspoon salt, and ¼ teaspoon pepper. When roll is cooked, place a sheet of buttered wax paper or foil, butter side down, over the roll and invert onto a warm cookie sheet. Carefully remove bottom paper. Spread mushroom mixture over hot spinach roll. Roll up, jelly-roll fashion, then ease roll onto warm platter. Serve immediately, with Hollandaise sauce. This can be made ahead. Cover with foil and heat until warmed through.

YIELD: 6–8 SERVINGS

Colorado Cache
THE JUNIOR LEAGUE OF DENVER, COLORADO

BLENDER HOLLANDAISE:
1 cup sweet butter (1 stick)
4 egg yolks
2 tablespoons lemon juice
¼ teaspoon salt
¼ teaspoon Tabasco

In small saucepan heat butter until very hot, but do not let it brown.

Into container of an electric blender put the egg yolks, lemon juice, salt, and Tabasco. Cover container and turn motor on low speed. Remove cover and pour in the hot butter in a steady stream. When all butter is added, turn motor to high for 3 seconds, then off.

Serve immediately or keep warm by setting container with the sauce into a saucepan containing 2 inches hot, not boiling, water.

YIELD: 1½ CUPS

Pâté en Croute

PASTRY FOR TWO CRUSTS:
2¼ cups flour
1 teaspoon salt
¾ cup chilled butter
1 egg, beaten
½ cup sour cream

PÂTÉ:
¼ cup butter
¾ cup finely chopped mushrooms
⅓ cup finely chopped onion
1 pound each of lean ground veal, pork, and beef steak
(grind together three times)
1½ cups freshly shredded Gruyère cheese
2 teaspoons salt
½ teaspoon pepper
½ teaspoon dill weed
½ teaspoon thyme
3 egg yolks, beaten

GLAZE:
1 egg yolk
1 teaspoon milk

To make pastry, sift flour and salt into chilled bowl; cut in butter until mixture is consistency of coarse meal. In a separate bowl, beat egg and sour cream. Mix into flour mixture. Work until dough can be gathered into a soft pliable ball. Wrap in plastic wrap and chill for 1 hour or more. Cut the chilled dough in half and roll each half into a 6 x 9-inch rectangle. Oil bottom of a jelly-roll pan and lay one pastry rectangle on it.

Melt butter and in it cook mushrooms and onion for 6–8 minutes. Remove to a bowl. Cook meat until done. Drain meat and cool slightly. Add vegetables, then cheese, seasonings, and egg yolks. If mixture is a little moist, add a little dry bread crumbs.

Gather the meat mixture in hands and pat into a narrow loaf down the center of the pastry from one end to the other. Lay the second sheet of pastry over the meat. Roll the bottom crust over the top crust and press the edges of the two sheets together.

To make glaze, combine egg yolk and milk. Dip a pastry brush into the mixture and moisten the edges of the dough. Press down on edges using the back of a fork, then prick the top of the pastry all over with the fork. Make thin strips or hearts, shamrocks, etc. using the leftover pastry. Brush entire pastry with glaze, then crisscross or place designs over the top in an attractive pattern. Now brush the designs. Bake in center of 375° preheated oven for 45 minutes, or until golden brown.

Serve on a large platter. Garnish attractively and serve with a bowl of cold sour cream.

YIELD: 12 SERVINGS

THE JUNIOR LEAGUE OF SPOKANE, WASHINGTON

· · · · · · · · · · · · · · ·

A Yard of Pizza

1 loaf unsliced French bread
1 6-ounce can tomato paste
⅓ cup grated Parmesan cheese
⅓ cup finely chopped green onion
⅓ cup chopped, pitted ripe olives
½ teaspoon crushed dried oregano
¾ teaspoon salt
Dash pepper
1 pound raw ground beef
2 tomatoes, sliced
1 green pepper, cut in rings
1 cup shredded American cheese

Cut loaf of bread in half lengthwise. In mixing bowl, combine tomato paste, Parmesan cheese, onion, olives, oregano, salt, and pepper. Add raw

Recipe continues . . .

beef and mix well. Spread mixture on top of loaf halves. Place on a baking sheet and bake at 400° for 20 minutes.

Remove from oven and top with tomato slices and green pepper rings. Sprinkle American cheese over all. Bake 5–10 minutes longer.

YIELD: 4–5 SERVINGS

THE JUNIOR LEAGUE OF SAN JOSE, CALIFORNIA

· ·

"Jiggs" Sandwiches

½ pound butter, softened
½ cup prepared mustard
25 hamburger buns, halved
2½ pounds ready-to-eat, garlic-flavored corned beef brisket, thinly sliced
25 1-ounce slices sharp, aged cheddar cheese
75 lengthwise slices dill pickle
1½ quarts finely shredded green cabbage
6 tablespoons mayonnaise-type salad dressing
1 tablespoon caraway seeds

Beat butter and mustard until light and fluffy. Spread on cut surfaces of buns, 1½–2 teaspoons per sandwich. Arrange approximately 1½ ounces of thinly sliced corned beef on 25 bun halves. On remaining 25, place a slice of cheese and 3 slices of dill pickle.

Blend cabbage, salad dressing, and caraway seeds together and place approximately ¼ cup on each cheese half.

Put bun halves together, place each sandwich on a piece of foil, wrap, and refrigerate.

These keep very well in the refrigerator for several days before baking.

As needed, bake foil-wrapped sandwiches in preheated 400° oven for 15–20 minutes.

YIELD: 25 SANDWICHES

Private Collection:
Recipes from The Junior League of Palo Alto
THE JUNIOR LEAGUE OF PALO ALTO, CALIFORNIA

. . . .

Onion Olé

1 13¾-ounce package hot roll mix
1 tablespoon chopped chives or instant minced onions
1 cup mayonnaise
4 cups shredded cheddar cheese (½ pound)
½ cup sliced green onions or chopped onions
¼ cup chopped stuffed green olives
1 teaspoon capers
2 tablespoons grated Parmesan cheese

Prepare hot roll mix as directed on package, adding chives. Cover and let rise in warm place until doubled in size, 30–45 minutes. Roll out or pat dough to fit a greased 10 x 15-inch jelly-roll pan.

Combine mayonnaise, shredded cheese, onions, olives, and capers. Spread mayonnaise mixture over dough in pan to within 1 inch from edges. Sprinkle top with Parmesan cheese. Bake at 375° for 30–45 minutes, or until bubbling and golden brown. Cut in squares and serve at once.

Dough may be divided in half and patted to fit 2 14-inch pizza pans. Spread half of mayonnaise mixture over each and sprinkle with Parmesan cheese. Bake at 375° for 15–20 minutes, or until bubbling and golden brown.

Can be made ahead and cooked at the last minute.

YIELD: 6 MAIN-DISH SERVINGS; 36 SNACKS

Gourmet Olé
THE JUNIOR LEAGUE OF ALBUQUERQUE, NEW MEXICO

. . . .

Santa Barbara Love Sandwich

4 slices dark pumpernickel bread (from round loaf)
2 avocados, peeled, seeded, and sliced
8 slices poached chicken breast (3 half-breasts of chicken)
8 mushrooms, sliced
4–8 slices Jarlsberg or Gruyère cheese

Prepare Mornay Sauce and reserve.

Heat broiler. Put slices of bread on broiler pan. Cover with avocado slices, then chicken slices. Put sliced mushrooms on chicken and cover with Mornay Sauce. Top with cheese. Put sandwiches under broiler until cheese melts.

MORNAY SAUCE:
2 tablespoons butter
1 tablespoon minced onion
2 tablespoons flour
Pinch salt
1 cup hot milk
¼ cup shredded Jarlsberg or Gruyère cheese

Melt butter in a saucepan and in it sauté onion until it is soft. Stir in flour and cook over low heat for 3 minutes, stirring. Remove pan from heat and add salt and milk, stirring with a wire whisk. Simmer over medium heat for 10 minutes, stirring occasionally. Add cheese and remove from heat as soon as the cheese is melted.

YIELD: 4 SANDWICHES

THE JUNIOR LEAGUE OF SANTA BARBARA, CALIFORNIA

Lido Sandwiches

2 whole chicken breasts, boned and skinned
¼ cup sautéed mushrooms
½ stick butter
1 cup chopped celery
1 tablespoon chopped onion
1 tablespoon chopped green pepper
2 tablespoons chopped pimento
1¼ cups Béchamel sauce
16 slices white bread
Soft butter for spreading
6 beaten eggs
4 tablespoons milk
2 cups crushed potato chips

Sauté chicken breasts and mushrooms in the ½ stick butter until tender. Dice chicken; add the celery, onion, green pepper, and pimento. Stir in the Béchamel sauce. Let cool.

Trim crusts from bread. Butter each slice and then spread half of the slices with some of the chicken mixture. Complete the sandwich, pressing halves firmly together. Wrap and chill in refrigerator overnight.

To serve: combine eggs and milk. Dip each sandwich in egg mixture. Roll in crushed potato chips. Arrange in a buttered baking pan and bake at 350° for 30 minutes, or until hot and crisp. Serve immediately.

YIELD: 8 SERVINGS

SAUCE BÉCHAMEL:
1¼ cups milk
1 thin slice onion
2 tablespoons butter
2 tablespoons flour
¼ teaspoon salt
¼ teaspoon white pepper
Nutmeg

Recipe continues . . .

Heat milk with the slice of onion until very hot. Set aside.

In saucepan melt butter over moderate heat. Stir in flour and cook, stirring, until butter and flour are thick and bubbling. Stir in salt and pepper.

Remove saucepan from heat, pour in hot milk, all at once, and stir rapidly with a wooden spoon or wire whisk for about 30 seconds, or until smooth. Return saucepan to stove and continue to stir rapidly over moderate heat until sauce is smooth and thickened. Discard onion slice, season with a pinch of nutmeg, and, if too thick, stir in a little half and half or cream.

YIELD: 1¼–1½ CUPS

THE JUNIOR LEAGUE OF BAKERSFIELD, CALIFORNIA

Spicy Shepherd Sandwich

4 pita bread or 8 flour tortillas
1 pound cooked roast beef, thinly sliced
1 4-ounce can chopped green chilies
½ pound longhorn cheese, shredded

If using pita bread, use scissors to open and cut three-quarters of the way around. If using tortillas, lay flat, and use as follows. Fill each pita with ¼ pound of beef; ⅛ pound per tortilla. Cover beef with green chilies and then with cheese. Close pita bread and cut in half; roll tortillas. Wrap each in foil. Bake at 325° for 20 minutes, or until cheese melts.

Serve half a pita or 1 tortilla per serving.

YIELD: 8 SERVINGS

Gourmet Olé
THE JUNIOR LEAGUE OF ALBUQUERQUE, NEW MEXICO

Sloppy Joes

1 pound ground beef
½ cup catsup
1 tablespoon vinegar
1 tablespoon sugar
1 tablespoon prepared mustard
1 tablespoon Worcestershire sauce
½ cup chopped onion
Salt and pepper to taste
1 package of four English muffins or hamburger buns

Do not brown ground beef. Put it and remaining ingredients except muffins into skillet; mix well. Cover and cook over medium heat, stirring frequently, for at least 20 minutes. Meat mixture can simmer longer if necessary.

Serve hot over English muffins or hamburger buns.

Recipe may be doubled or tripled as desired.

YIELD: 4 SERVINGS

THE JUNIOR LEAGUE OF LONG BEACH, CALIFORNIA

Tostadas
(Mexican Open-Face Sandwich)

12 tortillas
Refried beans, homemade or canned
Shredded cooked chicken or pork
Shredded lettuce
Shredded cheese
Mexican Hot Sauce
Sour cream
Avocado

Fry tortillas to a crisp golden brown in hot oil, keeping them flat. Spread tortillas with beans, sprinkle with chicken or pork, lettuce, cheese, hot sauce, and 1 tablespoon cream. Top with slice of avocado.

Pick up in hands to eat; they may break and are sure to be messy, but they're worth every morsel.

YIELD: 6 SERVINGS

MEXICAN HOT SAUCE:
4 ripe tomatoes, peeled
1 onion, coarsely chopped
3–4 fresh serrano chilies, seeded
(if chilies are not available, add 1 tablespoon Tabasco)
1 tablespoon chopped parsley
1 tablespoon salt
1 tablespoon cooking oil

Put all ingredients in blender and blend 1 minute. Pour in saucepan and cook sauce over low heat until the flavors are blended.

Serve with Mexican Tacos and Tostadas.

Que Sabroso!
THE JUNIOR LEAGUE OF MEXICO CITY, MEXICO

Family-Style Tostadas

MEAT SAUCE:
1 pound stew meat, cut in ½-inch cubes
½ cup peanut oil
1 onion, finely chopped
2 cloves garlic, minced
1 7-ounce can green chili salsa
½ teaspoon salt
1 10-ounce can enchilada sauce
¼ cup tomato juice

BEANS:
2 16-ounce cans refried beans
Dash Tabasco
4 green onions, chopped
6 ounces Monterey Jack cheese, shredded

SALAD:
3 green onions, chopped
6 pitted black olives, sliced
1 tomato, chopped
½ teaspoon salt
3 cups shredded lettuce
2 tablespoons Italian-style dressing

GARNISH:
12 tortillas
Cheddar cheese, shredded
Avocados, sliced
Sour cream
Taco sauce

Brown stew meat in ¼ cup peanut oil. Add onion and garlic. Sauté until onion is transparent. Add green chili salsa, salt, enchilada sauce, and tomato juice; cover and simmer for 4 hours.

Recipe continues . . .

Blend beans with Tabasco and green onions. Layer beans and cheese in buttered casserole with cheese on top. Cover and bake at 350° or ½ hour.

Mix green onions, olives, chopped tomato, salt, and lettuce. Toss with dressing and set aside.

Heat remaining peanut oil and fry tortillas one at a time until crisp, turning frequently.

To serve tostadas, top tortilla with hot bean mixture, meat sauce, and salad mixture. Garnish with avocado, cheddar cheese, sour cream, taco sauce. *Con cerveza! Qué otro?*

YIELD: 8–10 SERVINGS

Epicure
THE JUNIOR LEAGUE OF NEWPORT HARBOR, CALIFORNIA

· · · · · · · · · · · · · · · · · · ·

Beef Stroganoff Sandwich Loaf

1 ½ pounds ground beef
½ cup chopped onion
1 cup water
½ cup sour cream
¼ cup sliced ripe olives
1 envelope Stroganoff seasoning mix
1 large loaf French bread, cut in half lengthwise and buttered
¾ cup shredded sharp cheddar cheese
1 green pepper, sliced
Cherry tomatoes, halved

In skillet, cook beef until it is no longer red. Add chopped onion and cook until transparent. Add the water, sour cream, olives, and seasoning mix. Cook until well combined.

Toast the bread under broiler heat until it is slightly browned on the edges. Divide the hamburger mixture onto the two halves and sprinkle

with cheese. Arrange green pepper and cherry tomatoes on top. Bake in
a 375° oven for 7–10 minutes. Slice and serve.

YIELD: 6–8 SERVINGS

THE JUNIOR LEAGUE OF GREAT FALLS, MONTANA

· · · · · · · · · · · · · · · · · · · ·

Mexican Barbecued Beef Sandwiches

1½ pounds beef chuck

SAUCE:
¼ pound margarine
½ cup vinegar
½ cup catsup
Juice of 1 lime
1 tablespoon Worcestershire sauce
2 cloves garlic, minced
1 large onion, finely chopped
1 tablespoon prepared mustard
½ teaspoon cayenne
1 teaspoon black pepper
1 teaspoon salt
¼ cup sugar
2 bay leaves, crushed

Cook the chuck in water to barely cover until tender. Drain and shred or
cut into small cubes.

Combine all ingredients for sauce and simmer over low flame for 15
minutes. Add the meat and mix well. Marinate meat for 24 hours.

Reheat and serve on hamburger buns.

YIELD: 15–20 SERVINGS

Que Sabroso!

THE JUNIOR LEAGUE OF MEXICO CITY, MEXICO

· · · · · · · · · · · · · · · · · · · ·

Kofte Patties
(Ground Lamb Burgers in Pita Bread)

2 pounds ground lamb or beef
1½ cups finely chopped onion
1 cup finely chopped parsley
2 teaspoons salt
1 teaspoon cinnamon
1 teaspoon paprika
½ teaspoon cayenne
8 pita bread

Knead, gently, all ingredients except pita bread until well mixed. Shape into eight patties about ½ inch thick. Barbecue or broil.

Place pita bread in 450° oven for 1 minute, or until bread puffs. Split each pita in half and fill with patties as you would a hamburger bun.

Serve with sliced tomatoes, pickles, sliced red onions, etc.

YIELD: 8 SANDWICHES

Private Collection:
Recipes from The Junior League of Palo Alto
THE JUNIOR LEAGUE OF PALO ALTO, CALIFORNIA

. . . .

Crab-Burgers

1 7½-ounce can Alaska king crab
4 ounces shredded sharp cheddar cheese
3 green onions, finely minced
¾ cup mayonnaise
Dash cayenne
Dash prepared mustard
Dash coarse black pepper
Few drops lemon or lime juice
6 French rolls

Mix first eight ingredients thoroughly. Place in covered container in re-frigerator for several hours, preferably overnight, before serving.

Cut crisp French rolls in half lengthwise. Toast lightly. Spread with crab mixture at least ¼ inch thick. Place under broiler until bubbly and lightly browned. Serve at once.

YIELD: 6 SERVINGS

Something New Under the Sun
THE JUNIOR LEAGUE OF PHOENIX, ARIZONA

Soups

Sopa de Albóndigas

1½ pounds chorizo Mexican sausage meat
1½ pounds ground beef
2 cloves garlic, minced
1 tablespoon minced parsley
1 teaspoon salt
½ cup soft bread crumbs
1 egg, beaten
1 tablespoon chopped fresh mint (optional)
4 tablespoons oil
1 onion, minced
3 quarts beef bouillon or consommé
3–4 carrots, sliced
3–4 zucchini, sliced
Minced cilantro or parsley

Mix well the chorizo, beef, 1 clove garlic, parsley, salt, bread crumbs, egg, and mint. Shape into 1-inch balls and brown lightly in 2 tablespoons oil, turning carefully to preserve the round shape. Set aside and keep warm.

Heat remaining 2 tablespoons oil in large kettle. Add onion and remaining clove of garlic and cook until tender but not brown. Add the bouillon, carrots, and zucchini and bring to a boil. Carefully drop the meat balls into the boiling broth, cover, and simmer 30 minutes.

Ladle soup, vegetables, and meat balls into hot soup plates. Sprinkle with minced cilantro or parsley.

YIELD: 8 SERVINGS

Epicure
THE JUNIOR LEAGUE OF NEWPORT HARBOR, CALIFORNIA

Sopa de Tomate Con Tequila
(Tomato-Tequila Soup)

1 tablespoon finely chopped onion
1 clove garlic, minced
1 teaspoon chili powder
2 tablespoons butter
1 10½-ounce can condensed tomato soup
1 soup can water
2 tablespoons tequila

Sauté onion, garlic, and chili powder in butter until tender. Add soup, water, and tequila. Heat, stirring occasionally.

Serve hot with dollop of garnish.

YIELD: 2–3 SERVINGS

GARNISH:
½ cup mashed avocado
2 teaspoons lemon juice
¼ teaspoon salt
Dash Tabasco
¼ cup sour cream

Combine ingredients and mix well.

Something New Under the Sun
THE JUNIOR LEAGUE OF PHOENIX, ARIZONA

Avocado Soup Mexican-Style

1 large ripe avocado, peeled and seeded
¼ onion
1 clove garlic
1 tablespoon mayonnaise
Juice of 1 lime
⅛ teaspoon Tabasco
½ teaspoon Worcestershire sauce
½ fresh jalapeño pepper, seeded
Cold chicken broth, homemade or canned
Salt and pepper to taste

Put avocado, onion, garlic, mayonnaise, lime juice, Tabasco, Worcestershire, and chili pepper in blender container. Fill with *cold* chicken broth and blend until smooth. Add salt and pepper to taste.

Serve with corn chips or thinly sliced avocado.

YIELD: 6 SERVINGS

Que Sabroso!
THE JUNIOR LEAGUE OF MEXICO CITY, MEXICO

· · · · · · · · · · · · · · · · ·

Black Bean Soup

1 pound dried black beans
2 tablespoons butter
1 stalk celery, diced
1 large carrot, diced
2 onions, chopped
3 quarts water
Salt to taste
1 teaspoon black pepper
1 cooked ham bone
½ cup sherry
Lemon slices for garnish

Soak the beans overnight in water to cover generously. Drain and set aside. Melt butter in a large pot and in it cook vegetables until golden and soft. Add water, salt, pepper, beans, and ham bone. Simmer for 3 hours, or until beans are soft.

Discard ham bone and purée beans and liquid, 2 cups at a time, in blender. Return soup to pot and stir in sherry. Reheat, and serve. Garnish with lemon slice.

YIELD: 12 SERVINGS

Que Sabroso!
THE JUNIOR LEAGUE OF MEXICO CITY, MEXICO

· · · · · · · · · · · · · · · · · · · ·

White Russian Borscht

3½–4 pounds chuck roast
Bouillon cubes to taste
2 cups diced beets
4 cups shredded cabbage
2 large onions, chopped
3½ cups tomatoes
¾ cup fresh lemon juice
6 cloves garlic, minced
¼ cup chopped parsley
1 small bay leaf, crumbled
1 teaspoon paprika
2 tablespoons sugar
1 teaspoon salt
1 teaspoon pepper
Sour cream

Cover meat with 1½ quarts water. Bring to a boil, cover, and simmer 1 hour. Taste stock for flavor and add bouillon cubes as needed. Add vegetables, lemon juice, and seasonings and simmer, covered, 2 hours.

Recipe continues . . .

Remove the meat, take out bones, and cut meat into bite-size pieces. Return meat to soup.

Serve with a generous spoonful of sour cream per serving.

YIELD: 8 SERVINGS

Colorado Cache
THE JUNIOR LEAGUE OF DENVER, COLORADO

. . . .

Cream of Cauliflower Soup

1 2-pound head cauliflower
¼ cup margarine
¼ cup flour
4 cups chicken stock
1 small onion, chopped
1 stalk celery, chopped
2 sprigs chopped parsley
2 egg yolks
½ cup light cream
Salt and pepper to taste

Poach cauliflower in boiling salted water 5 minutes; drain.

Melt margarine in saucepan; add flour and cook, stirring, until a smooth paste is formed. Gradually stir in chicken stock and cook, stirring, until sauce is smooth and thickened. Add onion, celery, and parsley and simmer for 20 minutes. Add cauliflower and cook until soft.

Purée soup, 2 cups at a time, in blender for 15 seconds and return to saucepan. Bring to a boil; stir in egg yolks and cream. Do not boil after eggs are added. Stir in salt and pepper to taste.

YIELD: 4—6 SERVINGS

THE JUNIOR LEAGUE OF RIVERSIDE, CALIFORNIA

. . . .

Mexican Cheese Soup

5 medium potatoes, peeled and diced
3 tablespoons butter
1 medium onion, peeled and chopped
1 4-ounce can chopped green chilies
1 large tomato, peeled, seeded, and chopped
2½ cups milk or half and half
1 pound Monterey Jack cheese, cubed
Salt and pepper to taste
Chopped parsley or cilantro

Put potatoes in a saucepan and barely cover with salted water. Bring to a boil, cover, and reduce heat. Cook until potatoes are tender. *Do not drain.* Mash potatoes directly in saucepan. Add butter and mix. Add onion, chilies, and tomato. Add milk or half and half. Then add cheese and stir over low heat until cheese is melted. *Do not boil.* Add salt and pepper to taste. Add additional milk if required to achieve desired consistency.

Serve hot, garnished with parsley or cilantro.

YIELD: 6 SERVINGS

THE JUNIOR LEAGUE OF SACRAMENTO, CALIFORNIA

Homemade Chicken Noodle Soup

1 whole chicken
2 onions, sliced
2 stalks celery, chopped
1 tablespoon salt
¼ teaspoon pepper
3½ quarts water
1 egg
2 tablespoons water
¼ teaspoon salt
Dash pepper
1 cup flour

Simmer chicken with onions, celery, salt, and pepper in water for 3½ hours. Cool. Strain broth and discard vegetables. Cut chicken into bite-size pieces.

To make noodles, beat egg, water, salt, and pepper; gradually add flour and knead slightly. (Too much kneading makes tough noodles.) Roll out very thinly. Cut into thin strips. Add to broth and boil 15 minutes. Add chicken pieces.

YIELD: 8 SERVINGS

Heritage Cookbook
THE JUNIOR LEAGUE OF SALT LAKE CITY, UTAH

San Francisco Cioppino

1½–2-pounds freshly cooked whole crabs
24 clams, well scrubbed
3 cups dry white wine
⅓ cup olive oil
1 medium onion, finely chopped
3 large cloves garlic, minced
1 medium green pepper, coarsely chopped
2 pounds fresh tomatoes, peeled, seeded, and chopped
3 ounces tomato paste
1 teaspoon freshly ground pepper
½ teaspoon dried oregano
½ teaspoon dried basil or 1 tablespoon finely chopped fresh basil
2 pounds fresh white-fleshed fish such as sea bass, rock cod,
halibut, ling cod, cut into large pieces
¾ pound scallops
¾ pound raw shrimp, peeled and deveined
Fresh parsley, chopped

Remove the legs and claws from the crab and break the body in half, reserving as much of the soft, mustard-colored center ("crab butter") as possible. Set crab pieces aside and force the crab butter through a sieve into a small bowl. Set aside.

Place the clams in a pan, add 1 cup of wine, and steam, covered, over medium heat for 4–6 minutes, or until clams open. Remove clams, discarding any that do not open. Strain the stock through cheesecloth and reserve.

In an 8-quart heatproof casserole or a kettle, heat the oil. Add the onion, garlic, and green pepper and sauté over medium heat, stirring occasionally, for approximately 5 minutes, or until vegetables start to soften. Add tomatoes, tomato paste, remaining 2 cups of wine, pepper, herbs, and clam stock. Partially cover and simmer for 20 minutes. Add the fish, scallops, shrimp, crab, and crab butter. Simmer for approximately 5 minutes, or until seafood is cooked. Do not stir. Add the clams and heat for a scant 1 minute.

Sprinkle with parsley and serve immediately from the kettle.

YIELD: 8 SERVINGS

San Francisco à la Carte
THE JUNIOR LEAGUE OF SAN FRANCISCO, CALIFORNIA

· ·

Red Wine Cioppino

2 large onions, chopped
2 bunches green onions, chopped
2 green peppers, seeded and chopped
4 cloves garlic, minced
¼ cup olive oil
4 tablespoons butter
½ pound fresh, medium mushrooms, sliced
2 cups red wine
1 15-ounce can tomato sauce
1 1-pound 12-ounce can Italian pear tomatoes
1 bay leaf
1 teaspoon oregano
1 teaspoon basil
3 dashes Tabasco
Juice of 1 large lemon (optional)
Salt and freshly ground pepper
2 pounds red snapper, or any firm-fleshed fish, cut in large chunks
24 clams in shell, well scrubbed
24 large raw shrimp, shelled and deveined
2 Dungeness crabs, cooked and cracked, or 1 lobster
½ pound raw scallops

In a large kettle, sauté onions, green onions, green peppers, and garlic in oil and butter for 5 minutes, or until tender, stirring often. Add mushrooms and sauté 4–5 minutes more. Add wine, tomato sauce, tomatoes, herbs, and Tabasco. Cover and simmer 1 hour or more.

Add lemon juice and salt and pepper to taste. Add snapper and simmer 3 minutes. Add clams and shrimp and simmer 3 more minutes, or until clams open and shrimp are pink. Do *not* overcook. Add cooked crab or lobster at very last, just to heat through. (You may cook live lobster in Cioppino, but add it 5 minutes before the red snapper. Also, instead of lobster, you may use 2 frozen lobster tails, but split them in half lengthwise and add them at the same time as the snapper.)

Check seasoning and serve in large, warmed bowls with chunks of sourdough bread and a green salad. Have large napkins or bibs on hand.

YIELD: 6–8 SERVINGS

Private Collection:
Recipes from The Junior League of Palo Alto
THE JUNIOR LEAGUE OF PALO ALTO, CALIFORNIA

· · · · · · · · · · · · · · · · · ·

Consommé Suvorov

6 10½-ounce cans beef consommé, undiluted
Juice of 4 lemons
2½ cups V-8 juice
2½ cups red Burgundy

Combine all ingredients. Heat and serve.

YIELD: 10 SERVINGS

No Regrets
THE JUNIOR LEAGUE OF PORTLAND, OREGON

· · · · · · · · · · · · · · · · · ·

Iced Cucumber Soup

3 cucumbers
1 leek, white part only, chopped
2 tablespoons butter
1 bay leaf
1 tablespoon flour
3 cups chicken broth
1 cup sour cream
Juice of ½ lemon
1 teaspoon chopped dill
Salt and white pepper

Chop 2 cucumbers and sauté with the leek in butter. Add bay leaf and cook for 20 minutes. Stir in the flour. Gradually stir in chicken broth and bring to boil. Purée in blender, strain to remove seeds, and chill.

Add remaining cucumber, peeled, seeded, and grated, sour cream, and lemon juice. Stir in chopped dill and adjust seasonings with salt and white pepper to taste.

Chill until ready to serve.

YIELD: 6 SERVINGS

Que Sabroso!
THE JUNIOR LEAGUE OF MEXICO CITY, MEXICO

· · · · · · · · · · · · · · · · · · ·

Curried Cream

8 ounces cream cheese, softened
1 10½-ounce can beef consommé with added gelatin
1 teaspoon curry powder
Parsley

Blend the cream cheese, half the consommé, and the curry powder and divide into four sherbet glasses. Refrigerate. Once set, pour remaining can of consommé over the tops. Refrigerate. When set, garnish with parsley.

Serve as a first course in place of soup.

YIELD: 4 SERVINGS

THE JUNIOR LEAGUE OF CALGARY, ALBERTA

. . . .

Erbsin Soupse
(German Soup)

1 pound dried split peas
3–4 large potatoes, partially peeled and chopped
2 large white onions, peeled
8–10 whole carrots, unpeeled and sliced
1 tablespoon olive oil
4 cloves garlic, chopped
Whole thyme*
Whole bay leaves*
Cumin*
Cracked peppercorns (lots)*
Salt*
Oregano
Celery seeds
Caraway seeds
Dry mustard
Rosemary
Mace
Red pepper
Marjoram
2 pounds Polish sausage, or 1 pound sausage and 1 pound
frankfurters, sliced

* Essential!

Recipe continues . . .

Soak peas in 3 quarts of water in large pot for several hours, washing three times. Bring peas to a rolling boil and add chopped potatoes, onions, and sliced carrots. Boil for 3–4 hours, or until all of the peas and most of the potatoes are very soft and soup begins to thicken.

Heat olive oil in saucepan and add garlic and spices. Be liberal! Cook for about 10 minutes and add to soup. Cover and cook over low heat for 45 minutes. Add sliced sausage and cook 20–30 minutes, or until heated through.

Serve with German black bread, lots of butter, assorted cheeses, and dark beer. This soup gets better the longer you keep it.

YIELD: 10–12 SERVINGS

From an Adobe Oven . . . to a Microwave Range
THE JUNIOR LEAGUE OF PUEBLO, COLORADO

· · · · · · · · · · · · · · · · · · ·

Garden Soup

12 ounces plain yogurt
1 cup cucumber purée*
2 tablespoons minced onion
¼ cup chili sauce
¾ teaspoons salt
1 cup chilled chicken consommé
1 tablespoon olive oil
Pepper to taste
1 mild onion, chopped
1 green pepper, chopped
1 cucumber, chopped
1 tomato, chopped

Blend the first eight ingredients in blender.

Chill *thoroughly*. When ready to serve, add vegetables.

Serve in chilled cups.

This soup may be garnished with a scoop of sour cream and sprinkled with chives.

YIELD: 8 SERVINGS

* CUCUMBER PURÉE

To prepare purée, peel and seed cucumbers, cut into pieces, and blend in blender until puréed.

THE JUNIOR LEAGUE OF OAKLAND-EAST BAY, CALIFORNIA

· ·

Blushing Soup

2 cups tomato juice
1 1-pound can beets, drained
3 tablespoons lemon juice
1½ cups buttermilk
½ cup cream
2 tablespoons chopped chives
2 tablespoons chopped celery
2 tablespoons chopped cucumber
8–10 drops Tabasco
1 teaspoon salt

Combine ingredients and mix in blender. Refrigerate.

Serve cold. Keeps several weeks very well.

YIELD: 6–8 SERVINGS

Something New Under the Sun
THE JUNIOR LEAGUE OF PHOENIX, ARIZONA

· ·

Santa Barbara Gazpacho

This is an update of an ancient recipe originated by Spanish peasants. It can be a soup, a salad, or the main course, depending on the mood or the weather.

12 medium-size tomatoes
4 cups canned condensed beef consommé
½ teaspoon basil
6 tablespoons lime juice
4 tablespoons olive oil
1 cup chopped green onions, bulb and green stems
2 large avocados, cubed
Salt and coarse pepper to taste
Avocado slices
Thinly sliced onion rings
Sour cream or yogurt
12 slices cooked bacon, crumbled
Sunflower seeds
Croutons

Peel, seed, and chop tomatoes into large pieces. Put into blender and whirl until smooth. Put into a large crockery bowl and add broth. Stir in ingredients through salt and pepper and chill well. Ladle soup into shallow bowls. Allow guests to help themselves to any or all of the condiments.

YIELD: 12 SERVINGS

CROUTONS:
1 green pepper, diced (optional)
1 small loaf of bread, cut into cubes
¼ cup butter

Sauté green pepper and bread cubes in butter. Put on cookie sheet in a slow 300° oven until bread is dry and crisp.

THE JUNIOR LEAGUE OF SANTA BARBARA, CALIFORNIA

. . . .

Gourmet Halibut Soup

2 pounds halibut
1 onion, sliced
3 sprigs parsley
1 slice lemon
1 bay leaf
4 whole peppercorns
Pinch allspice
1 clove garlic, minced
1 quart water
¼ cup butter
¼ cup flour
2 teaspoons, salt
1 cup cream
1 tablespoon dry sherry
¼ cup chopped parsley

Discard fish skin and bones and cut fish into ¼-inch cubes. Put fish in heavy pot with the onion, parsley, lemon, bay leaf, peppercorns, allspice, garlic, and water. Cover and simmer for 30 minutes. Strain, reserving both the broth and the halibut.

In a saucepan, melt butter and blend in flour and salt. Gradually stir in the reserved broth and cook until it thickens and is smooth. Add fish and bring to a simmer. Add cream to soup and heat. Add sherry and serve.

Garnish each serving with chopped parsley.

YIELD: 6 SERVINGS

THE JUNIOR LEAGUE OF SEATTLE, WASHINGTON

Hot and Sour Soup

¼ pound lean boneless pork, very thinly sliced
1 tablespoon soy sauce
1 tablespoon cornstarch
1 quart chicken stock
1 teaspoon salt
4 Chinese mushrooms (1–1½ inches in diameter), slivered
½ cup slivered bamboo shoots
2 squares Chinese bean curd, slivered
¼ teaspoon pepper
2 tablespoons vinegar
2 tablespoons cornstarch
3 tablespoons water
1 egg, beaten
Sesame seed oil
Green onions, chopped

Marinate pork in 1 tablespoon soy sauce mixed with 1 tablespoon corn-starch for 15–30 minutes. Bring stock to a boil. Add salt, mushrooms, and bamboo shoots. Add the pork, bean curd, pepper, and vinegar. Bring to a second boil and stir in the 2 tablespoons cornstarch mixed with the water. Continue to boil until the pork is done and the soup is thickened. While stirring boiling soup, slowly pour in the beaten egg.

Garnish each bowl of soup with a drop of sesame seed oil and a few chopped green onions.

YIELD: 1½ QUARTS

THE JUNIOR LEAGUE OF BAKERSFIELD, CALIFORNIA

East Bay Minestrone

1 cup dried white beans
1 quart water
1 tablespoon olive oil
4 cloves garlic, minced
3 slices Canadian bacon, diced
2 cups chopped onions
8 cups chicken stock
½ cup red wine
1 cup chopped celery
1 cup diced potatoes
1 cup diced zucchini
1 cup diced carrots
2 cups canned, drained and chopped tomatoes
1 cup coarsely chopped cabbage
2 tablespoons chopped fresh parsley or 1 tablespoon dried
2 tablespoons fresh oregano or 1 tablespoon dried
2 tablespoons fresh basil or 1 tablespoon dried
½ cup elbow macaroni
Salt and pepper to taste
1 cup freshly grated Parmesan cheese

Soak beans for 6 hours in 1 quart water.

In large Dutch oven, heat olive oil. Sauté garlic and bacon until bacon begins to brown. Add onions and sauté until soft. Add beans and water and cook for 1½ hours, or until beans are tender.

Add chicken stock, red wine, vegetables, herbs, and macaroni and simmer until vegetables are tender, about 30 minutes. Do not overcook.

Season to taste with salt and pepper.

Serve with freshly grated Parmesan cheese.

YIELD: 8 SERVINGS

THE JUNIOR LEAGUE OF OAKLAND-EAST BAY, CALIFORNIA

Fresh Mushroom Soup

6 tablespoons butter
2 cups finely minced yellow onions
½ teaspoon sugar
1 pound fresh mushrooms
¼ cup flour
1 cup water
1¾ cups chicken broth
1 cup dry vermouth
1 teaspoon salt
¼ teaspoon pepper

In a large saucepan melt butter and in it cook onions and sugar slowly until golden, about 30–45 minutes. Slice one third of the mushrooms and finely chop the rest. Add all mushrooms and sauté for 5 minutes. Stir in flour until smooth. Cook for 2 minutes, stirring constantly. Gradually stir in water. Add remaining ingredients and heat to boiling, stirring constantly. Reduce heat and simmer, uncovered, 10 minutes.

May be prepared in advance, refrigerated, and reheated, covered, over low heat for 10 minutes.

YIELD: 6 SERVINGS

Colorado Cache
THE JUNIOR LEAGUE OF DENVER, COLORADO

Cream of Fresh Mushroom Soup

¼ cup butter
2 tablespoons chopped onion
½ cup all-purpose flour
½ teaspoon salt
⅛ teaspoon pepper
Dash cayenne
3 cups chicken broth
½ pound fresh mushrooms, sliced lengthwise
2 cups scalded milk
2 tablespoons dry sherry
Parsley

Heat butter in a saucepan. Mix in onion and cook until onion is tender. Stir in flour, salt, and pepper. Add the chicken broth gradually, stirring constantly. Continue to stir until soup is simmering, and cook 1 minute. Stir in the mushrooms. Cook over low heat 30 minutes, covered, stirring occasionally. Remove cover and add scalded milk. Cook, uncovered, over low heat 5–10 minutes.

Just before serving, stir in the sherry. Garnish with parsley.

YIELD: 4–8 SERVINGS

A Taste of Oregon
THE JUNIOR LEAGUE OF EUGENE, OREGON

Curried Fresh Mushroom Soup

4 tablespoons butter
1 onion, finely minced
1 pound fresh mushrooms, chopped
1 teaspoon curry powder
½ cup flour
2 quarts whole milk
10 chicken bouillon cubes
⅛ teaspoon ground coriander
5 tablespoons lemon juice
½ teaspoon grated lemon peel
2 tablespoons sherry
1 tablespoon plum or currant jelly
Lemon slices for garnish

In a large frying pan over medium-high heat, sauté in the butter the finely minced onion and mushrooms for 3 minutes. Add curry and flour and blend. Gradually add milk, stirring until smooth. Add bouillon cubes and coriander. Continue cooking, stirring occasionally, about 20 minutes, or until cubes are dissolved and soup has thickened. Add lemon juice, lemon peel, sherry, and jelly. Reduce heat; stir and keep warm for another 30 minutes to allow flavors to blend.

Serve with a very thin slice of lemon floating on top.

YIELD: 2½ QUARTS

THE JUNIOR LEAGUE OF BOISE, IDAHO

Fish and Mushroom Stew

2 teaspoons oil
½ cup chopped onion
1 clove garlic, minced
1 1-pound 12-ounce can tomatoes, chopped
1 12-ounce bottle clam juice
1 teaspoon salt
1 teaspoon crumbled oregano leaves
½ teaspoon ground black pepper
1 pound mushrooms, sliced
1½–2 pounds fresh or frozen halibut or cod steak
1 10-ounce can baby clams, drained
¼ cup chopped parsley

In a Dutch oven or large, heavy pan, heat oil. Add onion and garlic; sauté for 2 minutes. Add tomatoes, clam juice, salt, oregano, and pepper. Bring to boiling point. Reduce heat and simmer, covered, for 30 minutes.

Add sliced fresh mushrooms. Cut fish into 1-inch pieces, discard skin and bones, and add fish. Add clams and return to boiling point. Reduce heat and simmer, covered, for 10 minutes.

Sprinkle with parsley before serving.

YIELD: 6 SERVINGS

THE JUNIOR LEAGUE OF SEATTLE, WASHINGTON

Oaxaca Soup

10 chili poblanos*, fresh or canned
6 medium potatoes
6 medium tomatoes, peeled
½ large onion, chopped
2 cloves garlic, minced
1 tablespoon cooking oil
4–6 cups water, as necessary
Salt to taste
3 tablespoons granulated chicken broth
1 teaspoon parsley
½ teaspoon baking soda
2½ cups milk
1 pound Oaxaca or mozzarella cheese, diced

If chilies are fresh, first roast them on a hot griddle until the skin blisters and turns brown. Put them in a plastic bag to "sweat" for about 10 minutes, then peel, devein, and remove the seeds. If canned chilies are used, slit them and remove seeds. Rinse chilies in water and cut in long strips.

Peel and *cube* the potatoes. Purée tomatoes in the blender and pour through a sieve to remove seeds.

In a 6–8-quart pan, fry the onion and garlic, potatoes, and chili strips in the oil until the onion is soft. Add the puréed tomatoes and cook for 3–5 minutes. Add the water, salt, broth granules, parsley, and the soda.

In a separate pan, bring the milk to a boil, remove any "skin," and add to the other mixture. Add about one-third of the diced cheese and let it melt. In each individual soup bowl, put about 3 tablespoons diced cheese and pour the piping-hot soup over it.

* A dark green pepper, usually mild in flavor. Bell peppers may be substituted, but they are not as good. If used, add 1 tablespoon Tabasco to the soup.

This recipe is a little bit of trouble to make, but the results are well worth it.

YIELD: 6 SERVINGS

Que Sabroso!
THE JUNIOR LEAGUE OF MEXICO CITY, MEXICO

·   ·   ·   ·   ·   ·   ·   ·   ·   ·   ·   ·   ·   ·   ·   ·   ·

Authentic French Onion Soup

⅓ cup butter
5 onions, thinly sliced
2 tablespoons flour
7 cups stock or 3 cans beef consommé and 2 cans water
½ teaspoon pepper
6 slices toasted French bread
6 thin slices Gruyère cheese
4 tablespoons shredded Gruyère cheese

Melt butter in heavy saucepan, add the onions, and sauté over very low heat until tender. Add flour and mix until smooth. Add stock gradually, stirring constantly. Add pepper, cover, and cook over low heat 30 minutes. Cool and freeze at this point if desired.

To serve, place cheese slice on bread in bottom of individual soup bowls—you will need six bowls—and pour hot soup over. Place under broiler for 1 minute. Sprinkle with shredded cheese and serve.

YIELD: 6 SERVINGS

THE JUNIOR LEAGUE OF BOISE, IDAHO

·   ·   ·   ·   ·   ·   ·   ·   ·   ·   ·   ·   ·   ·   ·   ·   ·

Ann's Potato Soup

1 huge potato, peeled and coarsely cut
1 huge white Bermuda onion, peeled and coarsely cut.
¼ pound butter
¼ cup Sauterne
2–3 chicken bouillon cubes
1 tablespoon lemon juice
Chopped chives and freshly ground pepper for garnish

Combine all ingredients except garnish in saucepan and barely cover with water. Bring to a boil and cook until potato and onion are tender. Purée in blender until soup is smooth but thick. Chill thoroughly.

Sprinkle with chives and freshly ground pepper. Serve cold.

YIELD: 6 SERVINGS

THE JUNIOR LEAGUE OF OGDEN, UTAH

.   .   .   .

Puget Sound Salmon Chowder

1 cup cooked, flaked salmon, fresh or canned
½ cup chopped celery
½ cup chopped onion
½ cup chopped green pepper (optional)
1 clove garlic, minced
3 tablespoons margarine
1 cup diced potatoes
1 cup shredded carrot
2 cups chicken broth
1½ teaspoons salt
½ teaspoon pepper
½ teaspoon dill weed
1 17-ounce can cream-style corn
1 13-ounce can evaporated milk or cream

Sauté celery, onion, pepper, and garlic in margarine until onion is translucent. Add potatoes, carrots, chicken broth, and seasonings. Simmer for 20 minutes and add corn, salmon, and evaporated milk or cream. Heat thoroughly and serve.

YIELD: 4–6 SERVINGS

THE JUNIOR LEAGUE OF SEATTLE, WASHINGTON

· · · · · · · · · · · · · · · · · ·

Italian Sausage Soup

1½ pounds mild Italian sausage, cut in ½-inch lengths
2 cloves garlic, minced
2 large onions, chopped
1 28-ounce can whole tomatoes
3 13¾-ounce cans beef broth or 5 cups water and 5 beef bouillon cubes
1½ cups red wine
½ teaspoon basil
3 tablespoons chopped parsley
1 medium green pepper, chopped
2 medium zucchini, sliced ¼ inch thick
3 cups uncooked bow-tie noodles
Grated Parmesan cheese

In 5-quart saucepan or large Dutch oven cook sausage until medium-brown. Drain off fat. Add garlic and onions and cook until limp. Add tomatoes with liquid, breaking tomatoes into pieces with side of a spoon. Add broth, wine, and basil. Simmer, uncovered, 30 minutes. Add parsley, pepper, zucchini, and noodles and simmer, covered, for about 25 minutes longer, or until noodles are tender.

Recipe continues . . .

Serve in soup bowls with Parmesan cheese served separately to sprinkle over soup.

YIELD: 6 LARGE SERVINGS

THE JUNIOR LEAGUE OF SAN JOSE, CALIFORNIA

Seafood Bisque

1¼ cup butter
1 cup all-purpose flour
4 7½-ounce cans minced clams or 4 cups fresh clams minced
½ gallon milk
1 pint half and half
1 bunch green onions
1 clove garlic, minced
2 pounds crabmeat
1 pound shelled shrimp, diced
1 cup dry white table wine
⅓ cup pale dry sherry
Parsley sprigs for garnish

Melt ¾ cup of the butter in a 6-quart heavy-bottomed pan. Blend in flour and cook about 2 minutes. Drain liquid from clams (reserve clams). Stir liquid into butter-flour mixture in pan until blended. Slowly stir in milk and half and half and cook until soup is thickened.

Chop the onions finely, discarding half of the green stems. Using a large skillet, sauté onions and garlic in the remaining ½ cup butter, cooking until limp. Add the crab, shrimp, and drained clams, and cook in the butter, stirring lightly, until seafood is heated through. Add seafood to the soup mixture and stir in the white wine and sherry. Heat just to serving temperature.

Garnish with parsley.

YIELD: 16 SERVINGS

THE JUNIOR LEAGUE OF SACRAMENTO, CALIFORNIA

· · · · · · · · · · · · · · · · ·

Chupe de Camarones (Peruvian-Style Shrimp Chowder)

This is a meal in itself served with a green salad and hot French bread.

> *4 tablespoons oil*
> *1 clove garlic*
> *1 onion, finely chopped*
> *1 large tomato, chopped*
> *4 cups boiling water*
> *1 ear corn, cut in pieces*
> *¼ cup peas*
> *1 pound potatoes, peeled and diced*
> *2 tablespoons rice*
> *1 pound fresh shrimp*
> *Pinch oregano*
> *Salt and pepper to taste*
> *4 slices white-fleshed fish*
> *1 cup heavy cream*
> *Chopped parsley*
> *1 poached egg per person (optional)*

Heat 2 tablespoons oil in large saucepan and in it sauté the garlic, onion, and tomato. Add the water, corn, peas, potatoes, and rice; bring to a boil and boil for 10–15 minutes. When potatoes are cooked, remove from heat

Recipe continues . . .

and add the shrimp, oregano, salt, and pepper. Simmer for 5 minutes, or until shrimp are cooked.

Sauté the fish in remaining oil until flesh flakes easily. Just before serving, add cream and fried fish and sprinkle with parsley. Top each serving with a poached egg, if desired.

YIELD: 4 SERVINGS

THE JUNIOR LEAGUE OF CALGARY, ALBERTA

•   •   •   •   •   •   •   •   •   •   •   •   •   •   •   •   •   •   •

Spanish Soup

2 tablespoons butter
1 tablespoon olive oil
4 cups thinly sliced onions
3 tablespoons flour
1 16-ounce can tomato purée
4 14-ounce cans regular-strength beef broth
1 clove garlic, minced
1 tablespoon red wine vinegar
1 tablespoon Worcestershire sauce
1 tablespoon sugar
1½ teaspoons salt
¼ teaspoon pepper
¼ teaspoon oregano
¼ teaspoon tarragon
¼ teaspoon Tabasco
½ teaspoon ground cumin

CONDIMENTS:
Group No. 1: Meat
2 large linguica, chorizo, or kielbasa sausages,
sliced ¼ inch thick and browned
¼–½ pound tiny shrimp, cooked and shelled
¾ pound ham, cooked and cubed, sautéed until lightly browned

Group No. 2: Fresh Vegetables
1 cup diced red or green pepper
1 cup peeled and diced cucumber
1 cup diced fresh tomato
1 cup diced onion
½ pound fresh mushrooms, sliced and sautéed in butter
½ pound fresh carrots, sliced, cooked until tender, and drained

GARNISHES:
3 hard-boiled eggs, chopped
1 cup sour cream
¼ pound cheddar cheese, shredded
2 limes, cut into wedges
1 8-ounce can garbanzos, drained
1 2¼-ounce can sliced ripe olives, drained
½ cup chopped parsley

Melt butter in a 4–5-quart pot over medium-low heat. Add olive oil and onions. Slowly cook the onions, stirring occasionally, until they are limp and slightly golden, about 45 minutes. Sprinkle flour over onions and blend. Gradually stir in tomato purée and beef broth. Add garlic, vinegar, Worcestershire sauce, sugar, salt, pepper, oregano, tarragon, Tabasco, and cumin. Stir until well blended. Bring to a boil over high heat, reduce heat to low, and simmer, uncovered, for 30–40 minutes, stirring occasionally.

This soup is served with several condiments. Ask your guests to choose 2 or 3 from each of the condiment groups.

YIELD: 6–8 SERVINGS

Colorado Cache
THE JUNIOR LEAGUE OF DENVER, COLORADO

Maggie's Split Pea Soup

1 pound dried split peas
3 pounds very lean country-cut (thick) pork spareribs
2 stalks celery, cut in chunks
3 carrots, cut in chunks
1 large onion, diced
1 potato, diced
8–10 cups chicken broth or water if desired
1 teaspoon salt
Pepper to taste
½ teaspoon thyme
1 teaspoon cumin
¼ cup dried parsley
Cider vinegar and plain yogurt for garnish

Combine all ingredients except garnish in large soup kettle. Bake, covered, at 350° for 4 hours, or for 7–8 hours at 200°. When spareribs are fork-tender, strip meat from bones. Return meat to soup.

When ready to serve, stir 1 teaspoon cider vinegar into each serving. Add a dollup of yogurt.

Better the second day; also freezes well.

YIELD: 10 SERVINGS

THE JUNIOR LEAGUE OF BAKERSFIELD, CALIFORNIA

Fresh Tomato and Basil Soup

4 tablespoons butter
1 large onion, chopped
1 carrot, grated
5 medium tomatoes, peeled and quartered
½ cup packed, fresh basil leaves or ¼ cup dried basil
1 teaspoon salt
¾ teaspoons pepper
¾ teaspoons sugar
2 cups chicken broth

In saucepan, melt butter over medium heat; add onion and carrot and sauté until onion is limp. Stir in tomatoes, basil, salt, pepper, and sugar. Cover and simmer for 15 minutes.

Place mixture in blender and blend until smooth. Heat chicken broth, add to tomato mixture, and mix well. Heat until soup is hot.

YIELD: 6 SERVINGS

THE JUNIOR LEAGUE OF OAKLAND-EAST BAY, CALIFORNIA

. . . .

Winter Tomato Soup

½ cup butter
2 tablespoons olive oil
1 large onion, thinly sliced (about 2 cups)
1 teaspoon thyme
1 teaspoon basil
Salt and pepper to taste
1 2-pound 3-ounce can Italian tomatoes
3 tablespoons tomato paste
3¾ cups chicken broth
4 tablespoons flour
1 teaspoon sugar
1 cup heavy cream

Recipe continues . . .

In a saucepan, melt butter and add olive oil, onion, thyme, basil, salt, and pepper. Cook, stirring, until onion wilts. Add tomatoes and tomato paste. Simmer 10 minutes.

Blend together 5 tablespoons of the chicken broth and the flour. Add this to the soup, stir, then add the rest of the broth. Simmer 30 minutes, stirring often to prevent burning. Purée 2 cups at a time in the blender; return to heat. Add sugar and cream. Simmer 5 more minutes.

YIELD: 8 SERVINGS

A Taste of Oregon
THE JUNIOR LEAGUE OF EUGENE, OREGON

· ·

Tortilla Cheese Soup

4 cups chicken broth
2 cups vegetable broth
1 7-ounce can Mexican green chili sauce
2 cloves garlic, minced
2 cups shredded Monterey Jack cheese
1 bunch green onions, thinly sliced (green tops only)
2 cups tortilla chips, slightly crushed

Place chicken broth, vegetable broth, green chili sauce, and minced garlic in saucepan. Bring soup to a boil; lower heat and simmer, covered, for 1 hour.

When ready to serve, sprinkle each soup dish with ½ cup cheese. Pour soup over cheese and sprinkle with sliced green onions and tortilla chips.

YIELD: 4 SERVINGS

THE JUNIOR LEAGUE OF OAKLAND-EAST BAY, CALIFORNIA

· ·

Waterzooie Van Kip
(A Specialty of Belgium)

Salt and freshly ground pepper
2 broiling chickens, cut into serving pieces
1 tablespoon butter
2 leeks, finely chopped
2 celery stalks, finely chopped
3 carrots, peeled and sliced
1 large onion, finely chopped
¼ cup finely chopped parsley
4–5 cups heated chicken broth
2 pinches mace (optional)
4 egg yolks
¼ cup chopped parsley for garnish
1 lemon, thinly sliced, for garnish

Salt and pepper chicken pieces. Use 1 tablespoon butter to thoroughly grease bottom of a Dutch oven or heavy heatproof casserole. Layer leeks, celery, carrots, onion, and parsley in casserole. Arrange chicken pieces on top.

Tightly cover casserole and simmer over low heat for 10 minutes. Don't worry, it will not burn if properly covered and temperature is kept low.

Add hot broth and mace; cover and simmer 1 hour.

Remove chicken pieces. Beat egg yolks lightly and add to the broth and vegetables, stirring constantly. Immediately remove from heat.

To serve, divide broth among warm, shallow soup bowls. Top with pieces of chicken and garnish with chopped parsley and lemon slices.

Serve with hot, crusty, French bread and a green salad.

YIELD: 8 SERVINGS

Private Collection:
Recipes from The Junior League of Palo Alto
THE JUNIOR LEAGUE OF PALO ALTO, CALIFORNIA

Curried Zucchini Soup

5 medium zucchini, unpeeled
3 cups chicken broth
½ cup heavy cream
1–2 teaspoons curry powder
Salt and pepper to taste

Cook the squash until barely tender in the chicken broth. Liquefy all ingredients in blender and heat but don't boil. Season to taste with salt and pepper.

Serve with croutons.

YIELD: 6 SERVINGS

Que Sabroso!
THE JUNIOR LEAGUE OF MEXICO CITY, MEXICO

· ·

Cream of Zucchini Soup

1 cup chopped onion
1 tablespoon butter
2 cups unpeeled, diced zucchini
3 cups chicken broth
1 teaspoon dill weed
1 cup plain yogurt
Salt and pepper to taste

Sauté onion in butter until onion is limp. Add zucchini, chicken broth, and dill. Cover and simmer 15–20 minutes. Stir in yogurt and mix well. Then purée in blender and stir in salt and pepper to taste.

Serve either hot or cold.

YIELD: 4 SERVINGS

THE JUNIOR LEAGUE OF SPOKANE, WASHINGTON

· ·

Beef and Large Game

Franciscan Beef

6–8-pound rib roast of beef
¼ cup olive oil
¼ cup port
4 teaspoons onion powder
1½ teaspoons fines herbes
2 cloves garlic, minced
¼ cup butter
10 fresh artichoke hearts or
1 10-ounce package frozen artichoke hearts, thawed
Butter
1 cup Burgundy
⅔ cup port
2 beef bouillon cubes
1½ teaspoons onion powder
1 teaspoon fines herbes
1 clove garlic, minced
⅛ teaspoon ground cloves
⅛ teaspoon grated orange peel
1½ teaspoons cornstarch
1 cup water

Place roast on rack. Combine oil, ¼ cup port, onion powder, 1½ teaspoons fines herbes, and 2 cloves garlic and blend well. Rub into roast on all sides. Roast at 325° until done, about 2–2½ hours. Remove from oven and let stand in warm place for 20 minutes before carving.

To make sauce, sauté artichoke hearts in butter until golden; reserve. Remove all but 2 tablespoons juice in roasting pan. Combine remaining ingredients, except for the cornstarch and water. Stir into juices. Boil until liquid is reduced by half. Blend cornstarch into water; add to pan, stirring until sauce boils and thickens. Add artichoke hearts and heat 3–5 minutes.

YIELD: 8 SERVINGS

Epicure
THE JUNIOR LEAGUE OF NEWPORT HARBOR, CALIFORNIA

· · · · · · · · · · · · · · · · · ·

Beef Wellington

2 pounds fresh mushrooms
4 tablespoons minced shallots
2 tablespoons butter
½ cup Madeira
Salt and pepper
4–5 tablespoon foie gras
2 cups beef bouillon
1 tablespoon tomato paste
2 tablespoon cornstarch
¼ cup Madeira
Salt and pepper
Whole 4–6-pound tenderloin of beef
1 tablespoon cooking oil
Suet to cover beef
2 10-ounce packages frozen patty shells, thawed, or
1 pound puff pastry dough purchased from bakery
1 egg, beaten
½ tablespoon water

To make filling, clean, wash, and dry mushrooms. Chop them into small pieces, and twist a handful at a time in the corner of a dishtowel to remove as much moisture as possible. Set mushroom juice aside for sauce.

Sauté the mushrooms and shallots in butter for 7–8 minutes, or until they are dark and dry. Add the ½ cup Madeira and boil until liquid is evaporated. Add salt and pepper to taste. Beat foie gras into the mushrooms with a fork. Cover and refrigerate until ready to use. Beat again with fork to loosen mixture before using.

To make sauce, simmer mushroom juice, beef bouillon, and tomato paste together for 1 hour. When reduced to about 2 cups, thicken with cornstarch which has been mixed with the remaining Madeira. Salt and pepper to taste. Heat before serving and pour into preheated gravy boat.

Have the butcher trim the tough membrane from the tenderloin and save the suet. Have the tail of the filet tucked under the meat and tie at intervals to hold the meat in an oval shape. Have the filet at room tem-

Recipe continues . . .

perature and rub with oil. Cover with the suet and place in a shallow baking pan. Roast at 500° for 15 minutes, then let cool for at least 30 minutes.

Roll out the patty shells or puff pastry about ¼ inch thick, making one long piece of pastry large enough to wrap the beef. Cut off the ends and save for decorations. Spread the center of the pastry with half the mushroom mixture, leaving the sides free for wrapping the beef. Remove the string from the filet and spread the remaining mushroom mixture on top of the filet. Place the filet on the pastry. You now have the mushrooms on both the top and bottom of the filet. Wrap the beef with the pastry very carefully, as if you were wrapping a package. Seal the seam and ends with a beaten egg mixed with the water.

Cut leaves, flowers, diamonds, etc. with small hors d'oeuvre cutters for top of the Wellington. Carefully turn your Wellington so that the seam is on the underside. Cut diagonal slits about 2 inches apart down the length of the Wellington, decorate with pastry decorations, and paint the Wellington with the egg-water glaze. Bake for 20 minutes in the middle of a preheated 425° oven, or until the pastry begins to brown. Lower oven to 375° and bake for 20 minutes more. Allow to rest a few minutes before carving.

To serve, carve in 1½-inch-thick slices, using a sharp serrated knife. Serve with Madeira Sauce, fresh green beans, and sautéed cherry tomatoes.

YIELD: 8 SERVINGS

Epicure
THE JUNIOR LEAGUE OF NEWPORT HARBOR, CALIFORNIA

.   .   .   .

Tenderloin Deluxe

2-pounds tenderloin of beef
2 tablespoons softened butter
¼ cup chopped green onion
¾ cup dry sherry
2 tablespoons soy sauce
1 teaspoon Dijon mustard
Dash freshly ground black pepper

Spread meat with all but about 1 teaspoon of the butter. Place on a rack in a roasting pan. Roast, uncovered, in a preheated 400° oven for 20 minutes.

While tenderloin roasts, cook onion in remaining butter in a small saucepan. Stir in sherry, soy sauce, mustard, and pepper. Heat and pour over meat. Roast 20–25 minutes longer, basting frequently.

Serve sauce remaining in roasting pan with the meat.

YIELD: 4–6 SERVINGS

THE JUNIOR LEAGUE OF LONG BEACH, CALIFORNIA

·   ·   ·   ·   ·   ·   ·   ·   ·   ·   ·   ·   ·   ·   ·   ·   ·

Peppered Roast Beef

½ cup cracked peppercorns
½ teaspoon ground cardamom
5–6-pound boneless beef roast
2 tablespoons tomato paste
¾ cup red wine vinegar
½ teaspoon garlic powder
1 cup soy sauce
1 teaspoon paprika

Mix pepper and cardamom; rub well into all surfaces of meat, using heel of hand. Make a marinade of remaining ingredients. Marinate beef in refrigerator overnight, basting now and then.

Remove from the refrigerator 2–3 hours before putting in oven. Remove meat from marinade and wrap in aluminum foil. Roast in a shallow pan at 300° for 2 hours for rare meat, or until meat thermometer indicates proper temperature. When done, open foil. Brown, uncovered, at 350° while making gravy—if desired.

Especially good served with wild rice.

YIELD: 8–10 SERVINGS

THE JUNIOR LEAGUE OF OGDEN, UTAH

·   ·   ·   ·   ·   ·   ·   ·   ·   ·   ·   ·   ·   ·   ·   ·   ·

B-B-Q Brisket

Salt and pepper
4 pounds beef brisket or chuck
2 tablespoons liquid smoke
1 cup water
B-B-Q Sauce

Salt and pepper the meat. Mix liquid smoke and water. Pour over meat in heavy casserole and let stand overnight.

Cover and cook at 250° for 4 hours. Pour off liquid, slice meat thinly. Return slices to casserole, add B-B-Q Sauce, and bake, uncovered, for ½ hour longer.

YIELD: 4–6 SERVINGS

B-B-Q SAUCE:
¾ cup sugar
1 teaspoon salt
1 teaspoon ginger
½ cup soy sauce
½ cup sherry
½ cup catsup
2 cloves garlic, minced

Mix together all ingredients. Refrigerate until ready to use.

Sauce keeps for weeks and can be used on other meats, too.

YIELD: 1 PINT

THE JUNIOR LEAGUE OF BILLINGS, MONTANA

Oven-Baked Deep-Pit Barbeque

6–10 pound beef chuck roast
2 teaspoons liquid smoke (optional)
Salt
Pepper
Garlic salt

Rub meat with liquid smoke, then with salt, pepper, and garlic salt. Wrap tightly in heavy foil; place in roasting pan. Roast in slow 200° oven for at least 12 hours.

Serve with Salsa Sauce.

YIELD: 10–15 SERVINGS

SALSA SAUCE:
3 1-pound 12-ounce cans stewed tomatoes
2 4-ounce cans chopped green chilies
4 red onions, coarsely chopped
4 bunches green onions, including tops, coarsely chopped
Garlic salt to taste
Salt and pepper to taste

Mix ingredients together; let blend. Serve with beef.

YIELD: 15–20 SERVINGS

THE JUNIOR LEAGUE OF BAKERSFIELD, CALIFORNIA

Canadian Spiced Beef

3–7 cloves garlic
5 tablespoons mixed pickling spice
5 tablespoons sugar
3 tablespoons salt
2 teaspoons saltpeter
¼ teaspoon cinnamon
Meat tenderizer
5–7 pounds whole, boned beef brisket

Mix garlic with all spices in blender to the consistency of sugar.

Sprinkle meat with the spice mixture and rub in thoroughly all over. Wrap meat in wax paper, then in brown paper, then in foil, and finally put it in a plastic bag and twist to close. Store in refrigerator for 14 days.

Unwrap and cook in shallow pan with all the spice mixture and a small amount of water, lightly covered with foil, for 2½ hours at 300°–325°. Cool.

When cool, slice paper-thin. Can be reheated in foil or chafing dish. Serve warm with rye bread and mustard. Makes fantastic sandwiches.

YIELD: 12–20 SERVINGS

THE JUNIOR LEAGUE OF CALGARY, ALBERTA

·　·　·　·　·　·　·　·　·　·　·　·　·　·　·　·

Yang's Pot Roast

3 ounces oil
2 onions, coarsely chopped
Salt and pepper
3-pound boneless rump roast
2 carrots, broken
2 potatoes, peeled
2 tomatoes
8 ounces beef consommé
¾ cup water

Heat oil in heavy kettle and in it brown onions. Set onions aside. Salt and pepper the roast and brown it on all four sides in oil remaining in kettle. Add onions and other ingredients and cook for 2 hours over medium heat.

After 2 hours, purée the vegetables and liquid in a blender for sauce. Pour puréed vegetable sauce back over pot roast and cook ½ hour longer. Serve with buttered noodles.

YIELD: 6 SERVINGS

THE JUNIOR LEAGUE OF LOS ANGELES, CALIFORNIA

Marinated Pepper Steaks

¼ cup olive oil
1 tablespoon crushed peppercorns
2 teaspoons salt
2 teaspoons paprika
1 teaspoon crushed rosemary
1 teaspoon minced garlic
6 1½-inch-thick club steaks

Combine olive oil, peppercorns, salt, paprika, rosemary, and garlic and rub into the steaks. Marinate in the refrigerator for 24 hours. Broil for 7 minutes on each side, or until done to taste.

YIELD: 6 SERVINGS

THE JUNIOR LEAGUE OF SAN DIEGO, CALIFORNIA

Baked Steak

3¼-pound top sirloin steak or Châteaubriand, 2 inches thick
Salt and pepper to taste
3 tablespoons catsup
2½ tablespoons Worcestershire sauce
Juice of ½ lemon
1 lemon, sliced
Whole mushrooms (optional)
Onions, peeled and parboiled (optional)

Place steak in shallow baking pan; season with salt and pepper. Combine catsup, Worcestershire sauce, and lemon juice and pour over steak. Do not marinate! Arrange lemon slices on top. Place mushrooms and onions in the pan around the steak.

Place pan in middle of preheated 500° oven. Cook 30 minutes for rare, 45 minutes for medium-done meat. Turn onions and mushrooms once or twice.

YIELD: 4 SERVINGS

No Regrets
THE JUNIOR LEAGUE OF PORTLAND, OREGON

. . . .

Chinese Pepper Steak

1½-pound ½-inch-thick sirloin, cut into thin strips
½ teaspoon salt
2 onions, chopped
1 cup beef broth
2 tablespoons soy sauce
1 clove garlic, minced
2 green peppers, cut in 1-inch pieces
2 tablespoons cornstarch
¼ cup cold water

Grease skillet with a little of the fat from the meat. Brown meat strips quickly over high heat. Reduce heat and season meat with salt. Add onions and cook until onions are tender. Stir in broth, soy sauce, and garlic. Cover and simmer 10 minutes. Add green pepper; cover and simmer for 3 minutes, or until green pepper is crisply tender. Blend cornstarch and water and gradually stir into meat mixture. Cook, stirring, until sauce thickens.

Serve over hot cooked rice.

YIELD: 6 SERVINGS

THE JUNIOR LEAGUE OF BUTTE, MONTANA

. . . .

Chinese Beef

½–1 pound fresh mushrooms, sliced
Butter
2 tablespoons oil
¼-inch ginger root, peeled and thinly sliced
1½–2-pound flank steak
2 pounds fresh green beans, trimmed and Frenched
1 cup chopped green onion tops
3–4 cups water
4 tablespoons soy sauce
1 tablespoon beef bouillon

Brown mushrooms in butter and set aside. In skillet heat oil. When very hot, fry ginger for 1 minute. Turn heat to low.

Slice flank steak on the bias very thinly. It will slice more easily if partially frozen. Turn heat to high; put meat in, stir until brown.

Add green beans, mushrooms, and green onions. Add water, soy sauce, and bouillon. Cover; cook on highest heat for 20 minutes.

Serve over cooked rice.

YIELD: 4 SERVINGS

THE JUNIOR LEAGUE OF LONG BEACH, CALIFORNIA

. . . .

Fantastic Flank Steak

¼ cup soy sauce
3 tablespoons honey
2 tablespoons vinegar
1½ teaspoons garlic powder
1½ teaspoons powdered ginger
¾ cup salad oil
1 small onion, chopped
2-pound flank steak

Combine all marinade ingredients, pour over the flank steak, and marinate in refrigerator 1–3 days.

Bring steak to room temperature a few hours before cooking. Broil or barbecue 5 minutes per side. Slice thinly on the diagonal.

YIELD: 4–6 SERVINGS

THE JUNIOR LEAGUE OF SAN JOSE, CALIFORNIA

· · · · · · · · · · · · · · · · · · · ·

Long Beach Flank Steak

2-pound flank steak
1 cup peanut oil
1 cup soy sauce
2 cups apple cider or beer
1 small clove garlic, minced
Juice of 1 lemon
2 teaspoons horseradish

Wipe meat with a damp cloth. Combine oil, soy sauce, cider or beer, garlic, lemon juice, and horseradish. Pour this marinade over steak in low oblong ovenproof dish. Let stand for at least 3 hours.

Cook meat on barbecue or grill, for 8 minutes each side for medium; more or less as desired. Cut on diagonal when carved.

YIELD: 6 SERVINGS

THE JUNIOR LEAGUE OF LONG BEACH, CALIFORNIA

· ·

Beef in Burgundy

2 pounds lean beef, chuck or round, cut in 1½-inch pieces
⅓ cup flour
2 teaspoons salt
¼ teaspoon pepper
⅓ cup vegetable oil
¼ pound bacon, diced
1 onion, chopped
2 carrots, chopped
1 clove garlic, minced
1 6-ounce can tomato paste
2 cups water
1 cup Burgundy
¼ cup minced parsley
1 bay leaf
1 teaspoon thyme
1 pound small white onions
½ pound fresh mushrooms

Coat beef with mixture of flour, salt, and pepper. Brown meat in oil in large skillet. Pour off fat and transfer meat to large casserole. Add bacon to skillet; brown lightly. Add chopped onion, carrot, and garlic. Cook for about 5 minutes. Add onion mixture to meat along with tomato paste, water, Burgundy, parsley, bay leaf and thyme.

Bake, covered, at 350° for 2 hours, or until meat is tender. Discard

Recipe continues . . .

bay leaf and skim fat from surface. Add whole onions and mushrooms, cover, and bake for 30 minutes longer.

YIELD: 6 SERVINGS

THE JUNIOR LEAGUE OF BUTTE, MONTANA

Beer Beef Curry

2 pounds round steak, cut in ½ x 2-inch strips
1 onion, chopped
4 tablespoons butter
1 teaspoon salt
1 12-ounce can beer
1 tablespoon curry powder
½ cup chopped apple
½ cup shredded coconut
¼ cup chopped almonds

Brown meat and onion in butter. Add salt, beer, and curry. Simmer 45 minutes, uncovered. Add the apple, coconut, and almonds and cook 15 minutes longer.

Serve on a bed of cooked rice.

YIELD: 6 SERVINGS

THE JUNIOR LEAGUE OF BOISE, IDAHO

Hungarian Goulash

2 pounds round steak, cubed
¼ cup shortening
1 onion, sliced
1 green pepper, diced
2 teaspoons paprika
2 teaspoons salt
1 28-ounce can whole tomatoes
2 tablespoons flour
¼ cup water

Brown beef in hot shortening. Add onion and green pepper; cook until vegetables are tender. Add seasonings. Add tomatoes with liquid and simmer 2–2½ hours, or until meat is tender.

Blend flour and water; stir into meat mixture. Heat to boiling, stirring constantly.

Serve over rice, noodles, or mashed potatoes.

YIELD: 4–6 SERVINGS

A Taste of Oregon
THE JUNIOR LEAGUE OF EUGENE, OREGON

Estofado Sonorense

4 tablespoons lard or oil
2 pounds lean stew meat, cubed
1 large onion, finely chopped
1 16-ounce can tomatoes and juice
½ cup tomato sauce
1 4-ounce can green chilies (remove seeds and veins, chop)
1 clove garlic, minced
1 teaspoon oregano
1 tablespoon sugar
¼ teaspoon cumin
Salt and pepper to taste
½ cup red wine
3 medium potatoes, peeled and sliced
2 zucchini, sliced
1 cup sliced green beans

Heat lard or oil in heavy kettle and brown meat over moderate heat. Remove from kettle, add onion, and sauté until onion is lightly browned. Add meat, tomatoes, tomato sauce, chilies, all spices, and wine. Reduce heat, cover, and simmer gently 1–1½ hours, or until meat is fork tender. Add liquid if needed to keep from sticking.

The last 30 minutes of cooking, add vegetables, cover, and cook until vegetables are tender.

Serve with tortillas.

Note: This stew is very popular in northern Mexico. Corn on the cob, peas, and chili pods are added according to their availability and the cook's taste.

YIELD: 4–6 SERVINGS

THE JUNIOR LEAGUE OF TUCSON, ARIZONA

Carbonades à la Flamande
(Beer Stew)

4 pounds stew meat, cut into ½-inch cubes
½ cup flour
½ cup cooking oil
2 pounds onions, thickly sliced
6 cloves garlic, minced
3 tablespoons dark brown sugar
¼ cup red wine vinegar
½ cup chopped parsley
2 small bay leaves
2 teaspoons powdered thyme
1 teaspoon salt
Black pepper to taste
2 10½-ounce cans beef consommé
2 12-ounce cans beer
Packaged dumpling mix

Dredge meat in flour a few pieces at a time and brown evenly in large heavy skillet in hot oil. Do not crowd pan as this will prevent browning. As each batch is done, remove meat to a large casserole (about 5 quarts). Add onions and garlic to oil in pan and cook, stirring, until onions are limp and transparent (more oil might be needed). Empty onions on top of meat in casserole.

Add next seven ingredients to skillet and stir in enough beef broth to make a sauce. Cook, scraping up all browned bits from bottom and sides of skillet. Pour over onions and meat. Pour remaining beef broth and the 2 cans of beer on top. Cover and cook in 325° oven for 2 hours.

Prepare dumpling batter as per package directions. Remove casserole from oven to top of stove over medium heat. Drop batter by spoonfuls on hot stew; cover and simmer for 15 minutes.

Good also if served over buttered noodles in place of dumplings.

YIELD: 8–10 SERVINGS

THE JUNIOR LEAGUE OF SAN DIEGO, CALIFORNIA

Beef and Coffee

3 pounds lean beef, cubed
¾ cup flour
Salt and pepper to taste
½ cup cooking oil
1 cup dry red wine
3 cloves garlic, minced
2 medium onions, sliced
½ cup strong black coffee
2 cups fresh, chopped mushrooms
1 tablespoon Worcestershire sauce
1 pint sour cream

Put meat, flour, and salt and pepper in a paper bag. Shake until meat is evenly coated. Heat some of the oil in a skillet and brown the meat over medium heat. Add more oil as needed, placing browned meat in a 3-quart casserole as it is browned. Add remaining ingredients except the sour cream. Bake at 350° for 2 hours. Remove from oven. Cool and refrigerate until needed, or overnight.

One hour before serving, blend in sour cream. Reheat in 350° oven for ½ hour.

Serve over rice or noodles.

YIELD: 6–8 SERVINGS

THE JUNIOR LEAGUE OF SAN DIEGO, CALIFORNIA

Wine-Country Stew

2–3 pounds top sirloin, cut in 2-inch pieces
2 tablespoons bacon drippings
½ pound Westphalian ham, cut in 1-inch pieces
2 large onions, chopped
25 stuffed green olives, halved
5 cloves garlic, wrapped in cheesecloth
¾ teaspoon dried thyme
½ cup raisins, soaked in hot water for 5 minutes and drained
1 bottle (but not more than 3 cups) Petite Sirah, Zinfandel, or
any full-bodied red wine
2 tablespoons green peppercorns or 2 teaspoons freshly ground pepper
1 teaspoon salt
4 tablespoons brandy
¾ cup heavy cream
Flour and water

In a heavy 12-inch skillet brown the beef in the bacon drippings over moderate-high heat for 3–5 minutes. Add the ham and onions and sauté 3–4 minutes, or until golden brown. Transfer meat, onions, and ham to a large Dutch oven. Add the olives, garlic, thyme, raisins, and wine. Cover and bake in a preheated 350° oven for 40 minutes. Add the peppercorns, salt, brandy, and cream and cook 30 minutes longer. Strain the juices from the pot and reserve. Discard the garlic cloves.

Transfer meat mixture to a serving dish and keep warm. Return the juices to the pot. For each cup of juice mix 1½ tablespoons flour with 3 tablespoons water until smooth. Add this to the juices, stirring with a wire whisk over moderate heat 2–3 minutes, or until thickened. Continue cooking over low heat for another 5 minutes. Pour over the meat and serve with cooked rice and a buttered vegetable.

YIELD: 4–6 SERVINGS

The California Heritage Cookbook
THE JUNIOR LEAGUE OF PASADENA, CALIFORNIA

· · · · · · · · · · · · · ·

Crocked Beef

Flour
3–4 pounds beef stew meat, cubed
1 12-ounce can beer
1 cup diced ham
1 bay leaf
2 cups sliced mushrooms
½ medium onion, chopped
Pepper to taste
Salt to taste

Flour beef cubes. Place in greased slow-cooking crockery pot. Add all other ingredients except salt. Cook on low 8–10 hours. Salt to taste before serving.

Serve with sourdough bread and green salad.

YIELD: 6–8 SERVINGS

THE JUNIOR LEAGUE OF RIVERSIDE, CALIFORNIA

Sangre de Cristo Stewpot

2 pounds beef stew meat, cubed
4 cups water
2 beef bouillon cubes
½ cup coarsely chopped celery
½ cup coarsely chopped onion
2 cloves garlic, minced
1 tablespoon oregano
2 teaspoons cumin
1 bay leaf
1½ teaspoons salt
5 carrots, cut in chunks
4 ears of corn, cut in 2-inch pieces
1 15-ounce can garbanzo beans, undrained
8 cabbage wedges

Put first nine ingredients in a large Dutch oven and cook for 2 hours, or until meat is tender. Stir in the salt, carrots, corn, and garbanzo beans and gently lay the cabbage wedges on top. Cover and simmer for 30 minutes.
Serve in bowls and pass the sauce to spoon over each serving.

YIELD: 8 SERVINGS

CHILI SALSA:
1 16-ounce can tomatoes, drained and chopped
½ cup finely chopped onion
1 4-ounce can chopped green chilies
1 clove garlic, minced
½ cup chopped parsley
½ teaspoon salt

Mix all ingredients together.

Gourmet Olé
THE JUNIOR LEAGUE OF ALBUQUERQUE, NEW MEXICO

Boeuf en Daube
(French Stew)

3 pounds lean round of beef
¼ cup flour
1 teaspoon pepper
½ teaspoon salt
6 slices bacon
2 cloves garlic, finely minced
2 tablespoons warmed brandy
12 small mushrooms, sliced
1 10½-ounce can beef bouillon
1 cup red table wine
12 pearl onions, peeled
12 small carrots, sliced
6 peppercorns, slightly bruised
4 whole cloves
2 tablespoons chopped fresh parsley
1 bay leaf, crumbled
1 teaspoon salt
¼ teaspoon dried marjoram
¼ teaspoon dried thyme
½ cup red table wine

Cut beef into 1-inch cubes. Mix flour, pepper, and ½ teaspoon salt in a paper bag. Add beef cubes and shake. Remove cubes. Set aside.

Fry bacon until brown (not crisp). Remove bacon from skillet, leaving drippings. Cut bacon into 1-inch pieces. Set aside.

Add beef and garlic to skillet. Brown beef quickly on all sides. Pour warm brandy into skillet. Set on fire. When flame dies, remove meat. Put meat on top of bacon in casserole dish.

Brown mushrooms lightly. Layer over meat. Add bouillon and the one cup of wine to skillet. Bring to a boil, stirring to loosen bits from pan bottom. Pour liquid into casserole. Add onions, carrots, peppercorns, cloves, parsley, bay leaf, 1 teaspoon salt, marjoram, and thyme. Pour in remaining ½ cup wine. Cover tightly. Bake at 300° for 3 hours.

YIELD: 8 SERVINGS

Heritage Cookbook
THE JUNIOR LEAGUE OF SALT LAKE CITY, UTAH

· · · · · · · · · · · · · · · · · · · ·

Korean BBQ Beef Strips

⅓ cup soy sauce
2 tablespoons sugar
4 tablespoons white wine
4 tablespoons roasted and crushed sesame seeds
4 tablespoons water
4 tablespoons sesame oil
1 clove garlic, minced
2 green onions, chopped
¼ teaspoon pepper
·1 1 x 2-inch section fresh ginger root, chopped
2-pound cross rib roast, thinly sliced

Combine all ingredients except meat. Place meat in marinade for 2–3 hours. Weave onto skewers and barbecue or broil 3 minutes per side.

YIELD: 4 SERVINGS

THE JUNIOR LEAGUE OF SAN JOSE, CALIFORNIA

· · · · · · · · · · · · · · · · · · · ·

Special Beef Parmesan

1½ pounds round steak or chuck
1 egg
⅓ cup Parmesan cheese
⅓ cup bread crumbs
⅓ cup oil
½ cup chopped onion
1 teaspoon each salt and pepper
¼ cup sugar
1 6-ounce can tomato paste
2 cups hot water
½ pound mozzarella cheese, shredded

Trim fat from meat and cut meat into 6–8 pieces. Place between wax paper and strike with bottom of a large pan to flatten them, or use a meat pounder.

Beat egg with a fork. Mix Parmesan and bread crumbs. Dip meat in egg, then the bread mixture. Brown meat in a skillet in the oil, then transfer to a 9 x 13-inch baking dish.

In oil remaining in skillet, sauté onion until transparent. Add salt, pepper, sugar, tomato paste, and water. Boil 5 minutes and pour two-thirds of sauce over meat. Cover with mozzarella and top with remaining sauce.

Bake at 300° for 1½ hours.

YIELD: 6 SERVINGS

A Taste of Oregon
THE JUNIOR LEAGUE OF EUGENE, OREGON

Boeuf Bourguignon, Canadian-Style

4 pounds lean sirloin
6 slices bacon
2 cloves garlic, minced
2 pounds mushrooms, sliced
2 bay leaves, crushed
2 tablespoons chopped parsley
1 teaspoon salt
1 teaspoon thyme
⅛ teaspoon pepper
½ cup butter
½ cup flour
2 10-ounce cans beef consommé
¾ cup red wine

Cut meat in strips with the grain. In a large deep skillet or chicken fryer, fry bacon until crisp. Remove. Sauté the meat in same skillet, then add garlic and mushrooms. Season with bay leaves, parsley, salt, thyme and pepper. Turn off heat.

In a saucepan make a roux with butter and flour. Cook, stirring, until mixture turns brown. Add consommé, stir and cook until sauce is thick. Pour over beef and mushrooms. Cover and simmer for 1 hour, then add wine and simmer for half an hour longer, or refrigerate after cooking for 30 minutes. Before serving add wine, bring to a simmer, and cook for about 1 hour.

YIELD: 8–10 SERVINGS

THE JUNIOR LEAGUE OF CALGARY, ALBERTA

Chinese Beef-Tomato

¾-pound round steak

3 tablespoons dark soy sauce

1 tablespoon water

1 tablespoon peanut oil

2 tablespoons cornstarch

1 teaspoon sugar

1 clove garlic, minced

1 slice fresh ginger, shredded, or ¼ teaspoon ground ginger

1 cup water

3 tablespoons soy sauce

1 tablespoon sherry

1 teaspoon salt

2 teaspoons sugar

⅛ teaspoon monosodium glutamate

1 onion, sliced into wedges

1 cup diagonally sliced celery

1 green pepper, seeded and sliced into wedges

4 tablespoons peanut oil

½ teaspoon salt

2 tablespoons water

2 fresh tomatoes, sliced into wedges

Thinly slice round steak against the grain into strips (it is easier to slice the meat if partially frozen). Combine dark soy sauce, 1 tablespoon each water, peanut oil and cornstarch, 1 teaspoon sugar, the garlic, and ginger. Marinate meat in this mixture for 30 minutes.

Combine remaining cornstarch, the 1 cup water, soy sauce, sherry, salt, sugar, and monosodium glutamate and set aside.

Heat wok. Stir-fry onion, celery, and green pepper in 2 tablespoons peanut oil. While cooking vegetables, season with the ½ teaspoon salt. Add the 2 tablespoons water, cover, and steam 2 minutes at medium heat. Set vegetables aside.

To oil remaining in the wok add remaining peanut oil and the garlic from the marinade. Cook 1 minute. Discard garlic and add meat. Turn with spatula when brown on one side. Brown other side of meat. Set meat aside.

Pour cornstarch mixture into wok and stir over medium heat. Cook until it bubbles and thickens. Add cooked vegetables and meat and uncooked tomatoes. Cook over medium heat for 2 minutes.

Serve with cooked rice.

YIELD: 2 SERVINGS

THE JUNIOR LEAGUE OF OAKLAND-EAST BAY, CALIFORNIA

· · · · · · · · · · · · · · · · ·

Sukiyaki I

1 bunch green onions, sliced in 2-inch lengths
½–1 pound fresh mushrooms, sliced
½ pound fresh bean sprouts
1 8-ounce can bamboo shoots, sliced
1½–2 pounds top round or sirloin tip, thinly sliced
1½ cups soy sauce
½ cup sugar
⅓–½ cup chicken broth

Place onions on bottom of a heavy pan. Arrange other vegetables on top. Place sliced meat on top of vegetables. Pour soy sauce, sugar, and broth over all. Cover; turn heat on medium-high. Do not stir, but occasionally turn meat. Cook until meat is done, about 4–5 minutes.

Serve with cooked rice.

YIELD: 4 SERVINGS

THE JUNIOR LEAGUE OF OGDEN, UTAH

· · · · · · · · · · · · · ·

Sukiyaki II

3 pounds top sirloin, thinly sliced
1½ tablespoons salad oil
4 large stalks celery, sliced diagonally
1 green pepper, sliced diagonally
1 8-ounce can bamboo shoots
2 medium onions, thinly sliced
4 tablespoons soy sauce
2 cups beef boullion
1 teaspoon monosodium glutamate
2 tablespoons sake wine
3 tablespoons sugar
½ cup butter
1 8-ounce can sliced mushrooms
1 bunch green onions, sliced in 2-inch pieces

Brown meat lightly in large heavy skillet with the oil. When meat is rare-brown add celery, green pepper, bamboo shoots, and onions. Cook for 5 minutes with soy sauce, bouillon, monosodium glutamate, sake, and sugar. Add green onions, mushrooms, and butter. Cook, covered, for 1 more minute.

Serve over cooked rice.

For a party, add salted almonds and sliced water chestnuts.

YIELD: 8 SERVINGS

THE JUNIOR LEAGUE OF OGDEN, UTAH

California Chunky Chili

4 medium tomatoes, peeled and coarsely chopped
1½ cups water
1 large onion, chopped
2 stalks celery, chopped
½ teaspoon salt
½ teaspoon pepper
1 medium onion, chopped
1 green pepper, seeded and chopped
2 cloves garlic, minced
4 tablespoons lard or bacon drippings
2 pounds round steak, trimmed and cut into ¼-inch cubes
1 pound lean pork, cut into ¼-inch cubes
1 tablespoon flour
5 tablespoons chili powder
2 bay leaves
1 teaspoon salt
1 tablespoon brown sugar
1 tablespoon dried oregano
1 tablespoon red wine vinegar
1 cup pitted ripe olives, coarsely chopped
1 cup shredded Monterey Jack cheese

Simmer the tomatoes, water, the large onion, celery, ½ teaspoon salt, and pepper in a medium saucepan for 30 minutes covered and another 30 minutes uncovered. Set aside.

In a large Dutch oven sauté the medium onion, green pepper, and garlic in the lard for 3–5 minutes over moderate heat. With a slotted spoon remove the vegetables from the pan and set aside.

Add the meats to the Dutch oven and brown over moderate-high heat for 5–8 minutes. Add more lard if necessary. Add the flour to the browned meat, stirring well. Simmer for 2 minutes.

Return the vegetable mixture to the Dutch oven and add the chili

Recipe continues . . .

powder, bay leaves, 1 teaspoon salt, brown sugar, oregano, and vinegar. Add the tomato sauce. Cover and simmer over low heat for 2 hours.

Add the olives and cheese and simmer, covered, for an additional 45 minutes, stirring occasionally. Discard bay leaves.

Serve in chili bowls with a side dish of finely chopped onions, a tossed salad and hot corn bread.

Note: The flavor of this dish is enhanced if it is made 24 hours in advance.

YIELD: 6 SERVINGS

The California Heritage Cookbook
THE JUNIOR LEAGUE OF PASADENA, CALIFORNIA

. . . .

Chasen's Chili

¾ pound dried pinto beans
5 cups canned tomatoes
1 green pepper, chopped
¼ cup salad oil
1 pound onions, chopped (3 medium)
2 cloves garlic, minced
½ cup chopped parsley
½ cup butter
2½ pounds ground round
1 pound lean ground pork
½–¾ tablespoon chili powder
1 tablespoon salt
1½ teaspoons pepper
1½ teaspoons cumin seed
Diced onion and corn chips for garnish

Wash beans. Soak overnight in water. Cover and simmer slowly in same water for 1½ hours, or until tender. Add tomatoes and simmer 5 minutes.

In skillet sauté green pepper in salad oil for 5 minutes. Add onions and cook until tender, stirring often. Add garlic and parsley to onion mixture.

In another skillet melt butter and sauté meat for 15 minutes. Add meat to onion mixture, stir in chili powder, and cook 10 minutes. Add this mixture to the beans. Add remaining spices. Cover and simmer slowly for 1 hour. Cook, uncovered, for 30 minutes. Skim fat from surface.

Serve with diced onions and corn chips.

YIELD: 6 SERVINGS

Something New Under the Sun
THE JUNIOR LEAGUE OF PHOENIX, ARIZONA

.   .   .   .

Susie's Chili

2 pounds ground beef
1 medium onion, diced
2 cloves garlic, minced
Salt and pepper to taste
2 32-ounce cans stewed tomatoes
2 32-ounce cans chili with beans
2 cups hot water
2 teaspoons ground oregano
1 teaspoon cumin seed
1 teaspoon Tabasco
2 teaspoons Worcestershire sauce

In heavy saucepan brown beef, onion, garlic, and salt and pepper together.

Add the remaining ingredients and simmer for at least 4 hours, adding a little more water from time to time if needed.

YIELD: 8 SERVINGS

THE JUNIOR LEAGUE OF BUTTE, MONTANA

.   .   .   .

Hamburger Cheese Bake

1 pound ground beef
½ teaspoon garlic salt
½ teaspoon salt
½ teaspoon pepper
1 teaspoon sugar
2 8-ounce cans tomato sauce
4 ounces cream cheese, softened
1 cup sour cream
4 green onions, chopped
1 7-ounce package noodles
¾ cup shredded cheddar cheese

In skillet combine ground beef, garlic salt, salt, pepper, sugar, and tomato sauce. Bring to a boil and simmer for 20 minutes.

Mix cream cheese, sour cream, and green onions.

Cook noodles according to package directions. Drain and empty into a 7½ x 11½-inch shallow casserole. Cover with meat-cheese mixture and top with cheddar cheese. Bake at 350° for 30 minutes.

YIELD: 4 SERVINGS

THE JUNIOR LEAGUE OF BUTTE, MONTANA

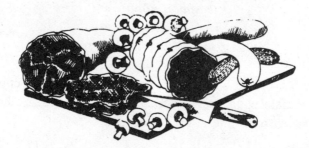

Alfred Lunt's Meat Loaf

1½ pounds lean ground chuck
Salt and pepper
½ cup raw rice
2 tablespoons butter
1 onion, chopped
1½ cups coarsely shredded green cabbage or unpeeled zucchini
1 cup sour cream
½ cup strong chicken broth
Paprika
Chopped parsley

Line the sides and bottom of a 9-inch pie plate with raw meat. Sprinkle with salt and pepper.

Cook the rice according to package directions. In the butter, sauté the onion until soft and combine with the rice and vegetable. Mix in the sour cream and season lightly. Put sour cream mixture in the meat shell. Just before baking, pour over chicken stock or as much as the dish will hold. Bake at 375° for 40–45 minutes.

Sprinkle with paprika and chopped parsley. Cut into wedges to serve.

YIELD: 6 SERVINGS

THE JUNIOR LEAGUE OF SACRAMENTO, CALIFORNIA

Stuffed Hamburgers

2 pounds lean ground round
1¾ cups tomato juice
¼ cup moist bread crumbs
1 egg
¼ cup red cooking wine
1 tablespoon instant minced onion
1 teaspoon salt
2 tablespoons butter
¼ teaspoon fines herbes
2 teaspoons cornstarch
2 tablespoons water

Mix meat with ¼ cup of the tomato juice, the bread crumbs, egg, wine, onion, and salt. Divide into twelve equal parts and flatten into circles. Place 1 tablespoon of filling on one side of each of the meat circles. Press meat mixture around filling.

In large skillet, sauté the hamburgers in butter until browned on both sides. Add remaining tomato juice and herbs, cover, and simmer for ½ hour. Blend cornstarch and water, add to skillet and cook, stirring until thick. Add more tomato juice if more gravy is desired.

FILLING:
1 cup thinly sliced fresh mushrooms
3 tablespoons butter
¼ cup moist bread crumbs
1 cup shredded Swiss cheese
¾ teaspoon fines herbes
1 teaspoon salt

Toss all filling ingredients lightly to combine.

YIELD: **6** GENEROUS SERVINGS

THE JUNIOR LEAGUE OF GREAT FALLS, MONTANA

· · · · · · · · · · · · · · · · · · · ·

Tamale Pie

1 medium onion, chopped
1 clove garlic, minced
2 tablespoons fat
1½ pounds lean ground beef
½ cup diced celery
¼ cup diced green pepper
1 14-ounce can whole kernel corn
1½ cups canned tomatoes
1 tablespoon chili powder
2 teaspoons salt
¼ teaspoon allspice
1 teaspoon cumin
¼ teaspoon freshly ground black pepper
1 cup shredded cheddar cheese

Cook onion and garlic in very hot fat for 5 minutes. Add ground beef and brown nicely. Add remaining ingredients, except cheese, and simmer for 10 minutes.

Line bottom and sides of a 2-quart casserole with corn meal mixture. Pour in meat filling. Bake at 350° for 45 minutes. Sprinkle with cheese and bake for 15 minutes more.

CORN MEAL CRUST:
1 cup corn meal
2 teaspoons salt
2½ cups boiling water
2 tablespoons butter
½ cup grated cheese

Stir corn meal and salt into boiling water. Cook until thickened, stirring constantly. Stir in butter and cook over hot water for 20 minutes.

YIELD: 6–8 SERVINGS

THE JUNIOR LEAGUE OF CALGARY, ALBERTA

· · · · · · · · · · · · · · ·

Hamburger Stroganoff

1 pound ground beef
1 cup chopped onion
1 cup sliced fresh mushrooms
1 clove garlic, minced
2 tablespoons chopped parsley
½ teaspoon dill weed
½ teaspoon salt
Pepper to taste
¾ cup beef broth
½ cup dry red wine
¼ cup catsup
1 cup sour cream
1 tablespoon flour
Grated Parmesan cheese

Brown beef with onion, mushrooms, and garlic. Stir in parsley, dill weed, salt, pepper, beef broth, wine, and catsup. Simmer for 10 minutes, stirring occasionally. Blend sour cream with the flour and stir into the meat mixture. Cook until very hot but do not boil.

Garnish with Parmesan cheese and serve over noodles.

YIELD: 4–6 SERVINGS

THE JUNIOR LEAGUE OF TACOMA, WASHINGTON

Mexican Sloppy Joes

1 pound ground round
1 onion, chopped
1 clove garlic, minced
1 tablespoon sugar
1 8-ounce can tomato sauce
1 6-ounce can tomato paste
1 6-ounce can water
1 teaspoon each oregano, chili powder, cumin, and salt

Combine all ingredients and simmer for 40 minutes. Serve as follows:
Start with a handful of tortilla chips.
Cover with meat sauce in amount desired.
Top with following condiments stacked high like a tostada—

Shredded lettuce
Shredded cheddar cheese
Chopped tomato
Chopped green onion
Chopped avocado
Sour cream
Chopped black olive

Arrange condiments in bowls and let each person build his own.

YIELD: 4—6 SERVINGS

From an Adobe Oven . . . to a Microwave Range
THE JUNIOR LEAGUE OF PUEBLO, COLORADO

Eldorado Casserole

1 pound ground beef
1 tablespoon chopped onion
1 teaspoon minced garlic
2 8-ounce cans tomato sauce
½ cup sliced olives
1 cup cottage cheese
1 cup sour cream
1 3½-ounce can whole chilies, seeded and chopped
¾ pound Monterey Jack cheese, shredded
½ pound tortilla chips

Mix ground beef, onion, and garlic in skillet. Cook until meat is browned. Add tomato sauce and sliced olives. Simmer for 10 minutes.

Mix cottage cheese, sour cream and chopped chilies.

Butter a 9 x 13-inch casserole and layer the ingredients in the following order: tortilla chips; meat sauce; cottage cheese mixture; Jack cheese. Repeat layers. Bake at 375° for 25–30 minutes.

YIELD: 6–8 SERVINGS

THE JUNIOR LEAGUE OF RIVERSIDE, CALIFORNIA

Mexi-Chili Casserole

1–1½ pounds ground beef
1 1-pound can kidney beans, drained
1 15-ounce can mild enchilada sauce
1 8-ounce can tomato sauce
1 tablespoon dried minced onion
1 6-ounce package corn chips
2 cups shredded cheddar cheese
1–1½ cups sour cream

In a skillet brown the ground beef. Drain off fat. Combine the beans, enchilada and tomato sauce in a bowl with minced onion.

Set aside 1 cup corn chips and ½ cup cheese. Add the remaining cheese and corn chips with the meat to the beans. Stir to blend. Empty into a lightly buttered 2-quart casserole. Bake, uncovered, at 375° for 20–25 minutes, or until heated through. Spread the top with the sour cream and sprinkle with the reserved cheese. Ring the remaining corn chips around the edge; return to the oven for 3–4 minutes, or until the cheese melts.

This will double or triple easily for a large group. May be made ahead and refrigerated.

YIELD: 4 SERVINGS

No Regrets
THE JUNIOR LEAGUE OF PORTLAND, OREGON

· · · · · · · · · · · · · · · · · ·

Chilaquilas
(Spicy Tortilla Casserole)

1 pound ground beef
1 medium onion
¼ teaspoon rosemary
½ teaspoon salt
⅛ teaspoon pepper
1 8-ounce can tomato sauce
1 19-ounce can enchilada sauce
½ pound cheddar cheese, sliced ¼ inch thick
8 corn tortillas
Ripe olives to garnish

In a large skillet cook ground beef and onion. Add seasonings and brown well.

In a saucepan, combine tomato sauce and enchilada sauce. Pour half

Recipe continues . . .

of the mixture over meat and seasonings. Simmer for 15 minutes. Simmer remaining sauce, also.

Place 4 corn tortillas in the bottom of a 9 x 9-inch or 10 x 10-inch casserole, overlapping. Pour meat mixture over tortillas. Top with half of the cheese slices. Top with remaining 4 tortillas and then remaining cheese slices. Pour sauce over all. Cover. Bake at 350° for 30 minutes. Garnish with ripe olives.

For a less spicy casserole, use 2 8-ounce cans tomato sauce and 1 10-ounce can enchilada sauce.

YIELD: 6 SERVINGS

THE JUNIOR LEAGUE OF RIVERSIDE, CALIFORNIA

· ·

Tortilla Beef Casserole

1½ pounds ground beef
1 onion, chopped
1 package dry taco seasoning
1 cup water
Garlic salt, salt, and pepper to taste
1 cup medium-hot red taco sauce
10 corn tortillas
2 10-ounce packages frozen chopped spinach
3 cups shredded Monterey Jack cheese
½ pound cooked ham, diced
1 cup sour cream

Cook ground beef with onion until meat is crumbly. Add taco seasoning and water. Cover and cook 10 minutes. Add salt, pepper, and garlic salt.

In a 9 x 13-inch casserole pour in ½ cup taco sauce. Turn 5 tortillas in it to coat and spread in bottom of dish.

Press water out of spinach. Add half of it to the beef mixture. Spoon mixture over tortillas. Sprinkle with half the cheese. Cover with remaining tortillas. Pour taco sauce over. Sprinkle diced ham on top. Spoon sour cream over and top with remaining spinach and cheese.

Cover and bake at 375° for 25 minutes. Uncover and bake for 25 minutes longer.

YIELD: 10–12 SERVINGS

THE JUNIOR LEAGUE OF LONG BEACH, CALIFORNIA

· ·

Swedish Meat Balls

2 eggs, beaten
1 cup milk
½ cup bread crumbs
½ cup chopped onion
3 tablespoons butter
1 pound ground beef
¼ pound ground pork
1 teaspoon salt
¼ teaspoon dill weed
¼ teaspoon allspice
⅛ teaspoon nutmeg
⅛ teaspoon cardamom
2 tablespoons oil
3 tablespoons flour
½ teaspoon dill weed
1 10½-ounce can beef consommé
½ cup cream

Combine eggs, milk, and bread crumbs. Set aside. Sauté onion in butter until onion is golden and stir into crumb mixture. Add beef, pork, and seasonings. Mix thoroughly. Refrigerate 1 hour, then shape into 1-inch balls. Sauté in oil in skillet until brown on all sides. Arrange in casserole as meat balls are done.

Stir flour into drippings remaining in skillet. Add ½ teaspoon dill

Recipe continues . . .

weed and gradually stir in consommé and cream. Cook, stirring, until sauce is thickened. Correct seasoning.

Pour sauce over meat balls and bake at 350° for 30 minutes, or until warm through.

Serve with rice, noodles, or mashed potatoes. Freezes well.

YIELD: 8–10 SERVINGS

THE JUNIOR LEAGUE OF VANCOUVER, BRITISH COLUMBIA

. . . .

Curried Meat Balls

1 onion finely chopped
3 tablespoons oil
3 tablespoons curry powder
¼ teaspoon coriander
¼ teaspoon cumin
¼ teaspoon dry mustard
¼ teaspoon mace
¼ teaspoon cloves
1 clove garlic, minced
¼ cup water
2 pounds ground beef
¾ cup bread crumbs
1½ teaspoons salt
¼ teaspoon pepper
1 8-ounce can tomato sauce
1½ cups water
½ teaspoon salt

In small skillet brown onion in 2 tablespoons of the oil. Mix the next seven ingredients together and stir in water to make a thin paste. Add to onion. Stir, brown, and set aside.

Mix ground beef, bread crumbs, the 1½ teaspoons salt, and pepper. Form into small balls. Heat remaining oil in a larger skillet and in it brown

the balls on all sides. Add tomato sauce, 1½ cups water, ½ teaspoon salt, and the browned spices. Blend until smooth. Cover and simmer 1 hour.
Serve over rice.

YIELD: 4—5 SERVINGS

THE JUNIOR LEAGUE OF TUCSON, ARIZONA

. . . .

Sweet-Sour Meat Balls

1½ pounds lean ground beef
½ pound ground pork
¾ cup fine dry bread crumbs
1 teaspoon salt
¼ teaspoon pepper
1 egg
½ cup milk

Combine all ingredients and mix thoroughly. Form into small meat balls, about the size of walnuts. Brown well in ¼ cup of hot cooking oil.
Add cooked meat balls to Sweet-Sour Sauce. Serve over hot rice.

SWEET-SOUR SAUCE:
1 20-ounce can sweetened pineapple chunks
¼ cup brown sugar
2 tablespoons cornstarch
¼ cup vinegar
2 tablespoons soy sauce
½ teaspoon salt
1 small green pepper, cut in strips
½ cup thinly sliced onion rings

Drain pineapple, reserving syrup. Combine brown sugar and cornstarch; add pineapple syrup, vinegar, soy sauce, and salt and heat until sauce

Recipe continues . . .

thickens, stirring constantly. Add pineapple, green pepper, and onion. Cook, stirring, for 2–3 minutes. *Do not overcook!*

YIELD: 6–8 SERVINGS

THE JUNIOR LEAGUE OF OGDEN, UTAH

. . . .

German Kraut Kuchen

1 cup milk
2 tablespoons butter
1 egg, beaten
2 tablespoons sugar
½ teaspoon salt
1 envelope active dry yeast
¼ cup warm water
3 cups flour
1 large onion, finely chopped
1 small green pepper, finely chopped
1 medium head cabbage, finely chopped
2 tablespoons cooking oil
1½ pounds ground beef
Salt
Pepper
1 stick butter, melted

Scald milk with butter. Cool to lukewarm. Add egg, sugar, salt, and yeast softened in the warm water. Stir in flour.

Let dough rise for 1 hour, then stir down. Roll out dough to about ½-inch thickness.

Sauté onion, green pepper, and cabbage in skillet with oil. Keep stirring and cooking until all is tender.

In another skillet, brown beef. Drain well, combine with the cabbage mixture, and add salt and pepper to taste.

Cut the dough into 3-inch squares; put a spoonful of cabbage and meat mixture on each. Fold together so mixture is sealed in. Dip each kuchen in melted butter, turn over to butter both sides, and place in large baking pan, allowing room for dough to rise. Pour over any remaining butter and let rise about ½ hour. Bake in 450° oven for 20 minutes.

YIELD: 10–12 SERVINGS

THE JUNIOR LEAGUE OF BILLINGS, MONTANA

Oxtail Stew

2 pounds oxtails
1 32-ounce can tomatoes
4 medium carrots, diced
1 cup diced celery
2 large onions, chopped
1 potato, diced
½ medium head cabbage, shredded
2 teaspoons salt
½ teaspoon freshly ground pepper
1 tablespoon paprika

Braise oxtails in a large Dutch oven. Add remaining ingredients and bring to a boil. Reduce heat to simmer and cook over low heat at least 6 hours or longer, adding a little water or beef stock if necessary.

YIELD: 4–6 SERVINGS

THE JUNIOR LEAGUE OF BAKERSFIELD, CALIFORNIA

Corned Beef Casserole

1 15½-ounce can corned beef hash
1 8-ounce jar meatless spaghetti sauce
1 3-ounce package cream cheese, cubed
1 cup shredded cheddar cheese
4 eggs, beaten
½ teaspoon crushed, dried oregano
Dash pepper

Line bottom and sides of a greased 1½-quart casserole with corned beef hash. Pour in spaghetti sauce; top with cubed cream cheese. Sprinkle with cheddar cheese.

Bake for 30 minutes at 350°. Combine eggs, oregano, and pepper; pour into casserole. Bake 20 minutes more.

YIELD: 4 LARGE SERVINGS

THE JUNIOR LEAGUE OF OGDEN, UTAH

· · · · · · · · · · · · · · · · · · ·

Calf's Liver Urbanstube

1½ pounds calf's liver, cut into ¼-inch strips
2 tablespoons olive oil
2 tablespoons butter
1 tablespoon chopped onion
1½ teaspoon chopped chives
1 teaspoon chopped parsley
½ teaspoon thyme
1 teaspoon marjoram
½ teaspoon basil
½ teaspoon sage

In a heavy skillet sauté the liver strips in olive oil, stirring, for about 1 minute. Transfer with a slotted spoon to a heated serving dish and keep warm.

Add the butter to the skillet and sauté onion, 1 teaspoon of the chives, parsley, thyme, marjoram, and basil until the onion is soft. Return liver to the skillet and stir over high heat until heated through.

Transfer to a serving dish and garnish with remaining chives and the sage. Serve immediately.

YIELD: 4 SERVINGS

San Francisco à la Carte
THE JUNIOR LEAGUE OF SAN FRANCISCO, CALIFORNIA

Cold Tongue with Oil and Vinegar

1 3–4-pound fresh beef tongue
2 cloves garlic
Parsley for garnish

MARINADA DE SAUCE:
3 cloves garlic, very finely chopped
4 tablespoons oil
2 tablespoons vinegar
Salt and pepper to taste

Boil beef tongue in salted water for about 2–3 hours, or until tender. Do not overcook, as tongue gets mushy. Remove skin while still warm. Cool and slice ⅛ inch thick.

Combine marinade ingredients and chill until needed.

To serve, pour marinade over tongue and sprinkle with chopped parsley.

YIELD: 6 SERVINGS

THE JUNIOR LEAGUE OF BAKERSFIELD, CALIFORNIA

Mexican Elk Steak

2 pounds elk or venison, trimmed and cut into 1-inch cubes
4 tablespoons vegetable oil
2 onions, cut in rings
2 large green peppers, cut in strips
1 1-pound 12-ounce can tomatoes
1 6-ounce can tomato paste
1 teaspoon chili powder
½ teaspoon paprika
1 10-ounce can mild enchilada sauce
1 clove garlic, minced
2 bay leaves
1 teaspoon ground cumin
½ teaspoon oregano
1 7-ounce can taco sauce
2 large potatoes, cubed
1 7-ounce can chopped green chilies

Brown meat in oil. Add onions and green peppers and simmer about 30 minutes. Add remaining ingredients and simmer slowly until meat is tender, about 1½ hours.

This is a favorite of hearty eaters served with a green salad and sopaipillas. Fresh pineapple for dessert is refreshing.

YIELD: 6 SERVINGS

Colorado Cache
THE JUNIOR LEAGUE OF DENVER, COLORADO

Sweet and Sour Elk Meat Balls

1 pound ground elk
½ pound ground pork
½ teaspoon salt
¼ teaspoon garlic powder
¼ teaspoon pepper
¼ teaspoon dry mustard
1 12-ounce jar chili sauce
1 10-ounce jar grape jelly

Place the meats in a large mixing bowl. Add salt, garlic, pepper, and mustard and knead with a fork or hands. Shape into cocktail-size balls about 1½ inches in diameter. Place on a cookie sheet and bake at 350° until brown, about 15 minutes.

Pour the chili sauce and jelly into a large saucepan over medium heat and stir until jelly melts. Add the meat balls, a few at a time, carefully stirring to cover the meat with sauce. Continue cooking over medium heat for about 20 minutes.

This improves when prepared a few days in advance and refrigerated or frozen. Reheat at serving time in a chafing dish or serve over brown rice with a green salad as a Sunday night supper.

YIELD: 4 SERVINGS

Colorado Cache
THE JUNIOR LEAGUE OF DENVER, COLORADO

Venison Stew

1 teaspoon salt
½ teaspoon pepper
2 pounds venison, cubed (add some neck bones for good flavor)
3 tablespoons oil
2 cloves garlic, minced
5 onions, 2 sliced and 3 quartered
Bay leaves
2 tablespoons wine vinegar
1 tablespoon Worcestershire sauce
6 carrots, quartered
6 potatoes, quartered

Salt and pepper venison. Brown in oil in heavy roasting pan or Dutch oven. Add garlic while browning. Add the 2 sliced onions, bay leaves, wine vinegar, and Worcestershire sauce. Add water to cover meat by about 2 inches. Bring to boil. Cover and simmer for 5–6 hours. During the last hour, add carrots, potatoes, and quartered onions. Continue cooking until done.

This is a recipe that has been enjoyed at Soda Flat, a remote camping spot in the Sierras, since early 1900.

YIELD: 6 SERVINGS

THE JUNIOR LEAGUE OF BAKERSFIELD, CALIFORNIA

Swiss Venison

2 pounds of venison round steak
1 6½-ounce can tomato sauce
2 tablespoons vegetable oil
1 teaspoon salt
1 teaspoon prepared mustard
¼ teaspoon pepper
1 4-ounce can mushroom pieces
1 bay leaf, crushed
½ cup diced onion

Place meat in baking pan on a large sheet of heavy-duty aluminum foil. Combine remaining ingredients and pour over meat. Bring ends of foil up over meat and wrap tightly so none of the marinade can leak out. Refrigerate for 1 hour or overnight, if possible.

Bake at 350° for 1½ hours, or until venison is tender.

YIELD: 5–6 SERVINGS

THE JUNIOR LEAGUE OF OGDEN, UTAH

· · · · · · · · · · · · · · · ·

Roast Venison

1 cup salad oil
½ cup wine vinegar
¼ teaspoon dry mustard
2 teaspoons salt
½ teaspoon pepper
2 cloves garlic
½ teaspoon Worcestershire sauce
½ cup diced onion
1 bay leaf, crushed
3–4 pound venison round steak or roast

Recipe continues . . .

Combine marinade ingredients. Marinate venison overnight in refrigerator, turning occasionally. Remove from refrigerator for 1 hour before cooking.

Roast, uncovered, in preheated 325° oven until meat thermometer registers 160°. Baste with marinade about every ½ hour.

Let roast or steak stand for about 15 minutes before carving.

YIELD: 4 SERVINGS

THE JUNIOR LEAGUE OF OGDEN, UTAH

Lamb, Pork, and Veal

Barbecued Butterflied Leg of Lamb

6-pound leg of lamb, boned and butterflied

MARINADE:
½ cup olive oil
1 cup dry red wine
1 teaspoon crushed rosemary
1 teaspoon crushed thyme
1 teaspoon crushed marjoram
½ teaspoon crushed oregano
2 tablespoons chopped green onion
¼ teaspoon coarse black pepper
½ teaspoon Worcestershire sauce
2 large cloves garlic, minced
1 teaspoon salt

Mix marinade ingredients thoroughly and pour over lamb. Let stand for 24 hours. Turn and baste occasionally.

Barbecue for 45 minutes, turning frequently and basting with marinade. Do *not* cook well done. The lamb should be crusty on the outside and pink in the center.

YIELD: 8 SERVINGS

THE JUNIOR LEAGUE OF SACRAMENTO, CALIFORNIA

Broiled Butterflied Leg of Lamb

6-pound leg of lamb, boned and butterflied

MARINADE:
1 clove garlic, minced
¾ cup olive oil
¼ cup red wine vinegar
½ cup chopped onion
2 teaspoons Dijon mustard
2 teaspoons salt
½ teaspoon basil
½ teaspoon oregano
⅛ teaspoon freshly ground pepper
1 bay leaf, crushed

Marinate boned leg for several hours at room temperature in combined marinade ingredients.

Remove meat from marinade and broil 10 minutes on each side, then roast in preheated 425° oven for about 15 minutes. Baste occasionally with some of the marinade.

To serve, cool for 5 minutes, then slice on the diagonal.

YIELD: 6–8 SERVINGS

Private Collection:
Recipes from The Junior League of Palo Alto
THE JUNIOR LEAGUE OF PALO ALTO, CALIFORNIA

Stuffed Lamb with Pan Gravy

1 12-ounce package frozen spinach
¼ cup butter (½ stick)
1½ cups soft bread crumbs
½ cup chopped fresh mint or ¼ cup dried mint flakes
1 teaspoon salt
¼ teaspoon pepper
⅛ teaspoon nutmeg
5-pound boned shoulder of lamb
1 tablespoon butter
1 cup peeled, diced tomatoes
1 cup coarsely chopped onion
1 cup coarsely chopped carrot
1 cup chopped celery
1 small piece bay leaf
2 tablespoons flour
2 cups water
Salt and pepper

Cook spinach according to package directions. Drain very well and chop.

Heat butter in a skillet. Add bread crumbs and brown lightly. Remove from heat and add spinach, mint, salt, pepper, and nutmeg and toss together with a fork. Lay lamb out flat and spread with spinach mixture.

Melt 1 tablespoon butter in skillet. Add tomatoes and cook gently, stirring, until hot, about 2 minutes, and spread over spinach. Roll lamb around stuffing and tie securely.

Put onion, carrot, celery, and bay leaf in the bottom of a shallow roasting pan. Place lamb on top of the vegetables. Roast 3–3½ hours, or until done to taste (175°F for medium and 182°F for well done). Remove roast from oven.

Discard all but 2 tablespoons of the drippings in the roasting pan. Heat this fat in a saucepan. Sprinkle in the flour and stir to blend. Remove from heat; add any cooking liquid left in the roasting pan and the 2 cups water. Return to heat and cook gently, stirring, for 5 minutes. Season with salt and pepper to taste. Serve the gravy with the roast.

YIELD: 6 SERVINGS

THE JUNIOR LEAGUE OF VANCOUVER, BRITISH COLUMBIA

· · · · · · · · · · · · · · · · · · ·

Swedish Leg of Lamb

6½-pound leg of lamb
1 teaspoon salt
1 teaspoon dry mustard
Clove garlic (optional)
1 cup strong coffee
2 teaspoons sugar
2 teaspoons cream
1 jigger brandy
1½ tablespoons flour
Salt and pepper to taste
2 tablespoons currant jelly

Prepare the lamb by sprinkling it with the 1 teaspoon salt and dry mustard (if desired, make three or four slashes and insert thin slices of garlic). Bake in a 325° oven for 2 hours, then add the coffee mixed with the sugar, cream, and brandy. Baste several times after adding the coffee and brandy.

Continue baking the lamb for 1½ hours (total cooking time, 3½ hours). Continue basting every 15 minutes, if possible. Meat will be well done. Remove the leg of lamb to a serving platter.

To make gravy to serve with the lamb, place roasting pan over direct heat and stir in flour, salt, pepper, and currant jelly. Add boiling water to make the gravy the consistency desired, stirring constantly.

YIELD: 6–8 SERVINGS

THE JUNIOR LEAGUE OF SEATTLE, WASHINGTON

· · · · · · · · · · · · · · · · · · ·

Leg of Lamb, Basque-Style

4–5 cloves garlic
1 6–6½-pound leg of lamb
Salt and pepper
Flour
Melted bacon drippings
1 cup water

Slice garlic cloves and insert into slits in lamb. Season entire leg with salt and pepper, and rub with flour. Place in roasting pan and pour over melted bacon drippings. Roast in preheated 450° oven for 15–20 minutes on each side. Add water to pan, cover, reduce heat to 300°, and cook slowly for 4–5 hours. Roast will be well done.

The Basque often add peeled, quartered potatoes during the last 45 minutes of cooking.

YIELD: 6–8 SERVINGS

THE JUNIOR LEAGUE OF BOISE, IDAHO

. . . .

Lamb Roast "Camargue"

½ cup olive oil
2 teaspoons rosemary
2 teaspoons pickling spice
2 1½–2-pound racks of fresh lamb, trimmed
Salt and pepper
2 tablespoons cooking oil
1 clove garlic, finely chopped
1 tablespoon chopped onion
2 tablespoons flour
1 cup beef bouillon
2 tablespoons red wine

Mix together olive oil, rosemary, and pickling spice and rub over lamb. Place in double plastic bag, push all air out, and seal end with a twist tie. Place in a dish and marinate in refrigerator overnight.

Remove lamb from marinade; dry, and salt and pepper all sides. Heat cooking oil in heavy skillet, add a little of the chopped garlic, and brown meat on all sides.

Transfer lamb to a shallow roasting pan. Roast, uncovered, at 425° for 18–20 minutes per pound for rare; 25 minutes for medium, and about 30 minutes for well done. Remove lamb to a warm platter.

Drain off some drippings if necessary. Brown remaining chopped garlic and onion lightly in pan drippings, then blend in flour. Stir in bouillon and wine and cook, stirring constantly, until thickened and smooth. Pour over lamb.

YIELD: 4 SERVINGS

THE JUNIOR LEAGUE OF VANCOUVER, BRITISH COLUMBIA

· · · · · · · · · · · · · · · · · · ·

Lamb Ragoût

3-pound boneless lamb shoulder or leg
Few teaspoons flour
Bacon drippings or oil
1 teaspoon salt
½ teaspoon each thyme, oregano, and pepper
1 onion, chopped
1 clove garlic, minced
1 cup peeled, chopped tomatoes
1 tablespoon tomato paste
½ teaspoon sugar
Parsley
1 bay leaf
1 cup brown stock or beef consommé
1 cup dry white wine

Recipe continues . . .

Cut lamb into 2-inch cubes. Flour and brown in a little bacon drippings or oil. Transfer browned cubes to a heavy casserole. Sprinkle with salt, thyme, oregano, pepper, and a little flour.

Cook onion, garlic, tomatoes, and tomato paste in some skillet until onion is tender. Add sugar and simmer 15 minutes. Add this mixture to lamb in the casserole with a few sprigs of parsley and 1 bay leaf. Pour over brown stock or consommé and white wine.

Bake, covered, at 325° at least 1½ hours, or until meat is tender. Add more liquid if it seems to be getting dry.

YIELD: 8 SERVINGS

THE JUNIOR LEAGUE OF EDMONTON, ALBERTA

Arni Avgolemeno
(Lamb Stew in Lemon Sauce)

3 pounds lamb shoulder, cut into cubes for stewing
2 tablespoons olive oil
Salt and pepper
3 small onions, chopped
4 celery stalks, chopped
3 carrots, cut in half lengthwise, then in ½-inch pieces
1 clove garlic, minced
2 cups water
Salt and pepper to taste

Brown meat in skillet with hot oil, adding some salt and pepper. Add onions, continuing to brown. Transfer to casserole, add celery, carrots, garlic, and water, plus more salt and pepper, if needed.

Simmer 1½ hours, or until meat is tender, adding a little water from time to time if needed. Remove from heat, skim off fat, and cool slightly.

Pour Lemon Sauce over slightly cooled stew, stir to mix, and serve at once.

YIELD: 6 SERVINGS

LEMON SAUCE:
4 eggs, separated
Juice of 1½ lemons

Beat egg whites until they form peaks. Gradually beat in the yolks. Add lemon juice slowly and continue beating.

Private Collection:
Recipes from The Junior League of Palo Alto
THE JUNIOR LEAGUE OF PALO ALTO, CALIFORNIA

· · · · · · · · · · · · · · · · · · ·

African Lamb Curry

2 pounds lean lamb, cubed
4 tablespoons butter
¼ cup all-purpose flour
¼ teaspoon thyme
¼ teaspoon ground ginger
1½ tablespoons curry powder
1 cup chopped onion
2 cloves garlic, minced
4–5 ounces dried apples, chopped
2–3 cups beef stock or consommé
1 teaspoon freshly grated lemon rind
Salt and freshly ground pepper to taste
½ cup chopped walnuts
½ cup seedless raisins, plumped in Madeira to cover
½ cup unsweetened shredded coconut

Brown meat in butter in a skillet; sprinkle with flour, thyme, ginger, and curry. Stir well and add onion, garlic, and apples. Cook and stir for 3 minutes.

Recipe continues . . .

Gradually add 2 cups of the stock, cook, and stir until slightly thickened and smooth. Add lemon rind, salt, and pepper. Cover and simmer for 1 hour, adding more stock if needed, until meat is tender. Stir in walnuts, raisins, soaking liquid, and coconut. Simmer for 30 minutes to heat thoroughly.

Serve with chutney, chopped hard-boiled eggs, and coconut. Cucumber, melon, and watercress salad is a refreshing accompaniment.

YIELD: 4 SERVINGS

San Francisco à la Carte
THE JUNIOR LEAGUE OF SAN FRANCISCO, CALIFORNIA

• • • • • • • • • • • • • • • • • • • •

Crown Roast of Pork with Cranberry Stuffing and Mustard Sauce Balchan

1 crown roast of pork, trimmed of any excess fat
(approximately 18 chops)
Cranberry Stuffing
Orange slices or spiced peaches
Watercress
Mustard Sauce Balchan

Cover the bone ends of the crown roast with foil to prevent burning in the oven. Place a piece of foil around the bottom of the roast so the stuffing will not leak through. Place the roast on a rack in a large roasting pan. Roast in a preheated 350° oven 20 minutes per pound.

One hour before the roast is cooked, fill the middle of the crown with Cranberry Stuffing, piling it quite high. Extra stuffing can be put in a buttered baking dish, covered, and baked with the roast for 30 minutes. Return the roast to the oven and roast an additional 1 hour. If the stuffing becomes too brown, cover it with foil.

Place roast on a platter, remove the foil tips, and decorate with paper frills. Garnish with the orange slices or spiced peaches and watercress. Pass Mustard Sauce Balchan separately.

CRANBERRY STUFFING:
4 cups cooked wild rice
2 cups raw cranberries, coarsely chopped
½ cup melted butter
3½ tablespoons sugar
2 tablespoons grated onion
1 teaspoon salt
½ teaspoon dried marjoram
1 clove garlic, finely minced
½ teaspoon pepper
½ teaspoon mace
½ teaspoon dried thyme
½ teaspoon dried dill weed

To prepare stuffing, in a large saucepan combine the stuffing ingredients and cook over medium-low heat 10–15 minutes, or until heated thoroughly. Stir the mixture often. Allow the stuffing to cool.

MUSTARD SAUCE BALCHAN:
4 tablespoons pan drippings or 4 tablespoons butter
4 tablespoons flour
1 cup dry white wine
½ cup chicken broth
¼ cup heavy cream
3 tablespoons Dijon mustard
1 teaspoon dry mustard
Salt and pepper to taste

To prepare sauce, in a medium saucepan blend the 4 tablespoons pan drippings or butter with the flour. Cook the roux over low heat 3 minutes. Add the white wine and cook until thickened, approximately 3 minutes. Add the chicken broth and cream and cook an additional 5 minutes. Stir in the Dijon mustard and dry mustard. Salt and pepper to taste.

Recipe continues . . .

The roast can be kept warm in a 200° oven while preparing the mustard sauce.

YIELD: 8–10 SERVINGS

The California Heritage Cookbook
THE JUNIOR LEAGUE OF PASADENA, CALIFORNIA

Polynesian Pork Roast

4–5-pound pork loin roast, boned and tied
Salt and pepper
Rosemary
½ cup soy sauce
½ cup catsup
¼ cup honey
2 large cloves garlic, minced
Preserved kumquats and watercress for garnish

Sprinkle roast with salt, pepper, and rosemary. Roast in a moderate 350° oven on rack for 35 minutes per pound, basting occasionally with soy sauce mixed with catsup, honey, and garlic.

Serve with preserved kumquats and watercress.

YIELD: 6 SERVINGS

From an Adobe Oven . . . to a Microwave Range
THE JUNIOR LEAGUE OF PUEBLO, COLORADO

Stuffed Pork Tenderloin

2 2–2½-pound pork tenderloins
1½–2 cups bread crumbs
Salt
Pepper
Garlic powder
Sage
Thyme
½ apple, diced
3 tablespoons milk, or enough to hold dressing together
1 10½-ounce can beef consommé
2 bay leaves
¼ cup oil

Remove excess fat from tenderloins. Split each down the middle, making a cavity for the stuffing.

Combine the bread crumbs with salt, pepper, garlic powder, sage, and thyme to taste. Add apple and milk. Mix well until dressing holds together loosely. Divide dressing into each cavity and sew each strip together with thread.

Place oil in a skillet and in it brown the tenderloins. Remove excess oil. Add consommé and bay leaves. Bring to a boil. Simmer for 1–1½ hours, basting and turning often.

Delicious served hot or cold.

YIELD: 6 SERVINGS

THE JUNIOR LEAGUE OF CALGARY, ALBERTA

Pork Roll Mexican-Style

3 chili poblanos or bell peppers, seeded and cut into strips
½ pound farmer's cheese or pot cheese, crumbled
2½-pound pork loin, slit open to make a flat rectangle approximately
9 x 15 inches
4 carrots, chopped
1 onion, chopped
2 stalks celery, chopped
2 bay leaves
Salt and pepper to taste
1 cup canned tomato purée

Place chilies and cheese on the meat; roll and tie. In large skillet cook meat in a little oil until evenly browned and remove from pan. Sauté the vegetables in oil in pan for 10 minutes. Add bay leaves, salt, and pepper. Place meat on top of vegetables and add water to barely cover. Cover skillet and cook over low heat for 3 hours, or until meat is tender.

Remove the meat, bay leaves, and chilies. Add the tomato purée and cook, uncovered, for 15 minutes.

Slice meat on platter and pour the sauce with vegetables on top. Serve with cooked white rice.

YIELD: 6 SERVINGS

Que Sabroso!
THE JUNIOR LEAGUE OF MEXICO CITY, MEXICO

· · · · · · · · · · · · · · · · · ·

Pork Loin in Chipotle

1 cup orange juice
3 large tomatoes, peeled
½ 4-ounce can chopped green chilies (preferably chipotle), or to taste
2-pound pork loin
Bacon drippings

Blend orange juice, tomatoes, and chilies in blender until smooth. Set aside.

Brown pork loin in a small amount of bacon drippings in a Dutch oven. When brown on all sides, add blended ingredients, cover with aluminum foil, and roast at 475° for 20 minutes. Remove aluminum foil, reduce oven temperature to 375°, and cook for 1 hour longer.

YIELD: 6 SERVINGS

Que Sabroso!

THE JUNIOR LEAGUE OF MEXICO CITY, MEXICO

. . . .

Porc en Croûte

PASTRY:
1¼ cups flour
¼ pound cold butter, cut into pieces
⅛ teaspoon salt
2 tablespoons cold water

MEAT:
3-pound boneless pork tenderloin
½ cup Dijon mustard
1 teaspoon crumbled dried tarragon
1 egg, lightly beaten

To make the pastry: Place the flour in a bowl and add pieces of butter, blending with a pastry blender until mixture is the texture of oatmeal. Add salt and water and mix lightly until dough can be gathered into a ball. Wrap in wax paper and chill for at least 1 hour, or overnight.

For the meat: In a large skillet or Dutch oven brown roast evenly on all sides over moderate to high heat. Set aside to cool. Preheat oven to 350°.

On a floured board, roll out pastry in a rectangle large enough to encase roast. Spread mustard on pastry and sprinkle with tarragon. Then

Recipe continues . . .

place roast in center and seal ends of pastry around roast, tucking them under. Place seam side down in a shallow baking pan. Brush pastry with beaten egg and bake for 1 hour, or until pastry is golden.

This recipe can be prepared in advance, refrigerated, then brought out about an hour or so before you wish to bake it.

YIELD: 6 SERVINGS

San Francisco à la Carte
THE JUNIOR LEAGUE OF SAN FRANCISCO, CALIFORNIA

• • • • • • • • • • • • • • • • • • • •

Pork Chops Veracruz

6 1–1¼-inch-thick pork chops
2 teaspoons dry mustard
1 teaspoon salt
¼ teaspoon freshly ground pepper
1 tablespoon butter
2–3 cloves garlic, minced
½ cup dry vermouth
½ cup dry white wine
¾–1 cup orange juice
1–1½ tablespoons flour
2–3 tablespoons cold water
Orange slices
Parsley

Rub pork chops with a mixture of dry mustard, salt, and pepper.

In a heavy skillet brown chops in butter with garlic. Add vermouth, wine, and orange juice. Cover and simmer over low heat for 1–1½ hours, or until chops are tender.

Remove chops to a warm platter. Make a paste of the flour and water (the amount of flour may vary according to the amount of liquid in the pan) and add to the pan, stirring with a wire whisk until gravy is smooth and thickened. Check seasoning.

Pour gravy over chops and garnish with orange slices and parsley. Brown rice is a good accompaniment.

YIELD: 6 SERVINGS

Private Collection:
Recipes from The Junior League of Palo Alto
THE JUNIOR LEAGUE OF PALO ALTO, CALIFORNIA

·   ·   ·   ·   ·   ·   ·   ·   ·   ·   ·   ·   ·   ·   ·   ·   ·   ·

Curried Pork Chops

8 ½-inch-thick pork chops
1 cup chopped onion
2 tablespoons peanut oil
2 tablespoons flour
2 tablespoons brown sugar
1 tablespoon curry powder
1 teaspoon salt
1 teaspoon cinnamon
1 beef bouillon cube
1 cup water
2 tablespoons catsup
1 4-ounce jar apples and apricots (baby food)

Brown chops and arrange in a single layer in a baking pan.

Sauté onion in oil and add flour, sugar, curry, salt, and cinnamon. Cook, stirring, until bubbly; stir in remaining ingredients. Cook until thick. Spoon half the mixture over chops and bake 20 minutes at 400°. Spoon remaining sauce on chops and bake 20 minutes more.

You can double sauce recipe if you wish to have plenty to serve over rice.

YIELD: 4 SERVINGS

THE JUNIOR LEAGUE OF SACRAMENTO, CALIFORNIA

·   ·   ·   ·   ·   ·   ·   ·   ·   ·   ·   ·   ·   ·   ·   ·   ·   ·

Baked Stuffed Pork Chops

1 cup bread stuffing
¼ cup hot water
2 tablespoons soft butter
6 double-rib pork chops with pockets
¼ teaspoon salt
½ teaspoon onion salt
1 16-ounce can applesauce
¼ cup water
¼ teaspoon salt
1 clove garlic, minced
Pinch each thyme, marjoram, and oregano

Mix bread stuffing with hot water and butter; fill pockets in the chops with the dressing. Season chops with the salt and onion salt and arrange in a shallow casserole.

Combine applesauce, water, salt, and garlic. Pour the mixture over the chops and sprinkle with the herbs. Bake at 350° for 1½ hours, covered. Uncover and continue baking for 20 minutes more, basting occasionally.

YIELD: 6 SERVINGS

THE JUNIOR LEAGUE OF GREAT FALLS, MONTANA

. . . .

Mandarin Stuffed Pork Chops

4 double-rib pork chops with pockets
1 10-ounce can mandarin oranges
1 cup dry seasoned stuffing
⅓ cup chopped onion
¼ cup seedless raisins
½ teaspoon salt
¼ teaspoon pepper
¼–½ cup orange juice

Open pork chops and pound one side at a time until thin.

Drain oranges, reserving juice. Mix oranges, stuffing, onion, raisins, salt, and pepper, reserving some orange sections for garnish. Add ¼ cup orange juice and mix. Stuff chops and fasten with wooden picks. Place chops in a shallow pan and add reserved mandarin orange juice.

Bake, covered, in a 350° oven for 1½ hours. Uncover and continue to cook, basting frequently, for 20–25 minutes, or until chops are golden.

Garnish with some orange sections.

YIELD: 4 SERVINGS

THE JUNIOR LEAGUE OF VANCOUVER, BRITISH COLUMBIA

· ·

Pork Chops in Chablis

10 medium fresh mushrooms
6 slices Swiss cheese
½ cup fresh parsley
Seasoned salt
4 1-inch-thick pork chops with pockets
½ cup flour, lightly salted
2 eggs, beaten
2 cups cracker crumbs
4 tablespoons lard or cooking oil
½ cup Chablis
3 tablespoons flour
2–3 cups hot milk
Salt and pepper to taste

Finely chop mushrooms, cheese, and parsley. Mix together and add seasoned salt to taste. Stuff mixture into pork chop pockets. Fasten securely with wooden picks.

Dip stuffed chops in flour, then in beaten eggs. Roll in cracker crumbs

Recipe continues . . .

and brown in shortening. Pour off most of the fat, add wine, cover, and simmer for 1 hour. More wine or a bit of water may be added if necessary.

Remove chops to a warm platter. Add flour to drippings and mix well. Gradually stir in milk and season to taste. Cook, stirring, until sauce is thickened and very hot. Pour over chops and serve with rice, buttered carrots, and fruit salad.

YIELD: 4 SERVINGS

THE JUNIOR LEAGUE OF BUTTE, MONTANA

· ·

Pork and Prune Casserole

1-pound boneless pork shoulder
1 ounce flour
½ teaspoon salt
½ teaspoon pepper
1 ounce margarine or butter
4 ounces prunes, pitted and soaked overnight in ½ pint water
1 cup prune juice
Juice of 1 lemon

Cut pork into 1-inch pieces. Mix flour with salt and pepper and dip pork pieces into the seasoned flour. Cook pork in butter or margarine until golden brown.

Arrange the pork and prunes in layers in a 2-quart casserole. Add the prune juice to the skillet, heat gently, and stir well to make a gravy. Add lemon juice and pour over pork and prunes. Bake at 375° for 1½ hours.

YIELD: 4 SERVINGS

THE JUNIOR LEAGUE OF VANCOUVER, BRITISH COLUMBIA

· ·

Chow Mein

1 pound lean pork
1½ tablespoons peanut oil
1 medium onion, thinly sliced
1 8-ounce can water chestnuts, drained and sliced
1 8-ounce can bamboo shoots, drained
1 4-ounce can mushrooms with liquid
1 8-ounce can bean sprouts, drained
4 cups diced celery
4 cups chicken broth, homemade or canned
2 tablespoons soy sauce
1 tablespoon bottled meat sauce
¼ teaspoon pepper
6 tablespoons cooked shredded chicken

Dice pork and brown lightly in oil; add onion and sauté for 15 minutes. Add water chestnuts, bamboo shoots, mushrooms, bean sprouts, celery, and all remaining ingredients except chicken. Simmer for 15 minutes longer.

Garnish with shredded chicken; serve on Chinese noodles or cooked rice.

YIELD: 6 SERVINGS

THE JUNIOR LEAGUE OF BUTTE, MONTANA

Korean Pork Platter

1½-pound lean boneless pork shoulder, cut in 1-inch cubes
2 tablespoons flour
4 tablespoons vegetable oil
3 teaspoons curry powder
1 tablespoon sugar
⅓ cup soy sauce
¾ cup water
2 large onions, peeled, sliced, and separated into rings
2 cups sliced celery
1 9-ounce package frozen, cut green beans
1 teaspoon celery salt

Shake pork cubes with flour to coat evenly. Brown cubes in 2 tablespoons vegetable oil in a large skillet; remove and set aside.

Stir curry powder into drippings in skillet; cook 3 minutes. Stir in sugar, soy sauce, and ½ cup of water. Cook until bubbly, stirring constantly and scraping cooked-on juices from bottom and sides of pan. Stir in pork and cover. Simmer 1¼ hours, or until pork is tender.

While meat cooks, sauté onion rings in remaining 2 tablespoons oil for 3 minutes in a second large skillet; set aside. Stir in celery; cook 3 minutes. Stir in frozen green beans. Sprinkle with celery salt; toss to mix. Add remaining ¼ cup water. Cover and steam 10 minutes, or until vegetables are crispy-tender; drain.

Spoon vegetables onto heated large platter; spoon pork on top. Serve with cooked rice.

YIELD: 6 SERVINGS

From an Adobe Oven . . . to a Microwave Range
THE JUNIOR LEAGUE OF PUEBLO, COLORADO

Shanghai Pork

2 pounds lean pork, cut in 2-inch strips about ½ inch thick
½ teaspoon garlic powder
½ teaspoon salt
¼ cup salad oil
2 tablespoons instant onion
2 tablespoons water
1 tablespoon salad oil
2 cups sliced carrots, cut in ½-inch pieces
1 6-ounce can sliced mushrooms
1 10¾-ounce can cream of celery soup
¼ cup soy sauce
¾ teaspoon ground ginger
¼ teaspoon ground pepper
3 cups shredded cabbage
¼ cup toasted slivered almonds

Rub pork with combined garlic powder and salt. Heat the ¼ cup salad oil in skillet. Add pork, a few pieces at a time, and brown on all sides. Transfer to 2½-quart casserole.

Combine onion and water; let stand 10 minutes for onion to soften. Add the 1 tablespoon salad oil to skillet. Add softened onion and carrots and cook until onion is golden. Stir frequently to keep from sticking. Add mushrooms and their liquid, soup, soy sauce, ginger, and pepper. Heat to boiling, stirring constantly. Pour mixture over pork and toss gently. Bake, covered, at 350° for 1 hour, or until meat is fork-tender. Top with shredded cabbage. Cover and cook for another 10 minutes.

Before serving garnish with slivered almonds. Serve with fluffy hot rice.

YIELD: 6 SERVINGS

From an Adobe Oven . . . to a Microwave Range
THE JUNIOR LEAGUE OF PUEBLO, COLORADO

Tourtiere

A traditional French-Canadian pork pie served on Christmas Eve.

1 pound lean ground pork
¼ cup chopped onion
½ teaspoon salt
1 clove garlic, minced
Dash pepper, cloves, and poultry seasoning
1 small bay leaf
½ cup boiling water
¼ cup dry bread crumbs
Pastry for a 2-crust pie (see Index)
1 egg, beaten

Mix pork, onion, seasonings, bay leaf, and water in a saucepan. Simmer, uncovered, for 20–30 minutes. Discard bay leaf. Drain meat, stir in bread crumbs, and cool.

Line pie plate with pastry. Fill with meat. Cover with pastry, sealing edges. Make steam vents on top. Brush with beaten egg. Bake at 425° for 30 minutes, or until golden brown.

May be frozen up to 6 weeks. Bake frozen pies for 25 minutes at 425°.

YIELD: 1 9-INCH PIE

THE JUNIOR LEAGUE OF EDMONTON, ALBERTA

Pork Pasties

2 pounds pork loin tips
1 1½-pound flank steak
5 medium potatoes
2 small onions
¼ cup chopped suet
Salt and pepper to taste
1 stick butter
2 batches pastry

Chop loin tips, flank steak, potatoes, and onions finely. Mix thoroughly and season with salt and pepper to taste. Stir in suet.

Roll out pastry thinly and cut into 8-inch circles. Place 1 heaping cup of mixture on each circle. Put a slice of butter on top. Fold pastry over mixture and seal edges securely. Arrange on baking sheet and bake for 1 hour in a 400° oven. Serve hot.

Cocktail pasties are delicious for parties. Just reduce the size of pastry circles to 4 inches.

YIELD: 8 LARGE OR 50 COCKTAIL PASTIES

PASTRY:
2 cups flour
1 teaspoon salt
¾ cup lard or shortening
6 tablespoons water

Mix flour and salt. Add shortening and cut in with pastry blender until mixture looks like coarse meal. Stir in water; gather dough into a ball.

THE JUNIOR LEAGUE OF BUTTE, MONTANA

Spareribs Gourmet

4 pounds small, meaty pork spareribs (25 ribs)

MARINADE:
5 tablespoons hoisin sauce
5 tablespoons soy sauce
1 teaspoon sherry
3 tablespoons brown sugar
3 cloves garlic, minced
1 teaspoon tomato paste
1 tablespoon brown bean sauce
Pinch Chinese five spice

Remove back flap and fat, chop off gristle and bone at end of each rib, and slit between each rib (not clear through). Combine marinade ingredients and marinate ribs for 3–4 hours or overnight in the refrigerator.

Preheat oven to 350°. Place ribs right on shelf in the oven. Place a pan of water underneath ribs on second shelf. Roast (steam) for 1–1½ hours.

Serve with Plum Brandy Sauce and hot mustard.

YIELD: 4–6 SERVINGS

PLUM BRANDY SAUCE:
¼ cup finely chopped chutney
¼ cup chili sauce
¼ cup plum preserves
½ cup apricot preserves
Pinch Chinese five spice
1 teaspoon brandy
¼ teaspoon salt
2 tablespoons honey
½ cup brown sugar
½ cup cider vinegar
½ cup applesauce

Combine the above ingredients and simmer 5–10 minutes.

THE JUNIOR LEAGUE OF SACRAMENTO, CALIFORNIA

· · · · · · · · · · · · · · · · · · · ·

Sweet and Sour Spareribs

Salt
12–16 country-style spareribs
1 tablespoon butter
1 onion, finely chopped
1 clove garlic, minced
1 cup brown sugar
½ cup vinegar
½ cup water
2–3 tablespoons soy sauce
1 tablespoon ground ginger
2 tablespoons cornstarch
2 tablespoons juice from pineapple chunks
1 16-ounce can pineapple chunks, drained
1 medium green pepper, sliced into long, thin slices
1 teaspoon toasted sesame seeds

Recipe continues . . .

Salt and cook ribs in a covered casserole at 350° for about 3 hours, pouring off the melted fat whenever necessary.

In a saucepan melt the butter and in it cook onions and garlic until soft. Add the brown sugar, vinegar, and water and pour over onions and garlic. Stir in soy sauce, ginger, and cornstarch mixed with pineapple juice. Cook, stirring, until sauce is smooth, bubbly, and thick.

An hour before ribs are cooked, pour off remaining fat and pour sauce over them. Add pineapple and green pepper and complete the cooking. Sprinkle with sesame seeds and keep warm in the oven until serving time.

Serve over cooked rice.

YIELD: 4–6 SERVINGS

THE JUNIOR LEAGUE OF TACOMA, WASHINGTON

· ·

Maple-Barbecued Spareribs

5 pounds spareribs
½ cup water
2 tablespoons butter
1 medium onion, chopped
1 clove garlic, minced
2 cups catsup
1 cup maple-blended syrup

Place ribs on rack in shallow roasting pan to which water has been added; cover tightly with aluminum foil and roast at 350° for 1 hour.

While spareribs are baking make the sauce: Melt butter in skillet. Add onion and garlic and cook until tender. Add remaining ingredients and simmer for 10 minutes.

Remove foil and roast for an additional 30–40 minutes, basting often with the sauce.

YIELD: 6 SERVINGS

THE JUNIOR LEAGUE OF EDMONTON, ALBERTA

Spareribs and Sauce

5 pounds spareribs
1 cup tomato sauce
½ cup vinegar
1 tablespoon chili powder
1 tablespoon celery salt
1 teaspoon paprika
3 tablespoons brown sugar
Salt, pepper, and Worcestershire sauce to taste
Chopped onion (optional)
Lemon juice (optional)

Bake ribs in roasting pan at 325° for 45 minutes.

While ribs are baking prepare sauce: Combine all remaining ingredients in a saucepan and simmer, covered, for 30 minutes.

When ribs are cooked, drain fat from roasting pan and cut ribs into individual ribs. Return to roasting pan. Raise oven temperature to 400° and cover the ribs with sauce. Bake 15 minutes longer.

YIELD: 4–6 SERVINGS

THE JUNIOR LEAGUE OF LONG BEACH, CALIFORNIA

Sausage and Cabbage Italian-Style

8 Italian sausages
1 head cabbage, cored and shredded
2 8-ounce cans tomato sauce

Cut sausages into 1-inch pieces and fry until lightly browned in large skillet. Drain off drippings, leaving 1 tablespoon in pan. Add shredded cabbage, tomato sauce, and sausages and simmer for 45 minutes.
Serve with French bread.

YIELD: 4 SERVINGS

THE JUNIOR LEAGUE OF BUTTE, MONTANA

Salsa de Naranja Cristina
(Orange Sauce for Ham or Pork)

4 oranges
3 tablespoons vinegar
3 tablespoons sugar
4 tablespoons water
Pinch salt
Pinch oregano
3 small chilies, finely chopped

Use only pulp and juice of oranges. Mix with other ingredients.
Serve with roast pork or ham.

YIELD: ENOUGH FOR A 5-POUND HAM OR PORK ROAST

THE JUNIOR LEAGUE OF TUCSON, ARIZONA

Veal Knots Piccata

2 pounds veal scallops, very thinly pounded
1 cup flour
½ teaspoon salt
¼ teaspoon white pepper
8 tablespoons butter
½ cup white wine
4 tablespoons fresh lemon juice
3 tablespoons drained capers
2 egg yolks, beaten
4 tablespoons chopped fresh parsley

Cut the scallops in long strips approximately 1 inch wide. Combine the flour, salt, and pepper and roll the veal strips in it. Gently tie each strip into a knot and reseason with flour mixture if necessary.

Melt the butter in a skillet and brown the knots on all sides. Add wine, lemon juice, and capers to the meat and simmer until tender, approximately 6 minutes. Remove meat from the skillet to a warm serving platter.

Make a sauce by adding egg yolks to the skillet and blending quickly with juices in pan until thickened. Pour sauce over knots and sprinkle with parsley to garnish.

YIELD: 4 SERVINGS

San Francisco à la Carte
THE JUNIOR LEAGUE OF SAN FRANCISCO, CALIFORNIA

Veal in Marsala Sauce

18 thin veal slices
1 cup flour
Salt and pepper to taste
8 tablespoons butter
2 teaspoons finely chopped shallots
3 cups thinly sliced fresh mushrooms
1½ cups dry Marsala
Lemon slices

Pound veal lightly between sheets of wax paper. Dip in flour; season with salt and pepper.

Heat butter in skillet and sauté veal over moderate heat for 3–4 minutes, or until brown on both sides. Place on platter and keep warm.

Cook shallots and mushrooms in butter remaining in pan for 3 minutes. Add wine and simmer to reduce to half the original quantity.

Pour sauce over veal and garnish with thin slices of lemon.

YIELD: 6 SERVINGS

THE JUNIOR LEAGUE OF LONG BEACH, CALIFORNIA

. . . .

Swedish Veal and Orange Casserole

3 pounds thinly sliced veal cutlets
½ cup grated Parmesan cheese
1 teaspoon salt
1 teaspoon pepper
1 teaspoon sugar
3 tablespoons butter
2 cups sliced carrots
3 oranges, sliced
1 cup beef stock
4 tablespoons orange juice or sherry

Pound cutlets until very thin. Combine cheese, salt, pepper, and sugar and sprinkle over veal. Melt butter in skillet and brown veal on both sides. Transfer to buttered shallow casserole.

Put carrots and orange slices over veal. Pour in beef stock. Cover and bake for 45 minutes. Add orange juice or sherry and bake 20 minutes more, or until veal is tender.

YIELD: 6 SERVINGS

THE JUNIOR LEAGUE OF GREAT FALLS, MONTANA

. . . .

Veal Cordon Bleu

6 thin slices veal steak
6 slices mozzarella cheese
6 thin slices cooked ham
Dry mustard
1½ cups fine dry bread crumbs
1 teaspoon salt
¼ teaspoon pepper
¼ teaspoon mixed herbs (sage, parsley, thyme, rosemary, and bay leaves)
2 eggs, lightly beaten
¼ cup olive oil
¼ cup butter
1 cup dry white cooking wine

Pound veal slices until paper-thin. Place 1 slice of cheese and 1 slice of ham on each veal slice; sprinkle a little mustard on the ham. Roll all three layers together and fasten with wooden picks. Set aside.

Combine bread crumbs, salt, pepper, and herbs. Dip each roll in the egg and then in bread crumbs. Refrigerate up to 8 hours, or until ready to use. Heat oil and butter in skillet. Brown rolls for 10–12 minutes on each

Recipe continues . . .

side. Remove rolls from pan, add wine, and simmer, stirring in all brown bits from bottom and sides of pan.

Pour pan sauce over rolls and serve.

YIELD: 6 SERVINGS

THE JUNIOR LEAGUE OF EDMONTON, ALBERTA

. . . .

Veal in Cream Sauce

3-pound boneless veal shoulder or leg
Salt and freshly ground black pepper
4 tablespoons butter
2 tablespoons olive oil
1 tablespoon flour
½ pint heavy cream
½ teaspoon paprika
2 tablespoons finely chopped onion
½ pound button mushrooms, quartered
1 green pepper, cut into strips
1 red pepper, cut into strips

Cut veal into 1½-inch cubes. Season generously with salt and pepper, rubbing seasoning well into meat.

Heat 2 tablespoons each butter and oil in skillet and sauté meat, 4–6 pieces at a time, until lightly browned on all sides. Transfer meat to a casserole.

Add flour to fat remaining in pan and cook, stirring constantly, until roux is smooth. Add cream and cook, stirring, until well blended and slightly thickened. Season to taste with salt, freshly ground pepper, and paprika.

Melt remaining butter in saucepan and simmer onion until golden. Add mushrooms and peppers. Cook over low heat for 5 minutes, stirring frequently.

Combine mushroom-pepper mixture with cream sauce and pour over veal. Cover casserole and bake for 1 hour at 325°, or until meat is tender. Serve with cooked rice.

YIELD: 8 SERVINGS

THE JUNIOR LEAGUE OF EDMONTON, ALBERTA

· · · · · · · · · · · · · · · · · · ·

Fricassoa di Vitello
(Veal Stew)

2 pounds lean, boneless veal, cubed
Salt, white pepper, and nutmeg
Flour
1 tablespoon salad oil
3 tablespoons butter
1 cup dry white wine
2 tablespoons fresh lemon juice
⅓ cup heavy cream
1 egg yolk, beaten

Sprinkle veal with salt, seasonings, and flour. Heat oil and butter in large skillet. Brown veal, a few cubes at a time. Remove from pan and when all are brown return to pan and add wine, lemon juice, and cream. Bring to a boil, reduce heat, cover and simmer for 1 hour. Stir a small amount of pan juices into egg yolk and stir into juices remaining in pan to make a rich sauce.

Serve with noodles.

YIELD: 4 SERVINGS

THE JUNIOR LEAGUE OF TUCSON, ARIZONA

· · · · · · · · · · · · · · · · · · ·

Poultry and
Game Birds

Roast Chicken with Mint Sauce

1 5–5½-pound roasting chicken
Salt and pepper to taste
3 large bunches fresh mint, washed and dried
4 tablespoons butter, cut into bite-size pieces
3 tablespoons melted butter
Mint sprigs

Rub the cavity of the chicken with salt and pepper. Stuff the chicken with the fresh mint leaves and butter, packing them in the cavity tightly. Truss the bird securely and brush completely with the 3 tablespoons melted butter.

Place the chicken breast side up in a roasting pan and roast, uncovered, in a preheated 450° oven for 20 minutes. Reduce the heat to 350° and roast for an additional hour. Baste regularly with the pan juices. Pierce the chicken with a fork, and if the juices are clear, the chicken is done.

Remove the chicken to a serving platter and keep warm, allowing it to stand 10 minutes before carving. Remove the trussing. Garnish with the fresh mint sprigs and serve with Mint Sauce.

YIELD: 4 SERVINGS

MINT SAUCE:
½ cup wine vinegar
½ cup dry white wine or vermouth
2 tablespoons minced shallots
¼ cup minced fresh mint leaves
½ teaspoon salt
¼ teaspoon freshly ground pepper
6 egg yolks, well beaten
4 tablespoons cold butter
1 cup melted butter

To prepare sauce, combine the vinegar, wine, shallots, half the mint leaves, salt, and pepper in a small saucepan. Bring to a boil over moderate heat and cook until liquid is reduced to 4 tablespoons. Cool and strain the mixture into the top of a double saucepan.

Place saucepan over simmering water and add eggs. Cut 2 tablespoons of the cold butter in small pieces and beat into egg mixture with a wire whisk. Beat in the remaining cold butter, a little at a time, in small pieces. Slowly add the melted butter, stirring constantly. When all the butter is incorporated and the sauce is thickened, remove the pan from the heat and beat in the remaining 2 tablespoons mint leaves.

YIELD: ABOUT 2 CUPS

The California Heritage Cookbook
THE JUNIOR LEAGUE OF PASADENA, CALIFORNIA

· ·

Leisure Chicken

½ cup butter
½ cup sherry
½ cup soy sauce
2 young broiling chickens, halved

Melt the butter in a saucepan and add sherry and soy sauce. Wash and pat dry chicken and brush with butter mixture. Broil for 30–40 minutes, turning chicken occasionally and basting with the sherry-butter sauce.

Serve with fresh fruit kabobs, cooked rice, and a tossed green salad.

YIELD: 4 SERVINGS

THE JUNIOR LEAGUE OF SPOKANE, WASHINGTON

· · · · · · · · · · · · · ·

Chicken Jardinière

2 2-pound broiler-fryers, quartered
1 clove garlic, minced
¼ cup vegetable oil
1 teaspoon salt
⅛ teaspoon pepper
2 cups chopped celery
5 small carrots, chopped
2 medium onions, sliced or chopped
½ pound fresh mushrooms (optional)
1 8-ounce can tomato sauce
½ cup water
1 cup dry white wine
¼ teaspoon marjoram

In skillet brown chicken with garlic in oil; sprinkle with salt and pepper. Transfer chicken to a large casserole.

In same skillet lightly brown celery, carrots, onions and mushrooms. Pour off excess fat. Stir in remaining ingredients; simmer 10 minutes. Pour vegetable mixture over chicken.

Bake, covered, at 350° for 40 minutes to 1 hour.

YIELD: 6–8 SERVINGS

THE JUNIOR LEAGUE OF SAN JOSE, CALIFORNIA

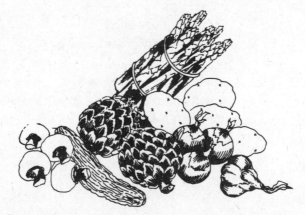

Poulet au Citron

2 tablespoons grated lemon peel
½ cup fresh lemon juice
2 cloves garlic, minced
2 teaspoons dried thyme
1 shallot, finely chopped
1½ teaspoons salt
1 teaspoon pepper
2 2½–3-pound fryers, quartered
¼ cup melted butter
2 lemons, thinly sliced
½ cup finely chopped fresh parsley

Combine the lemon peel, lemon juice, garlic, thyme, shallot, salt, and pepper in a mixing bowl. Place chicken pieces in a single layer in a shallow baking dish and cover with the lemon marinade. Turn chicken until it is thoroughly coated. Refrigerate, covered in the marinade, 3–4 hours, turning the chicken several times to marinate evenly.

Lift chicken from the marinade and drain well on paper towels, reserving the marinade. Place chicken in a single layer in a shallow 2-quart baking dish and brush with the melted butter.

Bake chicken, uncovered, in a preheated 425° oven for 25 minutes. Brush with reserved marinade, lower heat to 325°, and bake for an additional 30–35 minutes more, or until chicken is brown and thoroughly cooked.

Remove chicken from oven and strain off as much fat as possible. Arrange the chicken on a serving platter. Surround with the lemon slices and sprinkle with chopped parsley. Heat any remaining marinade and pass separately in a gravy boat.

YIELD: 6–8 SERVINGS

The California Heritage Cookbook
THE JUNIOR LEAGUE OF PASADENA, CALIFORNIA

Chicken with Lemon and Lime

1 2½–3 pound chicken, cut up
¼ cup lime juice
¼ cup lemon juice
⅓ cup dry white wine
1 clove garlic, minced
1 teaspoon salt
¼ teaspoon dried tarragon or ¾ teaspoon chopped fresh tarragon
⅛ teaspoon fresh ground pepper
¼ cup butter

Place chicken pieces in bowl. Combine next seven ingredients and pour over chicken. Let stand at room temperature for ½ hour or refrigerate for 2–3 hours. Stir occasionally.

Remove chicken from marinade. Reserve marinade. Arrange chicken pieces in a shallow, buttered casserole. Crowd them, if necessary, but do not put them in more than 1 layer. Dot chicken with butter. Bake, uncovered in 425° oven for 30–40 minutes. Baste with reserve marinade every 10 minutes.

Serve from the casserole and pour some of the sauce over each serving.

YIELD: 4 SERVINGS

Something New Under the Sun
THE JUNIOR LEAGUE OF PHOENIX, ARIZONA

Parmesan Chicken

½ pound butter
1 clove garlic, minced
2 cups bread crumbs
¾ cup grated Parmesan cheese
¼ cup chopped fresh parsley
2 teaspoons salt
⅛ teaspoon pepper
3 small fryers, halved, or 8 chicken breasts

Melt butter and add garlic. Mix together bread crumbs, Parmesan cheese, parsley, salt, and pepper.

Dip chicken into butter, then into crumb mixture. Place in baking dish and pour any remaining butter over.

Bake, uncovered, in 350° oven for 1 hour.

YIELD: 8 SERVINGS

THE JUNIOR LEAGUE OF TUCSON, ARIZONA

. . . .

Italian Chicken

2 tablespoons butter
1 fryer, cut into serving pieces
1 clove garlic, minced
1 medium green pepper, cut in strips
1 medium or large onion, chopped
2 tomatoes, skinned and chopped
Salt and pepper
¼ pound mozzarella cheese, sliced
2–3 anchovy filets
2 tablespoons Worcestershire sauce
Chopped parsley

Recipe continues . . .

Heat butter in skillet and add chicken. Cook until golden brown. Add garlic, pepper, onion, and tomatoes. Season with salt and pepper. Cover and continue to cook over low heat for 30 minutes. Place slices of cheese on chicken and place strips of anchovies on top of cheese. Cover until cheese melts. Transfer to heated serving dish.

Mix Worcestershire sauce with juices and vegetables remaining in pan. Heat and pour over chicken. Sprinkle with parsley.

YIELD: 2–4 PEOPLE

THE JUNIOR LEAGUE OF CALGARY, ALBERTA

Polynesian Chicken

2–3 teaspoons oil
2–3 teaspoons butter
1 fryer, cut up or equivalent of fryer parts
1 onion, quartered and separated into layers
1 green pepper, cut into strips
1 30-ounce can sliced cling peaches, undrained
1 teaspoon cornstarch
1 teaspoon soy sauce
3 teaspoons vinegar
2 tomatoes, cut into sixths

Heat the oil and butter in a heavy skillet. Sauté the chicken pieces on all sides in the butter-oil mixture until golden in color. Add the onion and green pepper, cooking until the onion is transparent and the chicken is tender.

Measure 1 cup of the juice from the peaches and mix with the cornstarch, soy sauce, and vinegar. Pour over chicken and cook until sauce is clear and thickened slightly. Add the sliced peaches and tomatoes. Heat through and serve with cooked rice.

Onions, peppers, peaches, and tomatoes may be prepared early in the day and added after the chicken is cooked.

YIELD: 4 SERVINGS

No Regrets
THE JUNIOR LEAGUE OF PORTLAND, OREGON

· ·

Spicy Barbecued Chicken

1 3-pound fryer, cut up, or chicken parts
4 tablespoons catsup
2 tablespoons vinegar
1 tablespoon lemon juice
2 tablespoons Worcestershire sauce
¼ cup water
3 tablespoons melted butter
2 teaspoons hickory salt
1 teaspoon dry mustard
2 teaspoons chili powder
1 teaspoon paprika
¼ teaspoon cayenne pepper

Arrange chicken in baking pan. Combine all other ingredients and pour the sauce over chicken. Cover pan and bake at 500° for 15 minutes. Reduce oven to 350° and continue baking for 1 hour longer.

YIELD: 4–6 SERVINGS

A Taste of Oregon
THE JUNIOR LEAGUE OF EUGENE, OREGON

· ·

Oven Barbecued Chicken

6–8 pieces chicken
1 large onion, sliced
⅔ cup catsup
⅓ cup vinegar
4 tablespoons margarine
1 clove garlic, minced
1 teaspoon rosemary, crushed
1 teaspoon salt
½ teaspoon dry mustard

Place chicken in single layer in shallow greased casserole. Mix rest of ingredients in small pan and heat to boiling point. Pour over chicken. Bake at 350° for approximately 1 hour, basting several times.

YIELD: 6–8 SERVINGS

THE JUNIOR LEAGUE OF CALGARY, ALBERTA

Sesame Chicken

1 cup soda cracker crumbs
1 cup grated Parmesan cheese
1 teaspoon salt
3 teaspoons parsley flakes
6–8 pieces chicken
½ cup melted butter or margarine
2–3 tablespoons sesame seeds

Combine crumbs, cheese, salt, and parsley flakes. Dip chicken into butter and roll in crumb mixture. Arrange chicken in foil-lined shallow baking dish. Pour over any remaining butter and sprinkle with sesame seeds. Bake, covered, at 350° for 30 minutes; remove cover and bake for 30 minutes longer.

YIELD: 6 SERVINGS

THE JUNIOR LEAGUE OF BILLINGS, MONTANA

· · · · · · · · · · · · · · · · · · · ·

Yellow Rice and Chicken

1 tablespoon salt
1 fryer, cut into serving pieces
½ cup olive oil
2 cloves garlic, sliced
1 onion, chopped
1 green pepper, chopped
3 cups water
1 15-ounce can whole tomatoes
1 teaspoon saffron
1½ cups raw rice
Salt to taste
1-pound can petite pois for garnish
1 4-ounce jar sliced pimento for garnish

Salt chicken. Heat olive oil in large pot or Dutch oven. Brown garlic in oil. Fry chicken in oil, turning frequently to brown on all sides. When chicken is light brown, add onion and green pepper. When these become glazed, drain off most of the oil.

Add water, tomatoes, and saffron. Boil 5 minutes. Add rice and boil for 5–10 minutes. Stir with a fork. Cover pan and bake in a 325° oven until rice has absorbed most of the liquid, about 25 minutes.

Recipe continues . . .

Stir with a fork and add salt to taste. Garnish with heated peas and sliced pimento.

YIELD: 4 SERVINGS

A Taste of Oregon
THE JUNIOR LEAGUE OF EUGENE, OREGON

. . . .

Easy Orange Chicken

1 fryer, cut into serving pieces
½ stick butter, melted
1 12-ounce can frozen concentrated orange juice, thawed
1 12-ounce can bourbon
Salt, pepper, and garlic salt
½ cup toasted slivered almonds

Arrange chicken pieces in shallow baking pan. Combine butter, orange juice, and bourbon and pour over chicken. Sprinkle lightly with salt, pepper, and garlic salt and bake at 350° for 1 hour. Baste three to four times.

Before serving, sprinkle with slivered almonds.

YIELD: 4—6 SERVINGS

THE JUNIOR LEAGUE OF SPOKANE, WASHINGTON

. . . .

Chicken Artichoke Casserole

1 3-pound chicken, cut into serving pieces
1½ teaspoons salt
¼ teaspoon pepper
½ teaspoon paprika
6 tablespoons butter
1 16-ounce can artichoke hearts, drained
¼ pound fresh mushrooms, sliced
2 tablespoons flour
⅔ cup chicken broth
3 tablespoons sherry
¼ teaspoon rosemary

Sprinkle chicken with salt, pepper, and paprika. In skillet brown chicken in 4 tablespoons of the butter and transfer to a 2-quart casserole. Arrange artichoke hearts between chicken pieces.

Melt remaining butter in the skillet and in it sauté mushrooms until barely tender. Sprinkle flour over mushrooms and stir in broth, sherry, and rosemary. Cook, stirring, until slightly thickened, then pour over chicken and artichoke hearts. Cover and bake at 375° for 40 minutes, or until tender.

YIELD: 4 SERVINGS

Gourmet Olé
THE JUNIOR LEAGUE OF ALBUQUERQUE, NEW MEXICO

Chicken Hawaiian

2 3-pound chickens, cut into serving pieces
¼ cup butter
2 cloves garlic, minced
2 tablespoons shredded fresh ginger root
2 cups coconut milk
1¼ cups cooked rice
2 teaspoons coarse salt
1 cup shredded coconut
½ cup chopped green onion

Brown chicken pieces in butter. When brown on all sides, sprinkle with garlic and ginger. Pour coconut milk over, cover, and simmer for 1 hour. Add cooked rice, salt, and coconut. Simmer for 15–20 minutes longer.
Before serving, sprinkle with green onion.

YIELD: 8 SERVINGS

COCONUT MILK:
2 cups boiling water
7 ounces flaked coconut

Combine water and coconut and let stand 30 minutes. Strain through a cloth, squeezing out all liquid.

YIELD: 2 CUPS

THE JUNIOR LEAGUE OF EDMONTON, ALBERTA

. . . .

Chicken Breasts with Apricots and Avocado

6 whole chicken breasts, about 1 pound each, split, boned, and skinned
Salt and pepper to taste
¼ teaspoon nutmeg
4 tablespoons butter
4 green onions, thinly sliced (about ¼ cup)
¼ cup dry vermouth
1 cup heavy cream
12 fresh apricots, halved (preserved apricots may be substituted*)
2 tablespoons minced parsley
1 large ripe avocado
1 tablespoon lemon juice

Sprinkle the chicken with salt, pepper, and nutmeg. Melt the butter over medium heat and in it brown the chicken on all sides. When brown, remove from pan. Add the green onion and brown lightly while the last breasts are browning. Return all the breasts to the pan and add the vermouth. Cover and simmer for 8–10 minutes, or until done. Do not overcook. Remove chicken from the pan and keep warm.

Add the cream to the pan and stir over high heat until reduced and thickened. Add apricots and parsley to the sauce to warm the fruit.

Arrange chicken on serving platter. Spoon the apricots around and pour the sauce over. Slice the avocado; drizzle with lemon juice and arrange around the chicken.

YIELD: 6–8 SERVINGS

* If preserved apricots are used they may be heated in their own syrup rather than in the sauce.

THE JUNIOR LEAGUE OF VANCOUVER, BRITISH COLUMBIA

·   ·   ·   ·   ·   ·   ·   ·   ·   ·   ·   ·   ·   ·   ·   ·   ·

Breast of Chicken Supreme

6 whole chicken breasts
Salt, pepper, and paprika
Flour
Butter
2 large onions, finely chopped
⅔ cup chopped green pepper
½ stick butter
¼ cup water
1 cup white wine
1 pint sour cream

Season breasts to taste with salt, pepper, and paprika. Flour lightly. Brown them quickly in butter and transfer to buttered baking dish.

Sauté onions and green pepper in butter until onion is golden. Combine water, ½ cup of the wine, onions, and green pepper and pour over chicken. Cover and bake in 350° oven for 1 hour. Just before serving, combine remaining wine and sour cream and pour over chicken. Bake 5 minutes longer.

Serve with cooked rice.

YIELD: 6 SERVINGS

Something New Under the Sun
THE JUNIOR LEAGUE OF PHOENIX, ARIZONA

Chicken Breasts in Ginger Cream

¼ cup flour
½ teaspoon ground ginger
1 teaspoon salt
¼ teaspoon white pepper
4 large chicken breasts, halved, washed, and dried
6 tablespoons butter
3 tablespoons flour
1¼ cups chicken broth
¾ cup light cream
2 tablespoons finely minced crystallized ginger
Parsley sprigs

Put the ¼ cup flour, ginger, salt, and pepper in a paper bag. Shake the chicken breasts in the paper bag, a few pieces at a time, and shake off any excess flour. In a 10–12-inch enameled skillet or casserole heat the butter until frothy and brown the chicken breasts skin side down over moderate heat for about 10 minutes. Turn the chicken and brown for 10 more minutes. Cover the pan and simmer until done, about 10 minutes more.

Remove the chicken to a heated platter and keep warm in the oven. Add 3 tablespoons flour to the juices in the skillet and stir over low heat about 5 minutes. Add the chicken broth and cream. Stir until smooth and thickened. Season with salt and pepper and additional ground ginger if necessary.

Pour the sauce over the chicken breasts on the platter and garnish with crystallized ginger and parsley sprigs. Serve with chutney and curried rice.

YIELD: 8 SERVINGS

The California Heritage Cookbook
THE JUNIOR LEAGUE OF PASADENA, CALIFORNIA

· · · · · · · · · · · · · · ·

"*Mother Loded*" *Chicken*

2 whole chicken breasts, skinned, boned, and halved
4 2 x 1½ ¼-inch pieces Monterey Jack jalapeño cheese
½ teaspoon oregano
2 eggs
1 tablespoon grated Parmesan cheese
¼ teaspoon salt
¼ teaspoon pepper
1 tablespoon minced fresh parsley
Flour
¼ cup peanut oil or 2 tablespoons butter and 2 tablespoons oil
1 lemon, cut in wedges

Cut pocket in each half chicken breast about 2 x 3 inches (do not cut through). Roll Jack cheese in oregano and insert in pockets. Chill.

In medium bowl beat eggs, Parmesan cheese, salt, pepper, and parsley. Roll stuffed breasts in flour and then in egg mixture.

Heat oil and sauté breasts until crisp and brown. You may do this early in the day before baking. Arrange in baking dish.

Bake at 375° for 8–10 minutes. Serve garnished with lemon wedges.

YIELD: 4 SERVINGS

THE JUNIOR LEAGUE OF SACRAMENTO, CALIFORNIA

·   ·   ·   ·   ·   ·   ·   ·   ·   ·   ·   ·   ·   ·   ·   ·   ·   ·

Orange Glazed Chicken

1 6-ounce can frozen concentrated orange juice
¼ cup water
2 tablespoons soy sauce
1 garlic clove, minced
1 teaspoon salt
¼ teaspoon pepper
2 tablespoons candied or preserved ginger, chopped
3 whole chicken breasts, halved

Combine orange juice, water, soy sauce, garlic, salt, pepper, and ginger. Place chicken breasts in a shallow buttered casserole. Pour sauce over chicken and marinate in refrigerator for 3 hours or overnight, turning at least once.

Bake in a 350° oven for about 1 hour, basting several times.

YIELD: 6 SERVINGS

THE JUNIOR LEAGUE OF CALGARY, ALBERTA

· · · · · · · · · · · · · · · · · · ·

Crocked Orange Chicken

4–6 chicken breasts or 2½ pounds chicken pieces
½ teaspoon ginger
1 teaspoon salt
Dash pepper
1 8-ounce can frozen concentrated orange juice
1½ cups shredded coconut
2 cups orange segments or canned Mandarin oranges
2 green onion stalks, chopped (optional)

Put chicken, ginger, salt, pepper, and frozen orange juice in slow-cooking crockery pot and cook on low 6 hours.

Serve chicken on hot cooked rice on platter. Top with coconut, orange segments, and green onions. Serve chicken liquid in gravy boat, if desired.

YIELD: 4–6 SERVINGS

THE JUNIOR LEAGUE OF RIVERSIDE, CALIFORNIA

· · · · · · · · · · · · · · · · · ·

Chicken-Grape Casserole

6 whole chicken breasts, split, boned, and skinned
2 tablespoons butter
2½ cups sour cream
½ teaspoon salt
2 10¾-ounce cans cream of chicken soup
1 8-ounce can water chestnuts, sliced
Bread crumbs
Slivered almonds
1 1-pound can Thompson grapes, drained

Wrap chicken in aluminum foil, dotting with butter before sealing foil. Bake in a 400° oven for 45 minutes. Unwrap, reserving a few tablespoons of the broth.

Mix sour cream, salt, soup, and water chestnuts together. Put half of the mixture on the bottom of a 3-quart rectangular casserole. Arrange the chicken breasts on top and sprinkle with a few tablespoons of the broth. Pour the remaining sour cream mixture over it. Sprinkle with enough bread crumbs to cover the surface and generously cover with slivered almonds.

Bake, uncovered, at 350° for 30 minutes, or until bubbly. Put grapes all over the top, and bake for 5 minutes longer.

YIELD: 8 SERVINGS

THE JUNIOR LEAGUE OF LOS ANGELES, CALIFORNIA

Chicken Momi

3 large chicken breasts, boned and halved
Salt
½ cup half and half
1 cup soft bread crumbs
⅓ cup finely chopped onion
1 5-ounce can water chestnuts, drained and finely chopped
2 tablespoons butter
¼ pound ground veal
½ pound ground pork
1 egg
1 tablespoon soy sauce
1 teaspoon ground ginger
2 tablespoons each soft butter and honey
1 tablespoon each soy sauce and sesame seeds
Papaya and lime slices for garnish

Pound inside of chicken breasts to flatten slightly, make a lengthwise slit in side of each breast and sprinkle with salt.

To make stuffing, pour half and half over bread crumbs. Sauté onion and water chestnuts in 2 tablespoons butter. Mix onion with bread crumbs, ground meats, egg, soy sauce, and ginger. Fill each breast with ½ cup of the stuffing and fasten with skewers or wooden picks. Place skin side up in a greased baking pan.

Cream butter with honey; slowly beat in soy sauce. Spoon mixture over chicken. Bake at 325° for 45 minutes, basting occasionally with pan drippings. Sprinkle with sesame seeds, increase temperature to 450°, and bake 10 minutes longer.

Garnish with papaya and lime slices. Serve with fried rice and crispy Chinese pea pods.

YIELD: 6 SERVINGS

Epicure
THE JUNIOR LEAGUE OF NEWPORT HARBOR, CALIFORNIA

Chicken Florentine

2 whole chicken breasts, boned and halved
1 teaspoon salt
¼ cup flour
2 eggs, beaten
2 tablespoons vegetable oil
1 10-ounce package frozen chopped spinach
1 tablespoon butter
2 ounces grated Parmesan cheese
4 ounces mozzarella cheese, sliced
⅓ cup white wine
Juice of ½ lemon
½ cup chicken broth

Dredge chicken in salted flour. Dip in beaten eggs. Sauté in vegetable oil 10 minutes on each side.

Cook and drain spinach. Top with butter. Set aside.

Place chicken in heavy metal baking dish. Cover each breast with spinach. Sprinkle Parmesan cheese over spinach. Cover with sliced mozzarella. Bake at 350° for 35 minutes. Remove chicken to heated platter. Keep warm. To make sauce, add wine and lemon juice to pan; simmer and scrape until liquid is half gone. Add chicken broth, stir, and simmer 2 minutes. Pour over chicken or serve separately.

YIELD: 3–4 SERVINGS

Heritage Cookbook
THE JUNIOR LEAGUE OF SALT LAKE CITY, UTAH

Chicken Kiev

4 whole chicken breasts
Salt
8 tablespoons each chopped green onion and parsley
1 stick chilled butter, cut into 8 pieces
Flour
2 eggs, beaten
Bread crumbs

Cut chicken breasts in half lengthwise. Remove skin and cut meat away from bone. Be careful not to tear meat; each half should be in one piece.

Place each piece between two pieces of clear plastic wrap, and working out from center, pound with wooden mallet to form cutlets less than ¼ inch thick; peel off wrap and sprinkle with salt.

Sprinkle 1 tablespoon each of onion and parsley over each cutlet. Put butter at one end and roll jelly-roll fashion, tucking in sides. Press ends to seal well. Dust each roll in flour; dip in egg, then in bread crumbs. Chill thoroughly at least 1 hour.

Fry chicken rolls in deep hot oil (340°) for about 5 minutes, or until golden brown.

YIELD: 4–6 SERVINGS

THE JUNIOR LEAGUE OF LONG BEACH, CALIFORNIA

Chicken-Wild Rice Casserole

2 3-pound whole broiler-fryer chickens
1 cup water
1 cup dry sherry
1½ teaspoons salt
½ teaspoon curry powder
1 medium onion, sliced
½ cup sliced celery
1 pound fresh mushrooms
¼ cup butter
2 6-ounce packages long grain and wild rice
1 cup sour cream
1 10¾-ounce can cream of mushroom soup

Put chicken in a deep kettle. Add water, sherry, salt, curry powder, onion, and celery. Bring to a boil, cover, reduce heat, and simmer for 1 hour. Remove from heat and strain broth. Refrigerate chicken and broth.

When chicken is cool, remove from bones. Cut into bite-size pieces.

Wash mushrooms, pat dry, and sauté in butter until lightly browned. Reserve enough to circle top of casserole.

Measure chicken broth; use as part of liquid for cooking rice, following package directions.

Combine chicken, rice, and mushrooms in a 4-quart casserole. Blend sour cream and mushroom soup. Mix with chicken mixture. Arrange reserved mushrooms on top of casserole. Bake at 350° for 1 hour.

YIELD: 8–10 SERVINGS

THE JUNIOR LEAGUE OF OGDEN, UTAH

Baked Chicken Breasts Supreme

6 12-ounce fryer breasts
2 cups sour cream
¼ cup lemon juice
4 teaspoons Worcestershire sauce
4 teaspoons celery salt
2 teaspoons paprika
½ teaspoon garlic powder
4 teaspoons salt
½ teaspoon pepper
1¾ cups packaged bread crumbs
½ cup butter or margarine

Cut chicken breasts in half, remove skin, and wipe well with damp paper towels.

In a bowl, combine sour cream, lemon juice, Worcestershire sauce, celery salt, paprika, garlic, salt, and pepper. Dip each piece of chicken in the mixture, coating well. Place in large bowl and let stand, covered, in refrigerator overnight.

Preheat oven to 350°. Remove chicken from refrigerator. Roll in crumbs, coating evenly. Arrange in single layer in large, shallow baking pan. This can be done early in the day, covered, and refrigerated again until ready to bake.

Melt butter in a saucepan. Spoon half over chicken. Bake, uncovered, for 45 minutes. Spoon rest of butter over chicken and bake 10–15 minutes more, or until chicken is tender and nicely browned.

YIELD: 8 SERVINGS

Gourmet Olé
THE JUNIOR LEAGUE OF ALBUQUERQUE, NEW MEXICO

Chicken Sesame

8 half breasts of chicken
8 thin slices ham
16 thin slices Swiss cheese
1 egg beaten with 1 tablespoon water
¾ cup bread crumbs
¼ cup butter
Sesame seeds

Bone and skin the chicken breasts. Cut a slit in each piece and insert 1 ham slice and 2 cheese slices. Press the edges of the chicken meat together firmly, dip each in the egg mixture, and roll in the crumbs. This may be done several hours before cooking. Cover and refrigerate.

When ready to cook, brown each piece of chicken in butter and arrange side by side in an ovenproof dish. Cover with the sauce and sprinkle generously with the sesame seeds. Bake at 350° for 35–45 minutes, or until tender.

SAUCE:
2 tablespoons melted butter
1 tablespoon soy sauce
½ cup chicken stock

Combine all ingredients.

YIELD: 8 SERVINGS

THE JUNIOR LEAGUE OF GREAT FALLS, MONTANA

Cheese-Stuffed Chicken Breasts

2 tablespoons butter
2 tablespoons flour
½ cup evaporated milk or light cream
¼ teaspoon salt
Dash cayenne, parsley, and rosemary
1 cup shredded cheddar or brick cheese
4 whole chicken breasts, boned and halved
Flour
2 eggs, beaten
1 cup finely crushed cornflake crumbs

In advance or early in the day, melt butter in saucepan and blend in flour. Stir in milk. Add seasonings. Cook, stirring, until mixture is thick. Stir in cheese and stir until cheese is melted. Spoon into shallow pan. Cover and chill. Cut into 8 wedges.

Place each chicken breast between two layers of plastic wrap. Pound to ¼ inch thickness. Peel off plastic. Place cheese wedge in center and, tucking in sides, roll jelly-roll fashion. Coat with flour, dip in egg, then roll in crumbs. Place rolls on a jelly-roll pan and refrigerate overnight or several hours.

Next day fry rolls in deep hot fat (375°) for 5 minutes, turning once. Drain on paper towels. Freeze until ready to use. Place frozen rolls on baking sheet. Bake 45 minutes at 350°.

YIELD: 8 SERVINGS

THE JUNIOR LEAGUE OF EDMONTON, ALBERTA

Curried Chicken

⅓ cup flour
½ teaspoon ground ginger
1 tablespoon curry powder
1 teaspoon salt
3 whole chicken breasts, boned and halved
¼ cup butter
1 8-ounce can sliced pineapple
1 8-ounce can mandarin oranges
1 tart apple, sliced
⅓ cup heavy cream
1 tablespoon lemon juice

Combine flour, ginger, curry, and salt. Put in a plastic bag with chicken and shake until chicken is well coated. Brown chicken on all sides in the butter. Add remainder of flour mixture while browning.

Grease a casserole. Arrange chicken in it. Drain pineapple and oranges, saving juice. Cut pineapple slices in half. Place pineapple, orange, and apple over chicken.

Pour fruit juices into skillet in which chicken was browned, add cream and lemon juice, and simmer, stirring, until sauce is thickened. Pour sauce over chicken, cover, and bake at 350° for 1 hour.

YIELD: 6 SERVINGS

THE JUNIOR LEAGUE OF BUTTE, MONTANA

Baked Chicken Pieces

2 tablespoons Dijon mustard
1 pint sour cream
½ teaspoon salt
¼ teaspoon white pepper
Wings, legs, and breasts to serve 4
Fine bread or cornflake crumbs

In a medium-size bowl combine mustard, sour cream, salt, and pepper.

Dip chicken pieces in the mixture and then coat them with fine bread crumbs or cornflakes. Arrange the pieces on a baking sheet in one layer and cover with aluminum foil. Bake at 400° for 30 minutes. Remove foil and bake at 450° for 20 minutes, or until chicken parts are golden brown and tender.

Serve with fresh fruit and wild rice.

YIELD: 4 SERVINGS

THE JUNIOR LEAGUE OF BUTTE, MONTANA

. . . .

Chicken Chow Mein

¼ cup cooking oil
1 teaspoon salt
½ teaspoon pepper
1 onion, sliced
3 cups thinly and diagonally sliced celery
1 17-ounce can bean sprouts
1 4-ounce can water chestnuts, sliced
2 teaspoons sugar
2 cups chicken stock, broth, or water
2½ tablespoons cornstarch
¼ cup cold water
¼ cup soy sauce
2 cups sliced cooked chicken

Recipe continues . . .

Heat oil in a deep skillet. Add salt, pepper, onion, celery, bean sprouts, water chestnuts, sugar, and chicken broth. Cook about 10 minutes. Do not overcook vegetables.

Blend together cornstarch, water, and soy sauce. Add to vegetables and stir until mixture thickens. Stir in chicken and serve immediately over chow mein noodles or rice.

YIELD: 5–6 SERVINGS

THE JUNIOR LEAGUE OF OGDEN, UTAH

·   ·   ·   ·   ·   ·   ·   ·   ·   ·   ·   ·   ·   ·   ·   ·   ·   ·   ·

Sandra's Chicken Cream Tortillas Casserole

12 corn tortillas
2 tablespoons oil
Salt
1 onion, chopped
1½ cups half and half
1 4-ounce can chopped green chilies
Salt and pepper to taste
Taco sauce to taste
3 cups cooked and boned chicken or 1½ pounds ground round, cooked
8 ounces sharp cheddar cheese, shredded

Pass tortillas through hot oil to soften. Drain on paper towel. Sprinkle with salt and tear into quarters. Set aside.

To make sauce, sauté onion in remaining oil. Add the half and half. Add chilies, salt, pepper, and taco sauce. Simmer 5 minutes.

In buttered 2-quart casserole layer tortillas, chicken or ground round, cheese and sauce. Bake, uncovered, in 350° oven 45 minutes.

YIELD: 6 SERVINGS

Something New Under the Sun
THE JUNIOR LEAGUE OF PHOENIX, ARIZONA

·   ·   ·   ·   ·   ·   ·   ·   ·   ·   ·   ·   ·   ·   ·   ·   ·   ·   ·

Sautéed Chicken Livers and Mushrooms

18 chicken livers
¼ pound mushrooms, sliced
1 tablespoon finely chopped green pepper (optional)
1 tablespoon finely chopped parsley
1 tablespoon finely chopped onion
4 tablespoons butter
1 tablespoon flour
1 cup white wine
1 cup chicken broth
1 small bay leaf
⅛ teaspoon each thyme and rosemary
Salt
Pepper
Grated nutmeg

Sauté the chicken livers, mushrooms, green pepper, parsley, and onion in the butter over low heat. Cook about 4 minutes, stirring frequently. Add the flour, and when lightly browned add the wine and broth gradually, stirring constantly. Add the bay leaf, thyme, and rosemary, cover, and simmer very gently for 10–15 minutes, stirring occasionally.

Season to taste with salt, pepper, and nutmeg. Serve at once with cooked rice or on triangles of hot buttered toast.

YIELD: 4 SERVINGS

No Regrets
THE JUNIOR LEAGUE OF PORTLAND, OREGON

Chicken Livers Elegant

12 chicken livers, cut into 1-inch pieces
6 slices bacon, cut into 1-inch squares
½ pound lean ground beef, pressed into miniature meat balls
4 tablespoons chopped onion
3 teaspoons fresh parsley
½ pound fresh mushrooms, sliced
1 tablespoon Italian herb seasoning
1 teaspoon salt
Freshly ground black pepper to taste
3 teaspoons tomato paste
6 tablespoons heavy cream

In a large skillet fry chicken livers, bacon, meat balls, onion, parsley, mushrooms, and seasonings until livers and beef are no longer pink. Stir in tomato paste and cream and cook until hot.

Serve with garlic bread and tossed green salad.

YIELD: 4–6 SERVINGS

THE JUNIOR LEAGUE OF TACOMA, WASHINGTON

· · · · · · · · · · · · · · · · · ·

Chicken Livers and Grapes

2 pounds chicken livers
6 tablespoons melted butter
½ pound green seedless grapes
½ cup port

In a skillet brown chicken livers in the melted butter over high heat. When brown and done to taste, preferably pink, remove to a warm platter.

Cook grapes in same skillet for 4 minutes over low heat. Pour over chicken livers. Pour wine into pan. Cook for a couple of minutes, stirring all brown bits from bottom and sides of pan, and pour over chicken livers and grapes.

Serve with cooked rice, wild rice, or rice pilaf.

YIELD: 4 SERVINGS

THE JUNIOR LEAGUE OF SAN DIEGO, CALIFORNIA

. . . .

Cuyama "Chicken" with Valley Mushrooms Pâté

4 tablespoons olive oil
2 cloves garlic, chopped
6 pheasant breasts or chicken breast halves, boned
½ teaspoon salt
4 cups sour cream (extra cream if breasts are very large)
½ cup dry red wine

Heat olive oil lightly in a large heavy skillet. Add chopped garlic and sauté for 3 minutes. Flour pheasant or chicken breasts, place in olive oil, sprinkle with salt, and brown gently on each side. Set aside each piece as it is browned. Arrange in layers in a stove-to-table casserole and cover each piece liberally with sour cream, especially the top layer.

Just before placing in oven, pour the wine gently around the breasts. Bake at 350° for 2 hours.

Garnish each serving with a Valley Mushroom and serve with steamed wild rice.

YIELD: 6 SERVINGS

VALLEY MUSHROOMS PÂTÉ:
6 very large fresh mushrooms
¼ pound fresh chicken livers
2 tablespoons olive oil
3 cloves garlic, minced

Recipe continues . . .

Wash mushrooms and remove stems. Set aside.

Cut chicken livers into small pieces and sauté gently in olive oil with the garlic, turning with a fork while cooking. Do not let pan overheat. Liver should be in tiny pieces. When nicely browned, remove from heat.

Fill cavity in each mushroom with pâté. Place mushrooms cap side down in small oiled casserole. Cook the mushrooms with the breasts for about 10 minutes before serving.

THE JUNIOR LEAGUE OF SANTA BARBARA, CALIFORNIA

Roast Rock Cornish Hens Montmorency

6 1¼–1½-pound Cornish hens
Salt and pepper
½ cup butter or margarine (1 stick)
1 1-pound can dark, sweet, pitted cherries
⅔ cup brandy
2 tablespoons lemon juice
1 13¾-ounce can chicken broth
2 teaspoons cornstarch
2 tablespoons water
Watercress for garnish (optional)

Heat oven to 425°. Rinse hens under cold water, drain, and pat dry. Sprinkle hens inside and out with salt and pepper. Brush with butter or margarine. Arrange hens on sides in a shallow open roasting pan. Roast 10 minutes; turn to other side and roast 10 minutes. Turn hens breast side up and roast until done, or until juices run clear when hen is pricked with a fork, 30–40 minutes. Remove hens to a platter and keep warm.

Drain cherries; reserve cherries and half the juice. Pour excess fat from roasting pan and place over medium heat. Add brandy and cook for 1 minute. Add reserved cherry juice and lemon juice. Cook until reduced by half. Add chicken broth and cherries. Simmer 3–4 minutes. Mix cornstarch with water; stir into sauce in pan. Bring to a boil, stirring constantly. Correct seasoning and pour over hens on platter. Garnish with watercress, if desired.

YIELD: 6 SERVINGS

THE JUNIOR LEAGUE OF VANCOUVER, BRITISH COLUMBIA

· · · · · · · · · · · · · · · · · ·

Cornish Game Hens with Polenta

1 Cornish hen per person
Salt and pepper
1 sprig rosemary per bird
1 leaf sage per bird
6 slices bacon, diced
Garlic salt
1 cup red wine
1 cup hot water
1 tablespoon flour

Rinse birds and pat dry. Sprinkle salt and pepper in body cavities. Stuff 1 sprig rosemary and 1 leaf sage into each bird.

Heat oven to 400°. Sprinkle diced bacon in a roasting pan and bake 5 minutes in oven. Add birds to bacon, sprinkle with salt, pepper, and garlic salt. Turn birds in bacon drippings to coat completely, then roast them in oven until lightly browned on all sides. Lower oven heat to 325°. Add wine and water to pan. Cover and cook birds for 1–1¼ hours, or until tender, basting often. Length of cooking time will depend on size of birds. More water should be added when necessary to keep pan juices at a constant level (2 cups).

When birds are done, remove to a warm platter. Skim fat from pan juices and thicken with flour. Add more salt and pepper to taste. Serve birds and gravy with Polenta.

This recipe may also be used with squab.

YIELD: 6 SERVINGS

Recipe continues . . .

POLENTA:*
6 cups water
½ tablespoon salt
1½ cups polenta meal
½ cup corn meal
½ stick butter, cut in pieces

In a heavy kettle bring water and salt to a full rolling boil. Mix polenta and corn meal together. Slowly add polenta-corn meal mix to water while beating constantly with a wire whisk to prevent lumps from forming. Cook, stirring, over moderate heat for about 5 minutes, or until it thickens. Cook over low heat for 30 minutes, stirring frequently. Stir in butter and turn polenta out onto a large platter. Slice and serve.

* Polenta is a staple in the cooking of Northern Italy. Polenta meal (a coarse corn meal) can be purchased in Italian grocery stores. Any leftover polenta is delicious the next day, diced and fried in butter. It can also be topped with slices of Monterey Jack cheese and sprinkled with Parmesan, then put in the oven for a few minutes until cheese is melted.

THE JUNIOR LEAGUE OF BAKERSFIELD, CALIFORNIA

Duckling aux Cerises

2 5-pound domestic ducklings
4 tablespoons butter
½ cup finely chopped onion
¾ cup dry Marsala
1½ cups chicken stock
1 bay leaf
2½ cups pitted black cherries with juice
3 tablespoons cornstarch
1 teaspoon salt
⅛ teaspoon freshly ground pepper

Preheat oven to 500°, then reduce to 350°. Rinse, pat dry, and quarter ducks. Brown quarters in butter in a skillet. When brown transfer pieces to a rack in a shallow pan and roast, uncovered, at 350°, for 90 minutes. Pour off all but 2 tablespoons fat from the skillet in which duck was browned. Sauté onions in skillet for 5 minutes, or until soft. Add Marsala, stock, and bay leaf.

Drain cherries and mix ¾ cup cherry juice with cornstarch, salt, and pepper. Stir into sauce in the skillet and simmer until thickened. Add cherries and simmer for 5 minutes.

Put duck on a warmed platter and cover with some sauce. Serve the rest of the sauce separately.

YIELD: 4 SERVINGS

San Francisco à la Carte
THE JUNIOR LEAGUE OF SAN FRANCISCO, CALIFORNIA

· ·

Duckling with Almond Gravy

2 4–4½-pound domestic ducklings
2 teaspoons salt
½ teaspoon pepper
3 oranges
10 slices raisin bread, toasted
2 oranges, sectioned, seeds and membrane discarded
1½ cups diced celery
2 teaspoons grated orange peel
¼ teaspoon dried thyme
Watercress
Orange slices

Recipe continues . . .

Rinse, dry, and rub the ducks with 1 teaspoon salt and ½ teaspoon pepper. Cut the three oranges in half and reserve them for the basting juice while the ducks are roasting.

To prepare stuffing, discard crusts from the toasted raisin bread and break the bread in small pieces into a large mixing bowl. Add the two sectioned oranges, celery, orange peel, remaining 1 teaspoon salt, and thyme. Stuff the ducks with the mixture, skewer closed, and truss.

Arrange the ducks on a rack in an open roasting pan. Roast in a preheated 325° oven for 2–2½ hours, or until tender. Drain the fat every 30 minutes. Baste frequently by squeezing half an orange over the birds. Rub the skin with same orange half. Add the orange skins to the roasting pan to add flavor while roasting.

Remove the ducks to a serving platter and keep warm while making the gravy. To serve, garnish the serving platter with sprigs of fresh watercress and orange slices. Pour Almond Gravy into a gravy boat and pass separately.

YIELD: 4 SERVINGS

ALMOND GRAVY:
1 cup water
1 cup fresh orange juice
2 tablespoons cornstarch
1 teaspoon molasses
2 teaspoons soy sauce
1 teaspoon salt
½ teaspoon pepper
½ cup slivered almonds
2 tablespoons butter

To prepare gravy, drain the fat from the juices in the roasting pan, reserving 1 tablespoon fat. Add the water to the pan, scraping the browned bits from the bottom, and strain the sauce into a 2-quart saucepan. Mix the orange juice with the cornstarch in a small bowl and add to the juices. Cook over low heat, stirring constantly, until the sauce is as thick as heavy cream, about 8–10 minutes. Add the molasses, soy sauce, 1 teaspoon salt, and ½ teaspoon pepper. Cook for 3 more minutes and strain the gravy again.

Meanwhile, in a small skillet sauté the almonds in the butter over medium heat for 2–3 minutes. Add the almonds to the gravy.

The California Heritage Cookbook
THE JUNIOR LEAGUE OF PASADENA, CALIFORNIA

· · · · · · · · · · · · · · · · ·

Canard au Poivre Vert
(Duck Breast with Green Peppercorns)

2 4–5-pound ducks
1½ teaspoons salt
½ teaspoon freshly ground white pepper
2 tablespoons flour
3 tablespoons sweet butter
2 tablespoons chopped shallots
2 tablespoons cognac
½ cup brown gravy, homemade or canned
3 tablespoons green peppercorns, mashed with the side of a heavy
knife into a purée
1½ cups heavy cream
2 tablespoons of chopped, mixed fresh parsley and tarragon

Ask the butcher to cut and bone out the ducks or do it yourself. The idea is to cut each bird into four pieces (two legs and two breasts), to remove the skin, and to bone each piece, leaving only a small piece of the wing bone at the first joint of the wing. Each boned-out piece should weigh about 4 ounces. Reserve the skin, bones, gizzards, necks, livers, etc. for another use.

Pound meat thinly and season with ½ teaspoon of the salt and the pepper, dredge with flour, and shake off excess. Melt butter in a large skillet and sauté meat over medium heat for about 3 minutes on each side, or until done to taste. The meat should be slightly pink inside. Arrange on serving platter and keep warm in a 180° oven.

Recipe continues . . .

Sauté shallots in the pan drippings for 30 seconds. Add cognac, brown gravy, crushed peppercorns, and remaining salt. Bring to a boil, add cream, and boil again. Reduce sauce over high heat for 4–5 minutes, or until it coats a spoon. Add parsley and tarragon. Coat meat with sauce and serve immediately.

The breasts have a nicer shape and are slightly more tender than the legs. Serve your guests the nicer pieces.

YIELD: 4–6 SERVINGS

THE JUNIOR LEAGUE OF LOS ANGELES, CALIFORNIA

Turkey Picatta

½ 2-pound turkey breast
2 tablespoons butter
2 tablespoons oil
½ cup flour
Salt and pepper to taste
1 clove garlic, minced
Juice of 2 lemons
Capers and lemon slices for garnish (optional)

Carefully skin and bone turkey breast. Place in freezer for 1 hour, or until firm but not frozen, then slice thinly.

Heat butter and oil in skillet over medium heat. Lightly dredge turkey slices in flour. Season with salt and pepper. Sauté in butter and oil until lightly browned, about 3–4 minutes on each side. Transfer to heated platter and keep warm. Continue browning remaining turkey slices, adding more butter and oil as necessary.

When all of the turkey is browned, turn heat to low and add garlic to juices remaining in skillet. Sauté for 1 minute. Add the lemon juice. Heat thoroughly, scraping pan to incorporate drippings into sauce. Adjust seasoning with salt and pepper to taste. Pour over turkey slices and garnish with capers and lemon slices, if desired.

YIELD: 4 SERVINGS

THE JUNIOR LEAGUE OF SAN JOSE, CALIFORNIA

· · · · · · · · · · · · · · · · · · · ·

Roast Wild Duck

6 medium ducks
Lemon juice
1 teaspoon salt
½ teaspoon pepper
1 cup each diced apple, celery, and onion

SAUCE:
Juice of 2 lemons
2 tablespoons Worcestershire sauce
2 tablespoons sugar

Rub cleaned ducks with lemon juice. Salt and pepper inside and outside. Stuff cavities with apple, celery, and onion. Arrange in baking pan and bake at 450° for 15 minutes. Cover ducks loosely with foil and continue cooking for 30–45 minutes.

Mix sauce ingredients; pour over ducks before serving.

YIELD: 6 SERVINGS

THE JUNIOR LEAGUE OF BAKERSFIELD, CALIFORNIA

· · · · · · · · · · · · · · · · · · ·

Wild Duck with Apricot Sauce

1 duck per person
Salt
Pepper
Soft butter
½ lemon per person
3 slices bacon per person
½ cup beer per person
½ cup apricot jam per person
1 tablespoon prepared mustard
1 teaspoon grated orange peel per person

Sprinkle ducks inside and out with salt and pepper and rub skin with softened butter. Tuck half a lemon inside each cavity. Place breast side up in roasting pan. Cut bacon slices in half and place over each bird. Roast in a 450° oven for 25 minutes so the birds brown lightly.

Meanwhile, combine in a saucepan the beer, apricot jam, mustard, and orange peel. Bring to a boil, stirring constantly, and remove from heat. Reduce oven to 425°. Spoon sauce on birds and cook 25–40 minutes longer for rare to medium.

YIELD: 1 SERVING

THE JUNIOR LEAGUE OF CALGARY, ALBERTA

. . . .

Wild Duck à la Duwall

4 small wild ducks
½ cup flour
Salt and pepper
2 tablespoons salad oil
1 medium onion, sliced
1½ cups apple juice
¼ cup soy sauce

Cut ducks into serving pieces; shake in flour, mixed with salt and pepper. Heat oil in heavy skillet and in it brown duck on all sides. Remove from skillet. Drain off oil leaving 2 tablespoons in skillet. Turn heat to low, add onion, and sauté until tender. Pour apple juice and soy sauce into the pan. Add browned duck pieces. Simmer 1 hour, or until tender, adding a little more apple juice if necessary.

Place the ducks on a serving platter. Spoon sauce over and serve.

YIELD: 4 SERVINGS

THE JUNIOR LEAGUE OF SEATTLE, WASHINGTON

·　·　·　·　·　·　·　·　·　·　·　·　·　·　·　·

Roast Wild Duck with Currant Sauce

2–3 wild ducks, ready to cook
Red wine
Water
1 stick butter, melted
6 tablespoons currant jelly
3 tablespoons sugar
Juice of ½ orange
2 tablespoons grated orange rind
¼ teaspoon salt
⅛ teaspoon Tabasco

Put ducks in a crock or bowl and cover with half red wine and half water. Refrigerate for 4–5 days before cooking.

When ready to cook, remove ducks from marinade and wipe dry with paper towels. Place on rack, breasts up, in large open roasting pan and roast at 350° for 2 hours, or until done to taste, basting occasionally with melted butter.

For the sauce, beat together the currant jelly, sugar, and orange juice.

Recipe continues . . .

Add remaining ingredients and stir over low heat until jelly is melted and sauce is hot. Serve with the ducks.

YIELD: 1 DUCK PER PERSON

THE JUNIOR LEAGUE OF SPOKANE, WASHINGTON

. . . .

Judy's Wild Duck

3 duck breasts
Salt and pepper
2 tablespoons olive oil
1 cup orange juice
1 cup red wine
1 onion, chopped
Juice of 1 lemon
½ teaspoon marjoram
½ teaspoon rosemary
Pinch oregano
2 apples, quartered
1 orange, quartered
1 cup consommé
1 tablespoon Cointreau

Season duck breasts with salt and pepper. Brown in hot olive oil. Remove to a 1½-quart casserole dish.

In the same pan, add orange juice, wine, onion, lemon juice, marjoram, and oregano. Bring to boil. Pour over duck. Add apple and orange pieces. Add consommé and Cointreau. Cover. Bake at 325° for 2½ hours, or until tender

YIELD: 2–3 SERVINGS

Heritage Cookbook
THE JUNIOR LEAGUE OF SALT LAKE CITY, UTAH

. . . .

Centennial Duck Breasts

10 duck breasts
Flour
½ cup butter
5 apples, chopped
5 oranges, chopped
5 onions, chopped
2 cups white wine

Roll duck breasts in flour and brown in butter. Then layer apples, oranges, and onions over the breasts and cover with wine. Cover pan and simmer for 45 minutes.

Serve with wild rice and fresh steamed broccoli.

YIELD: 6 SERVINGS

THE JUNIOR LEAGUE OF BUTTE, MONTANA

· · · · · · · · · · · · · · · ·

Quail Sullivan

8 quail, cleaned and halved lengthwise
2 tablespoons butter
¼ cup chopped onion
¼ cup chopped celery
½ pound fresh mushrooms, sliced
¼ teaspoon rosemary
½ cup dry white wine
1 10¾-ounce can cream of mushroom soup

Brown quail in butter. Add remaining ingredients and simmer over low heat for 45 minutes.

YIELD: 4 SERVINGS

THE JUNIOR LEAGUE OF BOISE, IDAHO

· · · · · · · · · · · · · · · ·

Pheasant Cumberland

2 pheasants
Flour seasoned with salt and pepper
½ cup butter
¼ cup dry vermouth
½ cup chicken stock
1 cup currant jelly
2 tablespoons Dijon mustard
½ teaspoon scraped onion
⅛ teaspoon powdered ginger
Grated rind of 1 orange
Grated rind of 1 lemon
½ cup orange juice
2 tablespoons lemon juice

Cut the pheasant into serving pieces, getting three pieces of breast per bird. Shake in seasoned flour and brown each piece in butter. Transfer to a shallow ovenproof dish. Deglaze the skillet with the vermouth. Add the stock and cook for a few minutes, scraping the brown bits from the sides of the pan. Whisk in the currant jelly, add the remaining ingredients and simmer another few minutes until blended.

Pour sauce over the pheasant, cover loosely with foil, and bake in a 325° oven approximately 1 hour, or until tender, depending upon the age of the birds. Uncover the last 20 minutes and baste the birds once in a while.

Delicious with wild rice.

YIELD: 6 SERVINGS

THE JUNIOR LEAGUE OF GREAT FALLS, MONTANA

Barbecue-Smoked Wild Duck

Wild ducks, plucked and cleaned
Vegetable oil
2 heads of garlic for every 2–3 ducks
Tabasco

For each 4–5 ducks, put 1 cup of oil in blender container. Remove garlic cloves from head and cut off hard ends but do not remove skin. Add to blender. Add a couple of dashes of Tabasco and blend on high speed for about 1 minute. Pour over ducks in glass, pottery, or stainless steel pot. Marinate at least 2 hours, or better yet, half a day, turning ducks frequently in the oil.

Use covered barbecue with a medium-hot fire. Roast, covered, 20 minutes for Teal, 30–35 minutes for Mallard. Meat should be cooked but not dry.

YIELD: ALLOW 1 LARGE MALLARD DUCK PER PERSON OR TWO SMALL TEAL DUCKS

THE JUNIOR LEAGUE OF SAN JOSE, CALIFORNIA

· · · · · · · · · · · · · · · · · ·

Pheasants in Wine

2 pheasants
1 stick butter
2 tablespoons chopped onion
½ cup chopped green pepper
2 tablespoons olive oil
Water
Salt and pepper
1 pound fresh mushrooms
1 tablespoon chopped parsley
1½ cups heated white wine

Recipe continues . . .

Clean and disjoint the pheasants. Brown the pieces lightly in 4 tablespoons butter in a skillet. Remove from heat.

In a separate pan, sauté the onion and green pepper in olive oil until brown. Add 3 tablespoons water, salt, and pepper. Add to pheasants, cover, and cook very slowly for about 2 hours, adding a few tablespoons of water at a time is necessary.

Sauté the mushrooms in remaining butter and add to pheasants. Add parsley and wine and simmer for 3 minutes.

Serve with wild rice.

YIELD: 4 SERVINGS

No Regrets
THE JUNIOR LEAGUE OF PORTLAND, OREGON

Burgundy Pheasant

1 pheasant or grouse, cut into serving pieces
Flour seasoned with salt and pepper
Oil
1 10½-ounce can consommé
1½ cups Burgundy
1 tablespoon celery salt
1 onion, diced
Salt and pepper to taste
1 stick butter
Cream (optional)

Shake pheasant in seasoned flour and sauté in hot oil until brown on all sides. Add consommé, Burgundy, celery salt, onion, and salt and pepper and dot with butter. Cover and simmer 1–1½ hours.

Transfer pheasant to serving platter and thicken gravy with 2 tablespoons flour mixed with 2 tablespoons water or wine. If desired, stir in a little cream. The gravy practically makes itself!

YIELD: 4 SERVINGS

THE JUNIOR LEAGUE OF SPOKANE, WASHINGTON

Simply Elegant Pheasant

1 cup flour
1 teaspoon salt
½ teaspoon pepper
1 pheasant, cut into serving pieces
½ cup butter
1 pint heavy cream

Combine the flour, salt, and pepper in a brown paper bag. Shake the pheasant pieces in this until well coated. In a heavy roaster melt the butter. Slowly brown the pheasant pieces on all sides. Add more butter if necessary. Cover and bake in 300° oven for 2 hours.

Remove from the oven and let cool a little. Now slowly add the cream to the pheasant. Cover and return to the oven for 1 more hour.

When cooked, you have a tender succulent pheasant in rich creamy gravy. Serve it with wild rice.

YIELD: 4 SERVINGS

THE JUNIOR LEAGUE OF GREAT FALLS, MONTANA

Arizona Game Birds

8–12 doves
1½ cups flour
½ teaspoon salt
½ teaspoon pepper
½ teaspoon seasoning salt
4 tablespoons butter
2 tablespoons vegetable oil
½ cup red wine
2 cups beef bouillon or homemade beef stock
1 medium onion, chopped
1½ cups pitted prunes (about 12)
2 large tart cooking apples, chopped
1 tablespoon brown sugar
2 stalks celery, chopped
1 tablespoon seedless raisins
Salt and pepper to taste
½ cup dry red wine
4 tablespoons soft butter
½ cup flour

Wash doves in cold water and pat dry. Coat doves in flour mixed with salt, pepper, and seasoning salt. Brown quickly in 4 tablespoons butter with the 2 tablespoons oil. Transfer to heavy pan.

Add ½ cup wine to pan used to brown doves and stir over high heat. When liquid is reduced by half, pour into pan with doves.

Add bouillon, onion, prunes, apples, sugar, celery, raisins, and salt and pepper. Bake in 325° oven for 2½ hours. At the end of 2 hours baking, add ½ cup red wine.

Remove from oven and strain broth into a saucepan.

Combine soft butter and ½ cup flour. Then stir 1 tablespoon at a time into the strained broth, cooking and stirring over moderate heat. This makes a rich gravy.

Serve doves with gravy over a bed of rice.

YIELD: 4–6 SERVINGS

THE JUNIOR LEAGUE OF TUCSON, ARIZONA

· · · · · · · · · · · · · · · · · · · ·

Baked Quail

12 quail soaked in salted water for several hours
¼ cup butter
¼ cup chopped onion
1 cup sliced mushrooms
1½ tablespoons flour
1 teaspoon salt
¼ teaspoon pepper
2 tablespoons chopped parsley
1 cup chicken broth
1 cup dry white wine

Sauté quail in butter in heavy roasting pan for about 10 minutes, or until brown on all sides. Remove quail and sauté onion and mushrooms in same butter until onions are transparent. Stir in flour, salt, pepper, and parsley. Slowly stir in broth and wine.

Return quail to pan, cover, and bake for 1 hour in a 350° oven.

YIELD: 2 QUAIL PER SERVING

THE JUNIOR LEAGUE OF BAKERSFIELD, CALIFORNIA

· · · · · · · · · · · · · · · · · · · ·

Fish and Seafood

Halibut Skillet Special

1 pound halibut filets
⅓ onion, sliced
Lemon wedge
Parsley sprigs
¾ cup chopped onion
¼ pound fresh mushrooms, sliced
1 clove garlic, minced
2 tablespoons butter
1 package fresh spinach or 10-ounce package frozen spinach,
thawed and drained
¾ teaspoon salt
3 eggs, beaten
Grated Parmesan cheese

Poach halibut by simmering for 5 minutes in salted water with onion slices, lemon, and parsley. Drain. Discard all but fish. Flake poached halibut.

Sauté chopped onion, mushrooms, and garlic in butter 5 minutes. Add halibut, uncooked spinach, and salt. Cook gently for 3–4 minutes. Stir in eggs and cook until eggs are set. Sprinkle with cheese.

YIELD: 5 SERVINGS

Heritage Cookbook
THE JUNIOR LEAGUE OF SALT LAKE CITY, UTAH

Halibut Steaks with Sauce

⅓ stick butter, melted
Juice of ½ lemon
½ cup sour cream
1–1½ pounds halibut steaks
Salt and pepper
1 onion, sliced and separated into rings
1 cup shredded medium-sharp cheddar cheese

Melt the butter and add the lemon juice and sour cream.

Sprinkle the halibut steaks with salt and pepper and place in a baking dish. Arrange the onion rings over the fish. Pour the sauce over fish and onion rings and sprinkle the cheese on top.

Bake at 350° for 35 minutes.

YIELD: 4–6 SERVINGS

A Taste of Oregon
THE JUNIOR LEAGUE OF EUGENE, OREGON

Red Snapper Creole

1 4–5-pound red snapper or 6 medium filets
Salt and pepper to taste
1 tablespoon butter
1–2 tablespoons flour
6 slices bacon
2 large onions, chopped
1 clove garlic, minced
2 16-ounce cans tomatoes
1 cup water
Parsley
½ teaspoon thyme
2 bay leaves
Lemon wedges
3 hard-boiled eggs, halved

Wash fish thoroughly, inside and out, and rub with salt and pepper. Put in baking pan, dot with butter, and sprinkle with flour. Bake at 350° for 15 minutes.

Fry bacon in skillet until crisp and set aside. Brown onions and garlic in bacon drippings, then add tomatoes, water, and seasonings. Cook until sauce is thickened. Pour over fish and bake 30 minutes more.

Garnish with bacon slices, lemon wedges, and hard-boiled eggs.

YIELD: 6 SERVINGS

THE JUNIOR LEAGUE OF LOS ANGELES, CALIFORNIA

Red Snapper Veracruzana

3 pounds red snapper filets (6–8 filets)
1 teaspoon salt
½ cup fresh lime juice
¼ cup olive oil
2 cloves garlic, minced
2 onions, thinly sliced
12 small tomatoes (or 6 large)
1 tablespoon tomato paste
1 large bay leaf
½ teaspoon dried oregano
18 green olives, pitted and cut in half
2 tablespoons minced capers
2 green chilies, seeded and cut in strips (chiles jalapeños en escabeche
preferred) *or 2 teaspoons Tabasco*
¼ cup fresh lemon juice

Place the red snapper in a shallow 2-quart casserole. Rub the fish with salt and lime juice. Prick the fish with a fork to aid in penetration of the lime juice and marinate for 3–4 hours, turning occasionally.

Pour the olive oil into a heavy 12-inch skillet. Add the garlic and onions to the skillet and sauté over moderate heat for 3–5 minutes, or until tender. Peel, seed, and coarsely chop the tomatoes. Add the tomatoes, tomato paste, bay leaf, oregano, olives, capers, chilies, and lemon juice to the skillet. Cook, stirring, over moderate heat for 10–15 minutes, or until the mixture is thick and some of the liquid is evaporated.

Place the red snapper filets in a shallow baking dish large enough to hold them in one layer and cover evenly with the tomato sauce. Bake, uncovered, in a preheated 325° oven for 20–30 minutes, or until the fish flakes easily when tested with a fork.

Serve with cooked rice and a crisp green salad.

YIELD: 6–8 SERVINGS

The California Heritage Cookbook
THE JUNIOR LEAGUE OF PASADENA, CALIFORNIA

· ·

Poached Salmon with Cucumber Sauce

1 whole salmon, cleaned (allow 4–6 ounces per serving)

COURT BOUILLON:
3 quarts water
3 cups white wine
2 carrots, chopped
2 stalks celery with leaves, chopped
1 onion, chopped
2 sprigs parsley
1 bay leaf
6 peppercorns
1 tablespoon salt
1 teaspoon thyme

A salmon may be poached, in any pan large enough to hold the fish, in court bouillon to nearly cover. A turkey roasting pan with its removable rack placed under the fish is a valuable assist when the cooked fish is removed from the pan.

Simmer the court bouillon ingredients for 15 minutes. Lower the cleaned fish into it. After broth comes back to a boil, simmer for 10 minutes per inch of thickness of the fish, measured at its thickest part. A 10-pound fish will take from 45 to 50 minutes.

Fish may be served hot or cold.

CUCUMBER SAUCE:
1 large cucumber
1 teaspoon salt
1 cup sour cream
1 cup mayonnaise
2 green onions, chopped
1 tablespoon dill weed

Peel, seed, and chop the cucumber finely. Sprinkle with salt and let sit for ½ hour. Discard any juices and stir in the sour cream, mayonnaise, onions, and dill weed. Let sauce sit for a while before serving.

It may also be served as a dip for raw vegetables.

YIELD: ABOUT 3 CUPS

THE JUNIOR LEAGUE OF TACOMA, WASHINGTON

Seattle Salmon

1 6-pound whole salmon
½ cup butter plus 12 small bits of butter to insert in slashes
Salt
¼ cup flour
1 cup chopped onion
1 quart stewed tomatoes
2 bay leaves
Salt
Paprika

Scale the fish if needed and rub with a wet cloth. Cut slashes on each side of fish and insert small bits of butter. Rub whole fish lightly with salt. Place salmon on a large enough piece of heavy-duty foil to encase it.

In saucepan melt the ½ cup butter. Stir in flour and brown lightly. Add the chopped onion and stir in the stewed tomatoes and the bay leaves. Season to taste with salt and pepper. Cook, stirring constantly, until sauce is slightly thickened.

Pour the sauce inside and over the fish. Wrap foil securely around fish and bake in 325° oven, for 15 minutes per pound.

YIELD: 8 SERVINGS

THE JUNIOR LEAGUE OF SEATTLE, WASHINGTON

Baked Pacific Northwest Salmon with Egg Sauce

1 5–7-pound fresh or frozen Pacific Northwest salmon
1 lemon, thinly sliced

Rinse fish and pat dry. Place lemon slices in the cavity and on the top skin side. Wrap tightly in heavy-duty foil so the juices do not escape. Place in a broiler pan or a 9 x 13-inch pan. Bake fish in preheated 450° oven for 45 minutes to 1 hour. When fish flakes easily it is done. Serve with Egg Sauce.

YIELD: 8–10 SERVINGS

EGG SAUCE:
3 tablespoons margarine
3 tablespoons flour
2 cups milk
½ teaspoon salt
⅛ teaspoon pepper
2 tablespoons chopped parsley
2 hard-boiled eggs, sliced

In a saucepan melt margarine over medium heat. Add flour and cook, stirring, for 2 minutes, or until mixture bubbles. Slowly stir in the milk. Continue stirring and cooking until sauce thickens and boils for 1 minute. Add salt, pepper, parsley, and sliced eggs. Heat to serving temperature.

THE JUNIOR LEAGUE OF SEATTLE, WASHINGTON

Salmon Steaks with Caper Sauce

2 tablespoons butter
¾ cup finely sliced carrots
½ cup finely sliced celery
¼ cup finely sliced shallots
4–5 sprigs fresh parsley, chopped
¾ teaspoon fennel seed
½ teaspoon thyme
6 salmon steaks
Salt and freshly ground pepper to taste
1 cup dry white wine
½ cup fish stock or clam stock

CAPER SAUCE:

3 egg yolks, lightly beaten
Salt and freshly ground pepper to taste
2 tablespoons capers
Chopped parsley for garnish

Preheat oven to 350°. In a large skillet melt butter and sauté the carrot, celery, shallots, parsley, fennel seed, and thyme for 2–3 minutes, stirring constantly. Cover the skillet and cook gently over medium heat for 10 minutes. Spread the vegetables in the bottom of a large heatproof dish. Season salmon steaks with salt and pepper and arrange on the vegetables. Cover with white wine and stock and bring liquid to simmer over low heat. Cover the dish tightly with foil and bake the salmon for 15–20 minutes, or until fish flakes easily.

Reserve braising stock. Transfer salmon to a heated serving platter and keep warm while making sauce.

To make the Caper Sauce, strain the braising stock into a saucepan and, over low heat, slowly beat in the egg yolks, using a wire whisk. Cook, stirring constantly, until sauce is thickened and smooth. Do not let sauce

Recipe continues . . .

boil. Add salt and pepper, fold in capers, and spoon sauce over salmon steaks. Garnish with chopped parsley.

YIELD: 6 SERVINGS

San Francisco à la Carte
THE JUNIOR LEAGUE OF SAN FRANCISCO, CALIFORNIA

. . . .

Cold Poached Salmon Steaks with Sauce Verde

8 salmon steaks
3 black peppercorns
1 bay leaf
2 slices lemon
½ cup dry white wine or vermouth
2 cups water
1 teaspoon salt
3 sprigs fresh dill weed or 1 teaspoon dried
Lettuce leaves
Sauce Verde
Hard-boiled eggs, sliced
Tomato wedges
Cucumber slices

Rinse and dry the salmon steaks. Combine the peppercorns, bay leaf, lemon slices, wine, water, salt, and dill. Bring to a simmer in a 14-inch skillet. Gently place the salmon steaks in the simmering liquid. Cover the pan and simmer gently over low to moderate heat for 10–15 minutes, or until the fish flakes easily when tested with a fork. Remove the salmon from the liquid with a slotted spoon and drain on paper towels.

Place the steaks in a shallow 9 x 13-inch dish, cover with foil or wax paper, and refrigerate until ready to use. The salmon may be prepared 4–6 hours before serving.

Line a large platter with lettuce leaves, arrange the salmon steaks over the lettuce, and coat with Sauce Verde. The platter may be garnished with sliced eggs, tomato wedges, and cucumber slices.

YIELD: 8 SERVINGS

SAUCE VERDE:

1½ cups spinach leaves, packed
½ cup watercress, packed
8–10 sprigs parsley
3–4 sprigs fresh chervil (optional)
6 sprigs fresh tarragon or 1 teaspoon dried
1 cup mayonnaise
2 tablespoons fresh lemon juice
1 cup sour cream
1 teaspoon cream-style horseradish
1 tablespoon finely minced parsley
1 tablespoon finely chopped watercress

Bring 2 quarts water to a boil in a 3-quart saucepan. Add the spinach, ½ cup watercress, parsley sprigs, chervil, and tarragon and boil for 5 minutes. Remove from heat, strain, cool, and press out all excess water.

In a 2-quart bowl combine the mayonnaise, lemon juice, sour cream, and horseradish and set aside. Force the cooled spinach mixture through a coarse strainer into a small bowl, and add to the mayonnaise mixture. Stir to blend well. These ingredients may also be blended for 2 minutes in a blender. Stir in the minced parsley and chopped watercress, cover, and refrigerate until ready to serve. The sauce will hold for 3–6 hours in the refrigerator.

YIELD: 3 CUPS

The California Heritage Cookbook
THE JUNIOR LEAGUE OF PASADENA, CALIFORNIA

Salmon Teriyaki

¼ pound onions
2 green peppers
¼ pound mushrooms
¼ pound tomatoes
2 pounds boned salmon, cut in 1¼-inch cubes

SAUCE:
½ cup soy sauce
½ cup sake or sherry
1 teaspoon sugar

Cube or slice onions, green pepper, mushrooms, and tomatoes. Place salmon on skewers alternately with onions, green pepper, mushrooms, tomatoes, or any other vegetable desired.

Combine sauce ingredients. Brush salmon with sauce and let sit for 30 minutes. Broil in oven or barbecue, turning often and brushing with sauce, for about 15 minutes.

YIELD: 8–10 SERVINGS

THE JUNIOR LEAGUE OF VANCOUVER, BRITISH COLUMBIA

· · · · · · · · · · · · · · · · · · ·

Salmon Mousse

1 envelope unflavored gelatin
¼ cup cold water
1½ teaspoons salt
1½ teaspoons dry mustard
2 tablespoons sugar
2 eggs
1 cup sour cream
¼ cup vinegar
1 15½-ounce can red sockeye salmon, flaked and boned

Sprinkle gelatin over cold water to soften. In the top of a double saucepan, mix salt, mustard, sugar, eggs, sour cream, and vinegar. Cook, stirring, until thickened. Remove from heat. Add gelatin and stir until it dissolves. Pour into salmon and mix thoroughly. Pour into 1-quart fish mold. Refrigerate overnight.

When ready to serve, unmold on cold serving plate and serve with Cucumber Dressing.

YIELD: 8 SERVINGS

CUCUMBER DRESSING:
3 peeled cucumbers, chopped
1 cup sour cream
3 tablespoons chopped chives or green onion
2 tablespoons lemon juice
1½ teaspoons salt
⅛ teaspoon pepper

Combine all ingredients. Chill.

THE JUNIOR LEAGUE OF BAKERSFIELD, CALIFORNIA

Crab-Stuffed Sole

1½ pounds sole filets
1 cup bread crumbs
1 cup crabmeat
1 green onion, minced
1 teaspoon minced parsley
½ teaspoon lemon juice
¾ teaspoon salt
¾ teaspoon white pepper
¼ cup melted butter
3 tablespoons lemon juice
1 cup flour
1 cup heavy cream

Trim filets evenly. Combine bread crumbs, crabmeat, onion, parsley, ½ teaspoon lemon juice, ½ teaspoon salt, and ¼ teaspoon pepper; spread on filets. Roll the filets and secure with wooden picks. Refrigerate for a few hours if desired.

When ready to cook, combine butter, remaining pepper, salt, and the 3 tablespoons lemon juice. Dip rolled filets in the butter, roll in flour, and arrange in a buttered casserole. Pour cream over, sprinkle with any leftover filling and bake 25–30 minutes at 350°, or until filets are firm.

YIELD: 6 SERVINGS

THE JUNIOR LEAGUE OF EDMONTON, ALBERTA

Low-Cal Sole

6–8 sole filets
Butter
Salt and pepper
Chopped parsley
1 large onion, sliced
1 green pepper, sliced into rings
2 cups white wine
Grated Parmesan cheese

Arrange sole in baking dish, dot with butter, and sprinkle with salt and pepper and lots of parsley. Cover with onion slices and green pepper rings, pour wine over all; cover and bake at 325° for 30–45 minutes.

Before serving, sprinkle with cheese and broil until lightly golden.

YIELD: 6 SERVINGS

THE JUNIOR LEAGUE OF SPOKANE, WASHINGTON

. . . .

Nutty Sole

4 large sole filets
½ cup flour
2 tablespoons fine cracker crumbs
2 tablespoons fine bread crumbs
1 cup chopped walnuts
3 egg whites
Salt, pepper, and celery salt
Cooking oil
Lemon wedges and broiled tomato halves for garnish

Rinse filets with cold water; leave moist. Coat with flour. On a piece of wax paper combine cracker crumbs, bread crumbs, and chopped walnuts.

Recipe continues . . .

Beat egg whites lightly in a shallow dish. Coat the floured filets first with egg whites, then with crumbs and nuts. Press nut mixture down onto filets with flat side of a bread knife.

Sprinkle filets with salt, pepper, and celery salt and sauté in a little hot oil in skillet for about 3 minutes on each side, or until golden brown.

Serve garnished with lemon wedges and broiled tomatoes.

YIELD: 4 SERVINGS

THE JUNIOR LEAGUE OF SPOKANE, WASHINGTON

·   ·   ·   ·   ·   ·   ·   ·   ·   ·   ·   ·   ·   ·   ·   ·   ·   ·

Filet of Sole with Asparagus Maltaise

16–24 asparagus spears, trimmed
8 sole filets
⅓ cup melted butter
Sauce Maltaise
2 tablespoons grated orange peel

Bring a 4-quart kettle of water to a boil. Drop the trimmed asparagus spears into the water, a few at a time, and boil for 6–7 minutes, or until barely tender. Remove the asparagus from the water with a slotted spoon and drain on paper towels. Place 2–3 asparagus spears lengthwise on each filet of sole. Roll the filet around the asparagus and place in a shallow 2-quart casserole, seam side down. Pour the ⅓ cup melted butter over the filets.

Cover the casserole with foil and bake in a preheated 350° oven for 20 minutes. Remove the casserole from the oven and drain all the juices from the fish. Set aside to keep warm.

When ready to serve, pour Sauce Maltaise over the filets and place under the broiler for 3–5 minutes, or until golden brown and bubbly. Garnish the filets with the 2 tablespoons grated orange peel.

YIELD: 8 FIRST-COURSE SERVINGS; 4 MAIN-DISH SERVINGS

SAUCE MALTAISE:
3 egg yolks
2 tablespoons fresh orange juice
2 tablespoons grated orange peel
¼ teaspoon salt
Dash white pepper
½ cup hot melted butter (1 stick)

To prepare sauce, place the egg yolks, orange juice, orange peel, salt, and pepper in the blender jar. With the lid on, blend at high speed for 1 second. Turn the blender off. Remove the center portion of the blender lid, turn to high speed, and slowly pour the hot butter into the blender. If the blender does not have a removable center in its lid, make a foil lid with a 2-inch hole in the center, as the mixture will splatter.

The sauce may be held until serving time by placing it in the top of a double saucepan over hot, not boiling, water. Stir occasionally.

The California Heritage Cookbook
THE JUNIOR LEAGUE OF PASADENA, CALIFORNIA

· · · · · · · · · · · · · · ·

Sole with Sauce

2 tablespoons butter
2 tablespoons olive oil
3 tablespoons wine vinegar
1 teaspoon dry mustard
1 teaspoon salt
1 teaspoon lemon juice
1 clove garlic, minced
3 drops Tabasco
Pinch summer savory
Grated ground pepper
1½ pounds sole filets

Recipe continues . . .

Combine all ingredients except fish in saucepan, bring to a boil, and simmer for 1–2 minutes.

Put the filets on a foil-lined broiler pan. Pour sauce over the fish and broil 4–5 minutes close to broiler heat. Serve immediately.

Sole is a thin fish so there is no need to turn.

YIELD: 4 SERVINGS

THE JUNIOR LEAGUE OF SEATTLE, WASHINGTON

· · · · · · · · · · · · · · · · · · ·

Filet of Sole with Crabmeat au Monblason

2 cups dry white wine
8 ounces clam juice
3 sprigs parsley
1 bay leaf
½ teaspoon thyme
½ pound mushrooms, sliced
5 tablespoons butter
5 tablespoons flour
2 tablespoons brandy
1 cup shredded Gruyère cheese
¼ cup cream sherry
½ pound crabmeat
½ cup heavy cream
Salt and freshly ground black pepper
1½ pounds gray sole filets

Simmer wine until reduced by half. Add clam juice, parsley, bay leaf, and thyme. Simmer for 15 minutes, then strain, reserving liquid.

Sauté sliced mushrooms in 2 tablespoons of the butter until most of the moisture is evaporated.

Melt the remaining 3 tablespoons of butter, stir in the flour, and cook gently until slightly browned. Stir in brandy; gradually add wine and clam juice to make a smooth sauce. Add mushrooms, ½ cup cheese, sherry, crab, and cream. Mix well and season with salt and pepper.

Spread half of the sauce in the bottom of an au gratin dish. Place the sole filets on top and cover with the balance of the sauce. Cover with the remaining cheese. Bake in a 400° oven for 15 minutes, then glaze under the broiler until a golden crust is formed.

YIELD: 4–6 SERVINGS

THE JUNIOR LEAGUE OF VANCOUVER, BRITISH COLUMBIA

Steamed Sea Bass

1 2-pound sea bass
1 tablespoon dry sherry
3 tablespoons peanut oil
2 tablespoons finely shredded fresh ginger
2 green onions, finely shredded
3 tablespoons soy sauce
1 teaspoon sugar
Fresh coriander (cilantro), or parsley, chopped

Have the fish cleaned and scaled, but leave on the head and tail. Rinse it in cold water and pat dry. Place on a shallow dish or foil and sprinkle with sherry. Let sit for 10 minutes. Put the fish on the rack of a steamer, making certain that the water level is below the rack. Cover and steam for 15 minutes.

Just before the fish is ready, heat a wok for 30 seconds over high heat. Add the oil and swirl around. Add ginger and stir-fry for 1 minute, then add green onions, soy sauce, and sugar. Stir mixture for a few seconds.

Remove the fish to a serving platter and pour the sauce over it. Garnish with fresh coriander and serve immediately.

YIELD: 4 SERVINGS

San Francisco à la Carte
THE JUNIOR LEAGUE OF SAN FRANCISCO, CALIFORNIA

Calamari Calabrese

TOMATO SAUCE:
1 large onion, chopped
1 clove garlic, minced
3 tablespoons olive oil
2 1-pound cans whole tomatoes
1 tablespoon tomato paste
2 whole bay leaves
½ teaspoon oregano
¼ teaspoon sage

WINE CREAM SAUCE:
3 tablespoons butter
3 tablespoons flour
1 cup milk
½ cup white wine
Salt and freshly ground pepper to taste

VEGETABLES AND SQUID:
1 large onion, coarsely chopped
2 cloves garlic, minced
½ pound fresh mushrooms, sliced
1 teaspoon crushed red pepper flakes
3 pounds squid
Flour
Olive oil

To make the tomato sauce, sauté the onion and garlic in the olive oil for 5–6 minutes. Add the other ingredients and cook, stirring occasionally, for about 30 minutes, or until the sauce thickens slightly. Set aside to cool.

To prepare the cream sauce, melt the butter over low heat until it bubbles, then gradually stir in the flour and cook, stirring, for 3–5 minutes. Slowly stir in the milk and continue to stir until the sauce is very thick and smooth. Add the wine and seasonings. Set aside.

In a skillet, sauté all the vegetables together for 5 minutes. Set aside.

In a large pan, combine the tomato sauce, cream sauce, and vegetables. Clean the squid by removing the ink sack, eyes, and cuttlebone. Cut squid into bite-size pieces, rinse, and drain thoroughly. Dredge the squid lightly in flour and fry in oil over high heat until well browned. Remove from skillet and drain thoroughly. Add the squid to the sauce, reheat slightly, and serve.

YIELD: 6–8 SERVINGS

San Francisco à la Carte
THE JUNIOR LEAGUE OF SAN FRANCISCO, CALIFORNIA

· · · · · · · · · · · · · · · · · ·

Lemon Soy Swordfish Steaks with Avocado Butter

⅓ cup soy sauce
1 teaspoon grated lemon peel
¼ cup fresh lemon juice
1 clove garlic, minced
2 teaspoons Dijon mustard
½ cup salad oil
8 small swordfish steaks or 4 large ones, cut in half
Lemon wedges
Parsley sprigs

Combine the soy sauce, lemon peel, lemon juice, garlic, mustard, and oil in a small bowl, blending well. Place the swordfish steaks in a shallow 9 x 13-inch baking dish. Pour the soy sauce marinade over the fish, pricking the fish thoroughly with a fork to assure penetration of the marinade. Turn the fish occasionally, again pricking it with a fork. Let the fish marinate for 1–3 hours in the refrigerator.

To cook, place the fish on a preheated broiler pan. Broil 5–6 minutes on each side, or until fish flakes easily when tested with a fork. This swordfish can also be barbecued on a charcoal grill over moderate coals for

Recipe continues . . .

5–6 minutes on each side. During the cooking, brush the fish often with the marinade sauce.

Garnish with lemon wedges and parsley and serve with Avocado Butter.

YIELD: 8 SERVINGS

AVOCADO BUTTER:
½ cup softened butter
½ cup mashed ripe avocado
4 tablespoons fresh lemon juice
2 tablespoons finely chopped fresh parsley
1 teaspoon Worcestershire sauce
½ teaspoon garlic salt

Whip the butter with an electric mixer in a small mixing bowl until soft and creamy. Beat in the remaining ingredients. Refrigerate until ready to serve. The butter will hold about 1 hour.

YIELD: ABOUT 1½ CUPS

The California Heritage Cookbook
THE JUNIOR LEAGUE OF PASADENA, CALIFORNIA

•   •   •   •   •   •   •   •   •   •   •   •   •   •   •   •

Trout in Cream

8 trout, cleaned
½ teaspoon salt
¼ teaspoon white pepper
¼ cup fresh lemon juice
3 tablespoons butter
⅓ cup dry vermouth
1 cup heavy cream
2 teaspoons dried tarragon
1 cup fresh soft bread crumbs
¼ cup melted butter
1 cup fine chopped fresh parsley

Wash and dry the trout thoroughly. Sprinkle inside and out with salt, pepper, and lemon juice. In a heavy 12-inch skillet melt the 3 tablespoons butter over low heat and place the trout in the skillet. Brown on both sides, approximately 3–5 minutes, over moderate heat.

Place the trout in a single layer in a shallow 9 x 13-inch baking dish. Pour the vermouth and cream over the fish and sprinkle with the tarragon. Cover the baking dish and bake in a preheated 350° oven for 30 minutes, or until the fish flakes easily when tested with a fork, basting occasionally.

Remove the fish from the oven and cover with bread crumbs. Pour the melted butter over the bread crumbs and place under a preheated broiler for 3–5 minutes, or until the crumbs are lightly browned. Garnish with the chopped parsley and serve at once.

This is a delicious first course when served with a dry white wine.

YIELD: 8 SERVINGS

The California Heritage Cookbook
THE JUNIOR LEAGUE OF PASADENA, CALIFORNIA

·   ·   ·   ·   ·   ·   ·   ·   ·   ·   ·   ·   ·   ·   ·   ·   ·

Sea Scallops in Wine Sauce

4 tablespoons butter
½–1 pound mushrooms, sliced
¼ cup finely chopped onion
2 tablespoons flour
1 cup dry white wine
2 teaspoons lemon juice
1 teaspoon salt
Fresh ground pepper to taste
2 tablespoons finely chopped parsley
1½–2 pounds scallops
Paprika

Recipe continues . . .

Wash and dry scallops.

In butter, sauté mushrooms and onion until tender. Stir in flour and cook for several minutes. Stir in wine, lemon juice, salt, pepper, and parsley. Bring to a boil; add scallops.

Spoon into shallow casserole or individual baking dishes. Sprinkle with the buttered bread crumbs and paprika. Bake at 400° for 25 minutes for the large casserole; 15 minutes for individual ones.

YIELD: 4–6 SERVINGS

THE JUNIOR LEAGUE OF SEATTLE, WASHINGTON

Scallop Casserole

7 tablespoons butter
2 tablespoons minced onion
¾ pound fresh mushrooms, chopped
1 cup dry white wine
1 tablespoon lemon juice
2 teaspoons chopped parsley
½ teaspoon salt
¼ teaspoon ground pepper
¼ teaspoon nutmeg
½ cup water
¼ teaspoon thyme
Sprig of parsley
1 bay leaf
2 pounds scallops, washed well and drained
4 tablespoons flour
1 cup light cream
6 tablespoons Parmesan cheese
Pinch cayenne

Melt 3 tablespoons butter and in it sauté onion until soft. Add mushrooms and cook until liquid evaporates. Add half the wine, lemon juice, chopped parsley, salt, pepper, and nutmeg. Cook until wine evaporates and set aside.

Heat remaining wine, water, thyme, parsley sprig, and bay leaf. Add scallops and poach gently, covered, until tender, about 5–6 minutes. Remove scallops; strain broth and reserve.

Melt remaining 4 tablespoons butter and blend in flour. Stir in cream and 1 cup of the broth. Cook, stirring, until sauce is thick and smooth. Mix ½ cup of the sauce with mushroom mixture and spread on the bottom of a shallow 1-quart casserole. Arrange strained scallops on top of mushrooms. Stir 4 tablespoons of the cheese and cayenne into remaining sauce and pour over scallops. Sprinkle with remaining cheese and bake in a 425° oven until lightly browned.

YIELD: 6–8 SERVINGS

THE JUNIOR LEAGUE OF LOS ANGELES, CALIFORNIA

· · · · · · · · · · · · · · · · · ·

Basque Clams

3–4 pounds small live butter clams
1 tablespoon cornmeal
Salad oil
1 large clove garlic, minced
¾ cup chopped fresh parsley
2 chorizo sausages, cooked and crumbled (optional)
Soft bread crumbs made from 3 slices white bread
1 hot red pepper, crumbled
Salt and pepper to taste

Scrub and soak clams overnight in salt water with cornmeal added. Rinse well several times and drain.

In a large dome-lidded skillet or Dutch oven with lid, heat enough oil to cover bottom. Toast garlic in the oil. Add clams and stir until shells open.

Recipe continues . . .

Add chopped parsley, cooked chorizos, bread crumbs, red pepper; cover and continue cooking for 3–4 minutes. Taste the broth that forms and add salt and pepper if needed.

YIELD: 4–6 MAIN-DISH SERVINGS; MORE APPETIZERS

THE JUNIOR LEAGUE OF BOISE, IDAHO

. . . .

Fresh Crabmeat and Mushrooms

1 medium onion, chopped
½ pound fresh mushrooms, thinly sliced
4 tablespoons butter
¼ cup all-purpose flour
1½ cups light cream
1 pound fresh crabmeat, flaked
Juice of ½ lemon
½ teaspoon paprika
Salt and white pepper to taste
Bread crumbs

Preheat oven to 375°. Sauté onion and mushrooms in butter until soft. Sprinkle with flour and cook and stir for 3 minutes. Gradually add cream and cook and stir until sauce is smooth and thickened. Fold in crabmeat. Add lemon juice and adjust seasonings with paprika, salt, and pepper to taste.

Fill six scallop shells or ramekins with mixture, sprinkle liberally with bread crumbs, and bake for 10 minutes, or until bubbly and golden brown.

Can also be served as a first-course appetizer.

YIELD: 4–6 SERVINGS

San Francisco à la Carte
THE JUNIOR LEAGUE OF SAN FRANCISCO, CALIFORNIA

. . . .

Crabmeat Delight

1½ cups scalded milk
1 cup soft bread crumbs
2 cups flaked crabmeat or diced shrimp
¼ cup melted butter
2 tablespoons chopped green pepper
2 tablespoons chopped pimento
4 tablespoons finely chopped onion
1 cup shredded American cheese
½ teaspoon salt
¼ teaspoon pepper
3 eggs, beaten

Pour milk over bread crumbs and stir in remaining ingredients. Pour into buttered casserole. Set in a pan of hot water and bake in a 300° oven for 60 minutes, or until a knife inserted in center comes out clean.

YIELD: 6 SERVINGS

A Taste of Oregon
THE JUNIOR LEAGUE OF EUGENE, OREGON

. . . .

Crab Gratinée

2 pounds King crab or snow crabmeat, fresh or frozen
½ cup sharp cheddar cheese, shredded
½ cup Monterey Jack cheese, shredded
½ cup fresh bread crumbs
¼ cup chopped parsley
1 teaspoon Tabasco
¼ cup dry white wine
Salt and pepper to taste

Recipe continues . . .

Mix together all of the above ingredients thoroughly. Turn into individual gratinée dishes or a 2-quart casserole. Sprinkle the top with crumb topping. Bake at 350° for 25–30 minutes, or until topping is browned.

YIELD: 6–8 SERVINGS

TOPPING:
1½ cups fresh bread crumbs
½ cup melted butter
¼ cup chopped parsley
½ cup grated Parmesan cheese

Combine all ingredients and mix well. Use as casserole topping.

THE JUNIOR LEAGUE OF SANTA BARBARA, CALIFORNIA

· ·

Deviled Crab

4 tablespoons butter
6 tablespoons flour
2 cups milk
⅔ cup chicken stock
2 egg yolks
2 tablespoons fresh chopped parsley
1 tablespoon sherry
1 teaspoon Worcestershire sauce
½ tablespoon dry mustard
2 heaping cups cooked fresh crabmeat
Grated Parmesan cheese for garnish

Melt butter in heavy saucepan, add flour, and cook for 2–3 minutes, stirring often. Gradually stir in milk and continue cooking until sauce is of medium consistency. Add stock mixed with egg yolks and cook, stirring, for 1 more minute. Remove from heat and add remaining ingredients except garnish. Serve in individual ramekins topped with grated cheese.

YIELD: 4–6 SERVINGS

VARIATION: Toast English muffins, top with crab mixture, 3 slices of avocado, and shredded Swiss cheese. Place under the broiler until browned and bubbly.

THE JUNIOR LEAGUE OF OAKLAND-EAST BAY, CALIFORNIA

. . . .

Spicy Lobster or Crab en Sauce

6 tablespoons butter
2 tablespoons shallots
1½ pounds lobster or King crabmeat
¼ cup warmed brandy
1 teaspoon salt
¼ teaspoon English mustard
¼ teaspoon paprika
¼ teaspoon curry powder
Dash cayenne
1 teaspoon lemon juice
1 tablespoon minced chives
1 tablespoon minced parsley
1½ cups cream sauce
½ cup whipped heavy cream

Heat butter and add shallots. Sauté the shallots until transparent and add the lobster or crab. Pour the warmed brandy over the seafood and ignite it. Stir until flame dies out. Mix the salt with the rest of the spices and add to

Recipe continues . . .

lobster along with the lemon juice. Add chives, parsley, and Cream Sauce. Cook over medium high heat, stirring frequently, for 3–5 minutes.

Remove from heat and stir in whipped cream.

YIELD: 6 SERVINGS

CREAM SAUCE:
2 tablespoons butter
2 tablespoons flour
½ cup chicken broth
½ cup heavy cream

Melt butter in saucepan. Stir in flour with wire whisk and cook for 2 minutes. Gradually add chicken broth and cream, stirring constantly with the whisk so sauce will remain smooth.

THE JUNIOR LEAGUE OF TACOMA, WASHINGTON

· · · · · · · · · · · · · · · ·

Shrimp Creole

½ stick margarine
2 stalks celery, chopped
6 green onions with tops, chopped
1 green pepper, chopped
2 pounds frozen raw shrimp, shelled and deveined
1 16-ounce can tomatoes
1 8-ounce can tomato sauce
1 bay leaf
Salt and pepper
Tabasco to taste

Melt margarine in large skillet and in it sauté onions, celery, and green pepper over medium heat until onion is transparent. Add shrimp and cook until shrimp turn pink. Add tomatoes and tomato sauce and all seasonings. Cover and simmer for 20 minutes over low heat.

Serve over rice. Great with tossed salad and hot French bread!

YIELD: 6–8 SERVINGS

THE JUNIOR LEAGUE OF BUTTE, MONTANA

· · · · · · · · · · · · · · · · ·

Quick Shrimp Jambalaya

2 tablespoons bacon drippings
2 tablespoons flour
1 cup cubed ham
1 onion, sliced
3 stalks celery, sliced
1 cup sliced green pepper
1 bay leaf
Pinch thyme (leaf)
1 tablespoon minced parsley
1 clove garlic, minced
Salt and pepper to taste
¾ pound small ready-to-cook shrimp, thawed
1 14½-ounce can stewed tomatoes
1¼ cups vegetable juice
1 cup frozen okra, thawed

Melt drippings in a heavy skillet over medium heat. Stir in flour, ham, onion, and celery. Simmer 5 minutes, stirring constantly. Add remaining ingredients, bring to a boil, then barely simmer for 5–10 minutes. Do not overcook, as green pepper and okra will lose fresh green color. Refrigerate and reheat at serving time.

Recipe continues . . .

Serve over rice with a simple green salad or a crisp cooked green vegetable.

YIELD: 6 SERVINGS

THE JUNIOR LEAGUE OF TUCSON, ARIZONA

Szechuan Shrimp

2 tablespoons peanut oil
1 pound extra-large raw shrimp, shelled and deveined
¼ cup minced green onion
2 tablespoons minced fresh ginger
3 cloves garlic, finely minced
2 tablespoons dry sherry
2 tablespoons soy sauce
2 teaspoons sugar
½ teaspoon salt
2–3 tablespoons catsup
2 tablespoons chili sauce
1 teaspoon red pepper flakes

Heat oil in a wok or large, heavy skillet. Add shrimp, green onion, ginger, and garlic. Stir-fry until shrimp are pink. Add sherry, soy sauce, sugar, and salt. Stir well and blend in catsup, chili sauce, and red pepper flakes.
Serve with piping hot rice.

YIELD: 6–8 SERVINGS

San Francisco à la Carte
THE JUNIOR LEAGUE OF SAN FRANCISCO, CALIFORNIA

Stuffed Butterfly Shrimp

8 large Guaymas shrimp (allow 4 per serving)
Lemon juice (optional)
Olive oil (optional)

STUFFING:
1 slice bread, crumbed
2 slices bacon, crisply cooked and crumbled
1 tablespoon chopped green onion
Lemon pepper
White wine to moisten
2 teaspoons olive oil
Additional bacon for wrapping shrimp

Shell and butterfly shrimp *raw*. If desired, marinate in lemon juice and a little olive oil for several hours.

To make stuffing, combine bread crumbs, crumbled bacon, onion, pepper, wine, and oil. Shortly before cooking, put as much stuffing as possible in each shrimp and wrap each with ½ slice of lean bacon. Fasten with wooden picks.

Broil about 5 minutes, or until bacon is crisp. Don't overcook.

YIELD: 2 SERVINGS

THE JUNIOR LEAGUE OF TUCSON, ARIZONA

Shrimp de Jonghe

½ cup softened butter
¼ teaspoon salt
1 teaspoon dried tarragon (optional)
1 clove garlic, pressed
1 cup fine bread crumbs
3 tablespoons minced parsley
½ cup dry sherry
2 pounds fresh raw shrimp, shelled and deveined

Blend all the above ingredients except shrimp. Layer the shrimp and the bread crumb mixture into individual shell dishes or an oblong casserole. Bake at 375° for 20 minutes.

YIELD: 6 SERVINGS

THE JUNIOR LEAGUE OF SAN DIEGO, CALIFORNIA

Curried Shrimp

4 tablespoons butter
½ medium onion, minced
4 tablespoons flour
1½ tablespoons curry powder
½ teaspoon garlic salt
½ teaspoon seasoning salt
⅛ teaspoon cayenne
½ cup beef broth
½ cup coconut milk
1 cup cream
½ teaspoon lemon juice
1 teaspoon grated lemon rind
½ medium green apple, grated
1 pound shrimp, cleaned and shelled

CONDIMENTS:
Thinly sliced green onions
Chutney
Chopped peanuts
Shredded coconut
Raisins
Crumbled crisp bacon
Chopped egg
Chopped tomatoes
Ginger marmalade
Chopped candied ginger

Melt butter in top of double saucepan over direct heat. Add onion and sauté until limp. Stir in flour mixed with the curry powder, garlic salt, seasoning salt, and cayenne.

Add beef broth, coconut milk, cream, and lemon juice gradually, stirring constantly, until sauce is smooth and thickened. Place saucepan over boiling water.

Add lemon rind, grated apple, and shrimp last. Cook for 20–30 minutes before serving.

Serve with cooked rice and condiments.

YIELD: 6 SERVINGS

THE JUNIOR LEAGUE OF OAKLAND-EAST BAY, CALIFORNIA

· · · · · · · · · · · · · · · · · · · ·

Shrimp Kabobs

2 pounds jumbo raw shrimp (approximately 9–10 per pound)
18 large mushroom caps
12 cherry tomatoes
12 slices green pepper

Recipe continues . . .

MARINADE:
1 ½ cups beer
½ cup soy sauce
1 clove garlic, minced

Shell and devein shrimp; rinse well. Wash mushroom caps. Marinate shrimp and mushrooms in marinade for approximately 3 hours. Drain.

Divide shrimp, mushrooms, tomatoes, and green pepper pieces evenly among six skewers. Broil approximately 5 minutes on each side, brushing often with marinade.

Serve kabobs over bed of cooked rice with heated soy sauce if desired.

YIELD: 4–6 SERVINGS

THE JUNIOR LEAGUE OF SANTA BARBARA, CALIFORNIA

· · · · · · · · · · · · · · · · · · · ·

Chinese Skewered Shrimp

30 large raw shrimp or prawns
⅔ cup dry sherry
⅔ cup soy sauce
⅔ cup olive or peanut oil
½ teaspoon powdered ginger
½ teaspoon grated lemon peel
1 clove garlic, minced
2 6½-ounce cans water chestnuts
30 fresh mushrooms, stemmed
½ pound bacon, cut into 2 x 2-inch squares
Tomatoes for garnish

Shell and devein the shrimp. In a 2–3-quart bowl combine the sherry, soy sauce, oil, ginger, lemon peel, and garlic. Add the raw shrimp and marinate in the mixture, stirring occasionally. This may be done in the refrigerator for 2 hours or at room temperature for 1 hour.

Thread the shrimp on metal skewers (5 per skewer), alternating with water chestnuts, mushroom caps, and bacon squares. This may be done ahead and refrigerated, covered, for several hours.

Place the skewers over medium coals on the barbecue, turning frequently and basting with the marinade. Cook for approximately 6–8 minutes, or until shrimp are pink.

Serve hot from the grill over rice pilaf, garnished with fresh or broiled tomatoes.

YIELD: 6 SERVINGS

The California Heritage Cookbook
THE JUNIOR LEAGUE OF PASADENA, CALIFORNIA

Shrimp or Crab à l'Amoricaine

2 onions, chopped
3 tablespoons vegetable oil
4 bay leaves
1 teaspoon thyme
Pinch tarragon
1 pint heavy or light cream
1 6-ounce can tomato paste
½ cup sherry
1½ pounds cooked, peeled shrimp or crabmeat, or half of each
Salt
Pepper

Sauté onions in vegetable oil until onions are golden brown. Lower heat. Add bay leaves, thyme, and tarragon. Blend in cream, tomato paste, and

Recipe continues . . .

sherry. Add seafood, salt, and pepper. Simmer 10 minutes, stirring occasionally.

Serve with cooked rice.

YIELD: 6 SERVINGS

Heritage Cookbook
THE JUNIOR LEAGUE OF SALT LAKE CITY, UTAH

• • • • • • • • • • • • • • • • • • • •

Lemon Oriental Shrimp

⅔ cup wild rice
1 cup chopped onion
2 cups chopped celery
2 tablespoons butter
1½ pounds large shrimp, shelled and deveined
1 pound fresh mushrooms, sliced
1 6-ounce package frozen pea pods
1 cup sliced water chestnuts

Cook the wild rice in water for 45 minutes. Drain and set aside.

Sauté the onion and celery in butter until onion is transparent. Simmer the shrimp in salted water for 1½ minutes. Drain and set aside. Combine the mushrooms, pea pods, and water chestnuts in a baking dish. Add to them the rice, celery, onion, and shrimp.

Pour Lemon Sauce over the shrimp mixture and bake for 20 minutes at 350°.

YIELD: 6 SERVINGS

LEMON SAUCE:
2 tablespoons cornstarch
½ cup lemon juice
2 chicken bouillon cubes
1 cup water
1 tablespoon grated lemon rind
1 clove garlic, minced
Dash soy sauce

In saucepan combine all ingredients and cook over medium heat until thick, stirring constantly.

THE JUNIOR LEAGUE OF GREAT FALLS, MONTANA

. . . .

Shrimp and Scallops Swiss

1 pound scallops
1 teaspoon lemon juice
1 pound fresh mushrooms, sliced
2 tablespoons butter
1½ pounds cooked shrimp, peeled and deveined
¼ cup minced parsley

Poach the scallops in water to cover with the 1 teaspoon lemon juice for 5–6 minutes. Set the scallops aside but reserve ½ cup of the broth.

Sauté the mushrooms in butter. Combine the scallops, mushrooms, and shrimp and add to the Swiss Sauce. Stir in the ½ cup of broth saved from cooking the scallops. Heat to blend flavors.

Garnish with parsley. Serve from a chafing dish on Melba toast or in patty shells.

YIELD: 8 SERVINGS

Recipe continues . . .

SWISS SAUCE:

¾ cup butter

¾ cup flour

3 cups milk

¾ pound imported Swiss cheese, grated

1 small clove garlic, minced

1 tablespoon salt

¼ teaspoon white pepper

¼ teaspoon dry mustard

2 teaspoons tomato paste

2 teaspoons lemon juice

In saucepan melt butter; stir in flour and cook, stirring, until mixture bubbles. Gradually stir in milk and cook over moderate heat, stirring constantly, until sauce is smooth and thick. Add the cheese and stir until melted. Add the remaining ingredients and cook over low heat for 5 minutes, stirring occasionally.

THE JUNIOR LEAGUE OF GREAT FALLS, MONTANA

Shrimp Dino

½ cup butter (1 stick)

1 medium onion, chopped

1 clove garlic, minced

1 bay leaf, crumbled

¼ cup flour

1 pint half and half

1 teaspoon curry powder

⅓ cup white wine

1 pound shrimp, shelled and deveined

1 pound fresh mushrooms, sliced

Shredded Swiss cheese

Melt 6 tablespoons butter and in it sauté the onion, garlic, and bay leaf until onion is very soft. Strain and use as the base for sauce.

Combine strained melted butter and flour. Stir in the half and half, wine, and curry powder. Cook until bubbling, stirring constantly. Set aside.

Cook shrimp in 1 quart boiling salted water for 2–3 minutes, or until shrimp are a light pink color (do not overcook as the shrimp will become tough and hard).

Sauté mushrooms in remaining 2 tablespoons butter. Combine cooked shrimp and mushrooms and divide into the bottom of four ramekins. Cover shrimp and mushrooms with curry sauce. Sprinkle with Swiss cheese. Bake in a 325° oven for 10 minutes, or until bubbly and cheese is melted.

YIELD: 4 SERVINGS

THE JUNIOR LEAGUE OF SPOKANE, WASHINGTON

Prawns and Mushrooms

⅓ cup white wine vinegar
Juice of 1 lemon
¼ cup soy sauce
⅓ cup oil
¼ teaspoon salt
1 garlic clove, minced
1 small piece crystallized ginger
1 pound fresh prawns, shelled and deveined
½ pound fresh mushrooms

Recipe continues . . .

Combine vinegar, lemon juice, soy sauce, oil, salt, garlic, and ginger in a deep bowl. Add prawns and mushrooms; let stand several hours in refrigerator.

Thread prawns and mushrooms on three skewers. Grill 10 minutes.

YIELD: 3 SERVINGS

Epicure

THE JUNIOR LEAGUE OF NEWPORT HARBOR, CALIFORNIA

Prawns Mimosa

48 prawns, cleaned and dried
Butter
1 cup dry Vermouth

Sauté prawns in butter; remove prawns to shallow baking dish and add vermouth to sauté pan. Cook until wine is reduced by one quarter.

Pour wine sauce over prawns and dot with Special Butter. Bake 4 minutes at 425°.

YIELD: 8 SERVINGS

SPECIAL BUTTER:
1 stick butter, softened
¾ cup bread crumbs
1 clove garlic, minced
2 tablespoons chopped shallots
2 tablespoons chopped parsley
Dash Tabasco
Dash Worcestershire sauce

Cream butter with all of the above ingredients.

THE JUNIOR LEAGUE OF OAKLAND-EAST BAY, CALIFORNIA

Tempura

2 pounds fresh shrimp
1 quart prepared vegetables: onions, zucchini, cauliflowerets,
broccoli buds, mushrooms, turnips, bean curd, etc.
2 egg yolks, beaten
2 cups ice water
2 cups flour

TEMPURA SAUCE:
1 cup dashi or chicken stock
⅓ cup soy sauce
⅓ cup sake wine

Clean and butterfly raw shrimp. Prepare and slice vegetables.

Mix egg yolks and ice water. Add flour all at once and mix lightly. The mixture should be thin and lumpy.

Dip a few shrimp at a time into the batter and drop into deep fat or oil heated to 350°. Fry 4–5 minutes, or until golden. Follow the same procedure with the vegetables. Drain well on paper towels and keep warm.

Combine ingredients for Tempura Sauce and bring just to a boil. Serve as a dip for shrimp and vegetables.

YIELD: 6 SERVINGS

THE JUNIOR LEAGUE OF LONG BEACH, CALIFORNIA

Egg and Cheese Dishes

California Cheese-Green Chili Strata

12 slices bread, trimmed, buttered, and cut into small cubes
1 pound cheddar cheese, shredded
1 pound bacon, crisply fried and crumbled (or ham or shrimp)
Chopped parsley
1 4-ounce can chopped green chilies (optional)
6 eggs, beaten
4 cups milk
1½ teaspoons minced onion
¼ teaspoon salt
Pepper
½ teaspoon dry mustard

Place cubed, buttered bread in 9 x 13-inch greased pan. Sprinkle with three-quarters of the cheese, all of bacon, parsley, and green chilies.

Mix eggs, milk, onion, and seasonings. Pour over other ingredients. Mix lightly with fork. Sprinkle remainder of cheese on top.

Allow to set in refrigerator overnight.

Bake, uncovered, at 350° for 45 minutes.

YIELD: 12 SERVINGS

THE JUNIOR LEAGUE OF LONG BEACH, CALIFORNIA

Mexican Green Chili Strata

6 slices firm bread
Butter
2 cups shredded sharp cheddar cheese
2 cups shredded Monterey Jack cheese
8 ounces minced green chilies
6 eggs
2 cups milk
2 teaspoons salt
2 teaspoons paprika
1 teaspoon crumbled oregano
¼ teaspoon pepper
½ teaspoon garlic powder
¼ teaspoon dry mustard

Trim crusts from bread and spread one side of each with butter. Arrange bread, butter side down, in a 9 x 12-inch baking pan. Sprinkle cheeses evenly over bread. Distribute the chilies evenly over the cheese layer.

In a bowl beat eggs with milk and all seasonings until well blended. Pour egg mixture over cheese. Cover and chill overnight or at least 4 hours.

Bake, uncovered, at 325° for about 50 minutes, or until top is lightly browned. Let stand 10 minutes before serving.

YIELD: 8 SERVINGS

Gourmet Olé
THE JUNIOR LEAGUE OF ALBUQUERQUE, NEW MEXICO

Sausage Strata

8 slices white bread, cubed
2 cups shredded sharp cheddar cheese
1½ pounds link sausage, cut into thirds and browned
4 eggs
2¼ cups milk
¾ teaspoon dry mustard
1 10¾-ounce can cream of mushroom soup
½ cup milk

Place bread in bottom of 8 x 12-inch baking dish. Top with cheese. Place browned sausage on top of cheese. Beat eggs with 2¼ cups milk and mustard; pour over. Refrigerate overnight.

Next day dilute soup with the ½ cup milk and pour over. Bake at 300° for 1½ hours.

YIELD: 6 SERVINGS

THE JUNIOR LEAGUE OF BILLINGS, MONTANA

· ·

Montezuma Tortilla Pie

1 medium onion, sliced
Cooking oil
4 fresh chili poblanos, cut into strips, or 1 tablespoon Tabasco
1½ cups tomato purée
½ cup water
1½ cups heavy cream
24 tortillas
2 cooked chicken breasts, shredded
1 cup shredded mild cheddar cheese

Sauté onion in 3 tablespoons cooking oil until onion is transparent. Add chilies and sauté for about 10 minutes longer. Add tomato purée and water and simmer for 15 minutes, stirring occasionally. Set aside. When cool stir in 1 cup of the cream.

Soften tortillas in hot oil. This takes about 30 seconds per tortilla. Do not let them get crisp. Put a layer of tortillas in a large baking dish, add a layer of chicken, another layer of tortillas, then a layer of chili-tomato mixture, then tortillas, and so on until all these ingredients have been used, finishing with a layer of tortillas. Sprinkle top layer with shredded cheese and pour in the remaining cream.

Bake in a 350° oven for about 30 minutes, or until very hot and bubbly.

YIELD: 6 SERVINGS

Que Sabroso!
THE JUNIOR LEAGUE OF MEXICO CITY, MEXICO

. . . .

Favorite Mexican Casserole

½ cup chopped onion
2 tablespoons butter
8 ounces tomato sauce
4 ounces diced green chilies
½ teaspoon celery salt
¼ teaspoon pepper
2 eggs
1 cup half and half
6 corn tortillas
¾ pound Monterey Jack cheese, shredded
8 ounces sour cream
4 ounces cheddar cheese, shredded

Sauté onion in butter until onion is transparent. Add tomato sauce, chilies, celery salt, and pepper. Simmer for 5 minutes.

Beat eggs and combine with half and half. Stir into tomato mixture.

Quarter tortillas and layer one-third of the tortillas, one-third of the tomato mixture, and one-third of the Jack cheese in a 4-quart casserole. Repeat three times.

Recipe continues . . .

Carefully frost with sour cream and sprinkle with cheddar cheese. Bake at 350° for 35–45 minutes.

YIELD: 6 SERVINGS

THE JUNIOR LEAGUE OF TUCSON, ARIZONA

. . . .

Chili-Cheese Casserole

2 7½-ounce cans whole green chilies
1½ pounds Monterey Jack cheese, sliced
Salt and pepper
2 green onions, minced
1 2¼-ounce can sliced black olives
1 7-ounce can pimentos
6 eggs, well beaten
1 13-ounce can evaporated milk
1 pound cheddar cheese, shredded
2 8-ounce cans tomato sauce

Butter sides and bottom of a 9 x 13½-inch baking dish. Preheat over to 350°.

Slit, wash, and remove seeds from chilies; pat dry with paper towel. Spread chilies on bottom of baking dish. Cover with a layer of half the Jack cheese. Sprinkle with salt and pepper to taste. Spread onions, olives, and pimentos over cheese; top with remaining slices of Jack cheese.

Beat eggs and milk together and pour over cheese. Sprinkle shredded cheddar on top. Bake for 45 minutes. Remove from oven, cover with tomato sauce, and bake an additional 15 minutes.

Good for Sunday brunch or late supper.

YIELD: 10 SERVINGS

Gourmet Olé
THE JUNIOR LEAGUE OF ALBUQUERQUE, NEW MEXICO

. . . .

Chili Casserole with Tomato Sauce

1 8-ounce can whole green chilies
½ pound Monterey Jack cheese, shredded
½ pound longhorn or cheddar cheese, shredded
2 eggs
2 tablespoons flour
1 13-ounce can evaporated milk
1 8-ounce can tomato sauce

Split and deseed chilies. Arrange a layer of chilies in the bottom of a 2½-quart casserole, then a layer of all the Jack cheese, another layer of chilies and, finally, all the longhorn cheese.

Beat eggs, flour, and milk together and pour over the top. Bake at 350° for 30 minutes. Remove from oven and pour tomato sauce over the top. Return to the oven and bake for 15 minutes longer. Let stand for 10–15 minutes before serving.

YIELD: 8 SERVINGS

THE JUNIOR LEAGUE OF RIVERSIDE, CALIFORNIA

· · · · · · · · · · · · · · · · · ·

Baked Chili

1 4-ounce can chopped green chilies
½–¾ pound Monterey Jack cheese, shredded
1 egg
1 cup milk
¼ cup flour
¼ teaspoon salt
¼ teaspoon onion salt

Recipe continues . . .

Butter a small, flat 8 x 8-inch baking dish. Spread chilies in the dish and cover with cheese. Beat egg and milk; add dry ingredients and pour over chilies and cheese.

Bake at 350° for 50 minutes.

YIELD: 4 SERVINGS

THE JUNIOR LEAGUE OF LONG BEACH, CALIFORNIA

. . . .

Chili Puff

6 4-ounce cans chopped or whole chilies
1 pound Monterey Jack cheese, shredded
1 pound longhorn or cheddar cheese, shredded
1 teaspoon salt
12 eggs
1 pint sour cream

Butter a 9 x 13-inch baking dish. Cover bottom with half the chilies and sprinkle with the Monterey Jack. Cover with remaining chilies and sprinkle with the other shredded cheese. Sprinkle with salt.

Separate eggs; beat whites until just stiff. Beat egg yolks until thick, then beat in sour cream. Fold yolks and whites together. Pour over chili mixture. Bake in 350° oven for 50–60 minutes. Serve hot and puffed.

YIELD: 8 SERVINGS

From an Adobe Oven . . . to a Microwave Range
THE JUNIOR LEAGUE OF PUEBLO, COLORADO

. . . .

Arizona Chili Casserole

4 eggs, separated
½ cup evaporated milk
3 tablespoons flour
½ teaspoon salt
16 ounces Monterey Jack cheese, thickly sliced
2 4-ounce cans chopped chilies

SAUCE:
1 small onion, diced
3 tablespoons olive oil
1 clove garlic, minced
2 8-ounce cans tomato sauce
2 teaspoons oregano
Salt and pepper to taste

Beat egg whites until stiff. Beat yolks and add milk, flour, and salt. Fold whites into yolk mixture. Arrange cheese and chilies in deep casserole and pour egg mixture over. Bake in 325° oven for 1 hour.

Sauté onion in oil with garlic. Add rest of ingredients and simmer for 10 minutes. Pour half the sauce over casserole and bake an additional 30 minutes. Serve remaining sauce on the side.

YIELD: 6–8 SERVINGS

THE JUNIOR LEAGUE OF TUCSON, ARIZONA

· · · · · · · · · · · · · · · · · · ·

Canned Chili Rellenos

1 8-ounce can whole green chilies
½ pound Monterey Jack cheese
4 eggs, separated
3 tablespoons flour
½ teaspoon salt
Cooking oil for frying

Recipe continues . . .

Remove seeds from chilies and wash in cold water. Drain on paper towel and pat dry. Cut cheese into narrow strips ½ x ½ x 2 inches. Wrap each piece of cheese tightly in a piece of chili.

Beat egg yolks and stir in flour and salt. Fold into stiffly beaten egg whites.

Heat oil in skillet. Using a large slotted spoon, dip a stuffed chili into the batter until thoroughly covered and then slide it into the hot oil. Turn at once and then turn again when brown. Remove from oil and drain on paper towel. Continue this procedure until all chilies are cooked. This can be done in the morning and reheated for dinner.

To heat, put chilies on a baking sheet and bake in 400° oven for 5 minutes. Allow 2 rellenos for each person. Serve with the tomato sauce.

YIELD: 4 SERVINGS

TOMATO SAUCE:
½ medium onion, thinly sliced
1 clove garlic, minced
1 tablespoon oil
1 cup canned whole tomatoes
2 cups chicken broth
Salt and pepper
½ teaspoon oregano

Cook onion and garlic in oil until tender. Add tomatoes, mashing them thoroughly. Add stock and seasonings. Bring to a boil and simmer 10 minutes. Serve over the rellenos.

Something New Under the Sun
THE JUNIOR LEAGUE OF PHOENIX, ARIZONA

Fresh Chili Rellenos

6 fresh green chilies
1 pound Monterey Jack cheese, slice to fit in chilies
Flour
2 eggs, separated
1 tablespoon flour
Hot oil for frying

SAUCE:
½ medium onion, chopped
1 tablespoon butter
1 8-ounce can tomato sauce
4 ounces water
Pinch salt
¼ teaspoon flour
Dash oregano
Pinch sugar

Wash and roast green chilies; peel and seed. (You may boil them to remove skins rather than roasting them.) Fill with strips of Monterey Jack cheese and roll in flour.

Beat egg whites until stiff; beat in 1 tablespoon flour. Beat egg yolks until creamy. Fold yolks and white together until well blended.

Dip chilies in the egg batter and fry in hot oil (365°) until brown. Drain on paper towel. Arrange in casserole.

Sauté onion in butter, then add remaining ingredients and cook *very slowly* for about 15 minutes.

Cover casserole with sauce and bake at 350° until sauce is bubbling.

YIELD: 6 RELLENOS

THE JUNIOR LEAGUE OF OAKLAND-EAST BAY, CALIFORNIA

Huevos Mexicanos
(Mexican Eggs)

4 canned whole green chilies
1 cup shredded Monterey Jack cheese
2 tablespoons butter
2 tablespoons oil
7 eggs, beaten
¼ cup diced hot green peppers
¼ cup shredded sharp cheddar cheese

Rinse whole chilies under running water. With thumbnail, gently slit each chilie lengthwise and rinse out seeds. Stuff each chili with shredded Monterey Jack cheese; press slit edges together.

Melt butter and oil together in large skillet, turning pan to coat part way up pan edges. Arrange chilies in pan and cook over moderate heat. When cheese just begins to melt, pour in beaten eggs. As the eggs cook, lift up egg mixture at pan sides to allow uncooked egg to run underneath. When eggs are firm, separate chilies with two spatulas and transfer to individual serving plates. Garnish with hot peppers and shredded cheddar cheese.

This is a good dish for weekend breakfast, lunch, or light supper. It can also be used as one of several dishes for a full Mexican dinner.

Serve with steaming hot corn tortillas and butter.

YIELD: 4 SERVINGS

THE JUNIOR LEAGUE OF SACRAMENTO, CALIFORNIA

Colorado Huevos Rancheros

Oil for frying
12 corn tortillas
4 chorizo* sausages, skinned and broken into pieces
6 4-ounce cans green chili salsa
1 15-ounce can tomato sauce
1 bunch green onions, chopped
1 4-ounce can sliced ripe olives
2 teaspoons ground cumin
½ teaspoon garlic powder
12 eggs

GARNISHES:
Chopped green onion tops
Chopped ripe olives
Shredded Monterey Jack cheese
Chopped avocado
Lime wedges

Heat ½ inch of oil in a small skillet. Dip each tortilla into hot oil for about 5 seconds, just to soften. Drain on paper towels. Set aside.

Brown sausages, drain off grease, and add green chili salsa, tomato sauce, green onions, olives, cumin, and garlic powder. Simmer, covered, for 1 hour.

Pour sauce into a large electric frying pan or top-of-the-stove skillet and heat. Poach eggs in sauce, cooking as many as will comfortably fit in the pan at one time. Remove eggs carefully from sauce and place one on each softened tortilla. Spoon some sauce over each egg and sprinkle with garnishes, ending with a squeeze of lime over all.

The sauce could also be used in omelettes.

YIELD: 12 SERVINGS

* A chorizo is a pork sausage seasoned with garlic and Spanish paprika.

Colorado Cache
THE JUNIOR LEAGUE OF DENVER, COLORADO

California Huevos Rancheros

12 eggs
¼ cup water
½ teaspoon salt
Dash pepper
Dash Tabasco
2 tablespoons butter
2 avocados
1 7-ounce can chopped green chilies
1 7-ounce can green chili salsa
¾ pound sharp cheddar cheese, shredded

Mix the first five ingredients in a blender. Melt the butter in the bottom of a 10-inch skillet. Add the egg mixture and cook, stirring constantly. When eggs are set but still moist remove from heat and spoon onto a warm platter.

Peel avocados, mash, and spread over the eggs. Sprinkle with the chilies and pour the salsa on top. Sprinkle with cheese and broil until cheese is bubbly.

YIELD: 6 SERVINGS

THE JUNIOR LEAGUE OF SAN JOSE, CALIFORNIA

Eggs Rio Grande

⅓ cup chopped tomato
2 tablespoons chopped celery
1 tablespoon chopped onion
1 4-ounce can chopped green chilies
½ teaspoon sugar
1 teaspoon vinegar
¼ teaspoon rosemary
6 eggs
½ teaspoon salt
⅛ teaspoon pepper
1 tablespoon butter
4 flour or corn tortillas

Mix tomato, celery, onion, green chilies, sugar, vinegar, and rosemary and let blend while preparing the eggs. Mix the eggs with salt and pepper and scramble with the butter, adding the tomato mixture before the eggs set.

Meanwhile, heat the tortillas slightly and pile the hot egg mixture on the warmed tortillas.

Serve with a chili salsa to pour over if desired.

YIELD: 4 SERVINGS

Gourmet Olé
THE JUNIOR LEAGUE OF ALBUQUERQUE, NEW MEXICO

·   ·   ·   ·   ·   ·   ·   ·   ·   ·   ·   ·   ·   ·   ·   ·   ·   ·

Western Green Chili Omelette

½ pound each Monterey Jack cheese and sharp cheddar cheese, shredded
3 4-ounce cans green chilies
12 eggs
¼ cup milk
1 pint sour cream
Salt to taste

Recipe continues . . .

Butter a large casserole and layer the cheeses on the bottom. Spread the chilies over the cheese layer.

In another bowl mix together the eggs, milk, sour cream, and salt. Pour this mixture over the chilies. Cover and bake at 350° for 50–60 minutes. The depth of the eggs in the casserole dish will determine the time. Uncover and cook for 10 minutes longer.

May be prepared ahead of time and refrigerated.

YIELD: 12 SERVINGS

THE JUNIOR LEAGUE OF BOISE, IDAHO

. . . .

Bacon and Eggs Casserole

1 pound bacon
¼ cup butter
¼ cup flour
1 cup milk
1 cup cream
¼ teaspoon thyme
¼ teaspoon marjoram
¼ teaspoon basil
¾ cup shredded cheddar cheese
1½ dozen hard-boiled eggs, sliced
¼ cup finely chopped parsley
½ cup fine bread crumbs
1 tablespoon butter

Fry bacon until crisp; crumble.

Make a white sauce: Melt ¼ cup butter in saucepan; add flour, stirring to make a smooth paste; add milk and cream gradually, stirring with wire whisk to make a smooth sauce. Add seasonings and stir in cheese until melted.

In a 2½ quart casserole dish, make layers as follows: sliced eggs, bacon, parsley, and sauce. Top with bread crumbs; dot with 1 tablespoon butter. Bake for 40 minutes, uncovered, at 350°.

YIELD: 8–10 SERVINGS

THE JUNIOR LEAGUE OF RIVERSIDE, CALIFORNIA

Scrambled Eggs and Lobster Sauce

2 shallots, minced
1 tablespoon butter
2 fresh mushrooms, sliced
½ cup heavy cream
2 ounces dry sherry
Paprika, salt, and pepper to taste
1 medium California lobster or equivalent of Australian lobster tails,
cooked and diced
4 eggs, scrambled
Chopped parsley

Sauté shallots in butter for 3 minutes. Add all other ingredients except lobster, eggs, and parsley. Bring sauce to a boil, add lobster, and cook just long enough to heat shellfish.

Serve with scrambled eggs. Sprinkle all with parsley.

YIELD: 2 SERVINGS

Epicure
THE JUNIOR LEAGUE OF NEWPORT HARBOR, CALIFORNIA

Joe Jost's Pickled Eggs

8 eggs
1 12-ounce jar yellow chili peppers
2 tablespoons pickling spice
1 cup wine vinegar
1½ scant cups water
1 tablespoon sugar
1 teaspoon turmeric
2 teaspoons salt

Hard cook eggs. Mix rest of ingredients. Peel eggs and put in liquid while still warm. *Don't refrigerate.*

Keep in sealed jar for 2 days. The marinade may be used again several times.

YIELD: 8 SERVINGS

Epicure
THE JUNIOR LEAGUE OF NEWPORT HARBOR, CALIFORNIA

•   •   •   •   •   •   •   •   •   •   •   •   •   •   •   •   •   •   •   •

Hangtown Fry

½ pound bacon, cut into large pieces
2 tablespoons butter
12 medium oysters
Flour for dredging
1 egg, lightly beaten, for dipping
1 cup bread crumbs
6 eggs, lightly beaten
Salt and freshly ground pepper to taste

Fry the bacon in a large skillet until crisp. Remove and drain. Pour off the bacon drippings from the skillet and add the butter.

Dip each oyster in flour, egg, and bread crumbs and fry over medium heat until golden brown. Add the 6 eggs and cook until set, stirring very carefully to cook eggs through. Arrange the bacon on top and serve immediately.

YIELD: 4 SERVINGS

San Francisco à la Carte
THE JUNIOR LEAGUE OF SAN FRANCISCO, CALIFORNIA

Stuffed Eggs au Gratin

6 hard-boiled eggs
¼ cup melted butter or margarine
½ teaspoon Worcestershire sauce
¼ teaspoon prepared mustard
2–3 green onions, including green tops, minced
1 teaspoon minced parsley
3 slices boiled ham, minced
Salt and pepper to taste
2 cups white sauce
Chopped parsley or chives
1 cup shredded American or mild cheddar cheese

Cut eggs in half lengthwise and slip the yolks out into a bowl. Mash the yolks with the butter, Worcestershire sauce, and mustard. Stir in minced onion, parsley, and ham. Season to taste with salt and pepper.

Fill the egg whites with this mixture and arrange in the bottom of a buttered casserole or pie plate. Pour white sauce over the eggs, sprinkle with the cheese and chopped parsley or chives for color.

Bake in a 325° oven for 25–30 minutes.

YIELD: 4 SERVINGS

Recipe continues . . .

MEDIUM WHITE SAUCE (BÉCHAMEL):
¼ cup butter or margarine
¼ cup unsifted all-purpose flour
Salt and pepper to taste
2 cups hot milk

Melt butter in saucepan over low heat. Blend in flour, salt, and pepper. Add milk all at once. Cook quickly, stirring constantly, until mixture thickens and bubbles.

YIELD: ABOUT 2½ CUPS

A Taste of Oregon
THE JUNIOR LEAGUE OF EUGENE, OREGON

Mexican Soufflé

2 cups shredded Monterey Jack cheese
2 cups shredded medium sharp cheese
3 4-ounce cans whole green chilies
6 large eggs
1 cup flour
4 cups whole milk, not skim milk
Salt and pepper to taste

Butter bottom of a 3-quart soufflé dish. Cut chilies into 1-inch pieces. Layer the cheeses and chilies in bottom of the soufflé dish. Beat together eggs, flour, milk, salt, and pepper. Pour over cheeses and chilies. (This should half-fill the dish.) Bake in preheated 350° oven for 1 hour. Let stand 5 minutes before serving.

Serve with guacamole, sour cream, Mexican salsa, and warm tortillas. This is an excellent brunch recipe.

YIELD: 8 SERVINGS

A Taste of Oregon
THE JUNIOR LEAGUE OF EUGENE, OREGON

Mexican Scrambled Eggs

½ large onion, chopped
2 teaspoons cooking oil
1 tomato, chopped
2 green serrano chilies, chopped
10 beaten eggs
Salt

Sauté onion in 2 teaspoons oil until transparent. Add tomato and chilies and cook for 5 minutes. Add eggs and salt to taste and scramble together until done to taste.

Serve with warm tortillas.

YIELD: 6 SERVINGS

Que Sabroso!
THE JUNIOR LEAGUE OF MEXICO CITY, MEXICO

Eggs Bonne Femme

3 ounces cream cheese
1 cup light cream
1 tablespoon butter
Salt and pepper to taste
6 drops Worcestershire sauce
1 tablespoon chopped chives or parsley
6 eggs

Into top of a double saucepan put cream cheese, cream, butter, salt, pepper, Worcestershire, and chopped chives or parsley. Cook over simmering water. When cheese and butter are melted, break in the eggs. Do not disturb until the whites have almost set, then stir until mixture is thick. Use a whisk for stirring.

Serve with crisp bacon and toasted English muffins for a delicious Sunday morning brunch.

YIELD: 4 SERVINGS

THE JUNIOR LEAGUE OF SEATTLE, WASHINGTON

· · · · · · · · · · · · · · · · · · · ·

Eggs MacSweeney

Bacon
Eggs
Milk
Salt
Paprika
Chopped chives
Chopped parsley

Into individual baking dishes, chop 2 tablespoons uncooked bacon. Put dishes under broiler until bacon is crisp. Into each dish break 1 or 2 eggs, add 1 tablespoon milk, and season to taste with salt, paprika, and, if available, chives and parsley.

Bake in 350° oven until whites are set (peek at them often).

What's Cooking
THE JUNIOR LEAGUE OF OGDEN, UTAH

. . . .

Eggs Supreme

10 hard-boiled eggs
½ pound fresh mushrooms
1 tablespoon butter
1 10¾-ounce can cream of mushroom soup
½ cup mayonnaise
½ cup milk
1½ teaspoons chopped chives
1 pound bacon
4–6 English muffins, split and toasted

Slice eggs and put in a 9 x 9-inch baking dish. Slice and sauté mushrooms in butter; spoon over eggs.

In blender, combine soup, mayonnaise, and milk; pour over eggs and mushrooms. Sprinkle chives on top.

Cook bacon and crumble over egg mixture just before baking. Bake at 350° for 20 minutes.

Serve over warm English muffins for excellent brunch or light supper. Can be made a day ahead.

YIELD: 4–6 SERVINGS

THE JUNIOR LEAGUE OF SAN DIEGO, CALIFORNIA

. . . .

Rice, Beans, and Pasta

Aroz Sopea
(Basque Rice)

Since many people of Basque origin have made their homes in Idaho, their customs and culinary traditions are very special to us. The Basques are neither French nor Spanish, and had, until about fifty years ago, a nation all their own.

Primarily a people of sheepherders, farmers, and fishermen, the Basques have learned to live off the land. They are also a people of strong traditions, and one of the most delightful of these is the pride all Basques take in their food. An invitation to a Basque meal, be it cooked in a ranch cookhouse or an elaborate home, is sure to be a memorable occasion.

2 tablespoons oil
1½ cups converted rice
3 chorizo sausage, sliced in thin rounds
1 medium onion, chopped
4½ cups water (half chicken broth, if desired)
1 cup tomato sauce
1 medium slice ham, cubed
3 hard-boiled eggs, chopped
Pimento for garnish

In Dutch oven or large ovenproof casserole heat oil and add rice. Toast rice until golden. Add chorizo and onion and cook about 3 minutes. Add water, tomato sauce, and ham cubes. Simmer gently over direct heat for 10 minutes. Cover and bake for 45–50 minutes in a 250° oven.

Remove from oven and stir gently; add chopped eggs. Garnish with pimento.

YIELD: 8–10 SERVINGS

THE JUNIOR LEAGUE OF BOISE, IDAHO

Russian Hill Pilaf

2 tablespoons butter
1 cup long-grain white rice
1 10½-ounce can beef consommé
¾ cup water
½ cup chopped green onion
¼ cup raisins
1 teaspoon salt
½ cup pine nuts or toasted slivered almonds

Melt butter in a skillet. Stir in rice and cook, stirring, until lightly browned and well coated with butter. Add consommé, water, onion, raisins, and salt. Bring mixture to a boil. Cover, turn heat to very low, and cook for 30 minutes, until all liquid is absorbed or rice is tender.

Just before serving, stir in pine nuts or toasted almonds.

YIELD: 3–4 SERVINGS

THE JUNIOR LEAGUE OF SPOKANE, WASHINGTON

. . . .

Nutty Rice

½ cup long-grain rice
1 tablespoon butter
6 mustard seeds
2 teaspoons coarsely chopped cashew nuts
1 tablespoon shredded coconut
2 green onions, finely chopped
½ teaspoon curry powder
½ lemon

Cook rice according to package directions. Set aside and keep warm.

In skillet melt butter, add mustard seeds, and cook until seeds swell.

Recipe continues . . .

Add cashew nuts, coconut, onions, and curry powder. Stir and cook over low heat for 2–3 minutes.

Remove mixture from heat and stir in a good squeeze of lemon juice. Toss with the hot rice, correct the seasoning with salt, and serve.

YIELD: 4 SERVINGS

THE JUNIOR LEAGUE OF SEATTLE, WASHINGTON

Lemon Rice

1 cup raw white rice
1½ cups boiling water
⅛ teaspoon salt
Juice and peel of 1 lemon
¼ cup butter
¾ cup heavy cream, slightly warmed
2 tablespoons chopped parsley

Add rice to boiling water. Season to taste with salt. Cook, covered, over medium heat for about 20 minutes, stirring occasionally with a fork. Do not overcook.

Sauté peel of lemon in butter for about 3 minutes. Remove peel. Add butter to cooked rice. Gently toss in lemon juice. Add half the warmed cream, stirring gently. Add remaining cream, stirring just enough to coat grains. Empty into ovenproof serving dish and set in 250° oven to keep warm until serving time. Garnish with the chopped parsley.

Delicious with fish dishes.

YIELD: 6 SERVINGS

THE JUNIOR LEAGUE OF SAN DIEGO, CALIFORNIA

Mexican Rice and Variations

1 cup raw white rice
3 cups very hot water
⅔ cup oil
½ medium onion, chopped
1 carrot
1 small clove garlic, chopped (optional—you can add any combination
of the following: chopped potato, chopped green pepper, corn, peas)
3 cups boiling water and 1 teaspoon salt or 3 cups
well-flavored chicken broth

Put rice in the hot water and let soak for 20 minutes. Drain and rinse well. Let stand in strainer to dry for at least 30 minutes.

Heat oil in a heavy saucepan. When hot add the rice and fry, stirring occasionally, until transparent (don't let it brown). Drain off excess oil and add the vegetables. Stir-fry together for about 5 minutes. Add water or broth. Bring to a boil, cover, and lower heat to simmer. Cook 20–30 minutes, or until water is absorbed and rice is tender.

YIELD: 6 SERVINGS

VARIATION—GREEN RICE:

Follow directions for Mexican Rice but cook with only 2 cups water for 15 minutes. Prepare buttered casserole. Put 2 chili poblanos*—peeled and deveined—in blender with ½ cup cream and ½ cup chicken broth. Blend well. Put rice in casserole and mix in the chili sauce. Sprinkle with ½ cup shredded cheese. Cover and bake at 320° for 20 minutes.

* If not available, use green peppers and add 1 tablespoon Tabasco to rice in the casserole.

Recipe continues . . .

VARIATION—RED RICE:

Follow directions for Mexican Rice but fry rice until a light golden color. Along with the vegetables add ½ cup tomato purée and continue as for white rice.

Que Sabroso!
THE JUNIOR LEAGUE OF MEXICO CITY, MEXICO

Pepper Rice

1½ cups white rice, cooked in salted water
2 pints sour cream
1 3-ounce can sliced olives
1 6-ounce can chopped chili peppers
½ pound mozzarella cheese, shredded
⅓ pound cheddar cheese, shredded

Beginning with cooked rice, layer ingredients in a greased 2-quart casserole. Bake at 325° until cheese is melted, about 25 minutes. Cover casserole and continue baking for 5 more minutes.

YIELD: 6 SERVINGS

THE JUNIOR LEAGUE OF SANTA BARBARA, CALIFORNIA

Cheese-Rice Casserole

1 cup raw rice
2 eggs, well beaten
2 cups milk
⅛ cup olive oil
2 cups shredded sharp cheddar cheese
1 medium onion, minced
1 cup minced parsley
1 clove garlic, minced
1½ teaspoons salt
Dash cayenne

Prepare rice to make 2–3 cups fluffy cooked rice. While still warm, carefully stir in remaining ingredients. Pour into a greased and floured 3-quart round casserole.

Bake at 350° for 35–45 minutes.

YIELD: 10–12 SERVINGS

THE JUNIOR LEAGUE OF OAKLAND-EAST BAY, CALIFORNIA

. . . .

California Ranch Rice

1 cup chopped white onion
2 cloves garlic, minced
4 tablespoons butter
4 cups cooked white rice
2 cups sour cream
1 cup small-curd cottage cheese
1 bay leaf, crushed
Salt and pepper to taste
2 7-ounce cans whole green chilies, rinsed, seeded, and cut into strips
2½ cups shredded cheddar cheese

Recipe continues . . .

In a large skillet sauté onion and garlic in butter until limp. Add rice, sour cream, cottage cheese, bay leaf, salt, and pepper. Mix together.

In a greased 3-quart casserole put a layer of rice mixture, a layer of chilies, and a layer of cheese. Repeat, ending with a layer of rice and leaving approximately ½ cup cheese to be used later.

Bake at 375° for 25 minutes. Remove from oven and sprinkle remaining cheese over top. Return to oven to bake 10 minutes longer.

This is a great casserole to serve with tacos or other Mexican food.

YIELD: 8–10 SERVINGS

THE JUNIOR LEAGUE OF SACRAMENTO, CALIFORNIA

·   ·   ·   ·   ·   ·   ·   ·   ·   ·   ·   ·   ·

Eggs and Rice Casserole

1 medium onion, chopped
2 cups raw white rice
6 tablespoons butter
6 cups chicken stock
4 tablespoons flour
1 cup light cream
12 hard-cooked eggs, sliced
1 4-ounce jar chopped green chilies
1 cup diced cheddar cheese
½ cup diced Monterey Jack cheese
Salt and pepper
Paprika

Sauté onion and rice in 4 tablespoons butter until onion is limp; add 3½ cups chicken stock and bring to a rapid boil. Reduce heat, cover, and cook about 20 minutes.

Meanwhile, melt remaining 2 tablespoons butter; blend in flour, slowly stir in cream and 2 cups chicken broth; continue to stir and cook until sauce is thick. Cool.

Arrange half the cooked rice in a 3½-quart casserole, top with half the eggs, half the chilies, half the cheese, and half the sauce. Repeat. Pour ½ cup chicken broth over all. Cover casserole and bake at 350° until hot and bubbly.

Serve with Mexican salsa.

YIELD: 12–16 SERVINGS

THE JUNIOR LEAGUE OF RIVERSIDE, CALIFORNIA

. . . .

Rice Casserole with Almonds and Mushrooms

1 clove garlic, minced
3 tablespoons minced green onion
1 stick plus 2 tablespoons butter
2 cups raw white rice or 1¾ cups white and ¼ cup wild rice
½ cup raisins, plumped 5 minutes in broth
4 cups chicken broth
2 tablespoons grated Parmesan cheese
1 cup sliced mushrooms
½ cup slivered almonds
2 tablespoons minced parsley

In casserole sauté garlic and onion in ½ stick butter until onion is soft. Add rice; stir until well coated. Stir in raisins. Add broth, bring to boil over high heat, cover, and transfer to a 350° oven for 25 minutes, or until all liquid is absorbed. Add remaining half stick of butter, cut in slices, and add the Parmesan cheese. Fluff with a fork and keep warm.

While rice is cooking, sauté the sliced mushrooms in 1 tablespoon butter. Sauté the slivered almonds until golden in remaining 1 tablespoon butter. Stir mushrooms and almonds into the rice along with the minced parsley.

YIELD: 8–10 SERVINGS

THE JUNIOR LEAGUE OF LOS ANGELES, CALIFORNIA

. . . .

Lee's Meatless Meal

1 cup raw rice
3 medium zucchini, thinly sliced
1 4-ounce can chopped green chilies
12 ounces Monterey Jack cheese, shredded
1 large tomato, thinly sliced
Salt to taste
2 cups sour cream
1 teaspoon oregano
1 teaspoon garlic salt
¼ cup chopped green pepper
¼ cup chopped green onion
2 tablespoons chopped parsley

Cook rice according to directions. Cook zucchini until barely tender, drain, and set both aside.

In a 3-quart buttered casserole, put a layer of cooked rice, cover with chilies, and sprinkled with half the cheese. Add zucchini, tomato slices, and salt. Combine rest of the ingredients, except parsley, and spoon over the tomato layer. Add remaining cheese and bake in a 350° oven for 45 minutes.

Remove from oven and sprinkle with chopped parsley.

YIELD: 8 SERVINGS

THE JUNIOR LEAGUE OF OAKLAND-EAST BAY, CALIFORNIA

California Paella

4 Italian sweet sausages
1 9-ounce package frozen artichoke hearts, partly thawed
1 10-ounce package frozen peas, partly thawed
1 pound frozen, ready-to-cook shrimp, partly thawed
½ cup cooking oil
8 chicken thighs (1¼ pounds)
1 cup coarsely chopped green pepper
1 onion, coarsely chopped
1 1-pound can tomatoes, drained and chopped
1 6½-ounce can minced clams
1 cup boiling water
2 6-ounce packages yellow rice with saffron
1 4-ounce jar pimentos, drained

Parboil sausages in water to cover for 3 minutes, cool, and cut into ¾-inch slices. Remove artichoke hearts, peas, and shrimp from freezer, and allow to thaw at room temperature while preparing paella.

In a 4-quart Dutch oven, heat oil; add chicken and brown well on both sides. Remove from Dutch oven. Add sausage, green pepper, onion, and tomatoes to Dutch oven and cook about 5 minutes, stirring constantly.

Stir in clams with juice, water, and rice. Return chicken to the Dutch oven, cover, and bake at 350° for 30 minutes.

Uncover, add artichoke hearts, peas, and shrimp; stir to blend, cover, and bake 30 minutes longer.

Garnish with pimento slices before serving.

YIELD: 8 SERVINGS

THE JUNIOR LEAGUE OF LONG BEACH, CALIFORNIA

Canadian Wild Rice and Mushroom Casserole

1 cup wild rice
½ cup minced onion
1 ½ pounds fresh mushrooms, sliced
Butter
1 egg
Salt and pepper to taste
1 teaspoon Worcestershire sauce
¼ cup sherry
1 cup cream
1 cup cooked, puréed chestnuts

Wash rice and drain. Bring to a boil in 3 cups water, cover, and cook over low heat until kernels burst. Remove from heat and drain.

Sauté onion and mushrooms in small amount of butter. Combine egg, seasoning, Worcestershire, sherry, and cream and stir in cooked mushrooms, onion, wild rice, and chestnuts. Refrigerate until ready to cook, then bake at 350° for 30–45 minutes.

Serve with game, fowl, or any roast.

YIELD: 6–8 SERVINGS

THE JUNIOR LEAGUE OF EDMONTON, ALBERTA

· · · · · · · · · · · · · · · · · · · ·

Wild Rice Casserole

1 ½ cups wild rice
3 cups bouillon
1 cup water
½ cup chopped onion
½ cup chopped green pepper
3–4 cups chopped chicken livers
1 cup chopped mushrooms
½ cup soft butter
1 cup cream

Soak wild rice for 6 hours and drain well. Boil rice in bouillon and water until liquid is absorbed.

Sauté onion, pepper, chicken livers, and mushrooms in all but 1 tablespoon butter. Mix rice with sautéed ingredients and stir in cream and remaining butter. Refrigerate for at least 2 hours.

Cover and bake at 325° for 30 minutes, or until thoroughly heated.

YIELD: 6–8 SERVINGS

THE JUNIOR LEAGUE OF BOISE, IDAHO

Barley Pilaf

½ pound fresh mushrooms, sliced
2 medium onions, chopped
¼ pound butter
1¾ cups pearl barley
4 cups chicken broth or bouillon

Sauté mushrooms and onions in half the butter. Remove to 2-quart buttered casserole when tender. Cook barley in remaining butter over low heat until almond-colored. Add to casserole. Pour broth over all.

Bake at 350° for 1½–2 hours. Cover for first half of cooking time.

If mixture should become dry, add a little water. May be prepared ahead. In that case, add liquid at cooking time.

YIELD: 8 SERVINGS

No Regrets
THE JUNIOR LEAGUE OF PORTLAND, OREGON

Barley and Pine Nut Pilaf

1 cup pearl barley
6 tablespoons butter
¼–½ cup pine nuts
1 medium onion, chopped
½ cup minced, fresh parsley
¼ cup minced chives or green onion
¼ teaspoon salt
¼ teaspoon pepper
2 13¾-ounce cans beef broth or 1 can beef broth and 1 can dry white wine

Rinse barley in cold water and drain.

In skillet heat butter and brown pine nuts. Remove with slotted spoon and reserve. Sauté onion and barley until lightly toasted. Remove from heat. Stir in nuts, parsley, chives, salt, and pepper. Spoon into 1½-quart casserole.

Heat broth to boiling and pour over barley mixture. Stir to blend well. Bake, uncovered, for 1 hour and 10 minutes at 350°.

YIELD: 6 SERVINGS

Private Collection:
Recipes from The Junior League of Palo Alto
THE JUNIOR LEAGUE OF PALO ALTO, CALIFORNIA

True Grit Soufflé

6 cups water
1½ cups grits
1½ sticks butter
1 pound mild cheddar cheese, shredded
2 teaspoons salt
3 eggs, beaten

Bring water to a rapid boil. Gradually stir in the grits and boil for 10 minutes, uncovered, stirring frequently. Remove from heat and stir in the butter, cheese, salt, and eggs.

Empty into 9 x 13-inch baking dish and bake for 1½ hours at 350°.

YIELD: 10 SERVINGS

Epicure
THE JUNIOR LEAGUE OF NEWPORT HARBOR, CALIFORNIA

Susan's Hominy Casserole

2 16-ounce cans yellow hominy, drained
1 2-ounce jar chopped pimento
1 4-ounce can chopped green chilies
½ stick butter, melted
1 cup sour cream
½ cup shredded longhorn cheese

Mix first five ingredients and turn into a 2-quart casserole. Sprinkle cheese on top. Bake, uncovered, in a 350° oven for 45 minutes to 1 hour.

This is especially good with roast meat or as an accompaniment to any main-dish Mexican recipe.

YIELD: 4 SERVINGS

Gourmet Olé
THE JUNIOR LEAGUE OF ALBUQUERQUE, NEW MEXICO

Basque Garbanzos

2 chorizo sausages, sliced
½ cup chopped onion
2 cloves garlic, minced
1 tablespoon oil
2 cups canned garbanzo beans
2 8-ounce cans tomato sauce

Sauté meat, onion, and garlic in oil until lightly browned. Add the beans, including the liquid, and tomato sauce and simmer gently for 1 hour.

YIELD: 4 SERVINGS

THE JUNIOR LEAGUE OF BOISE, IDAHO

· · · · · · · · · · · · · · · · · · ·

Spanish Beans

2 pounds dried cranberry or pinto beans
1 cup olive oil
2 cloves garlic, minced
2 onions, chopped
1 ham hock, quartered by butcher
2 large tomatoes, peeled and quartered
1 8-ounce can tomato sauce
1 tablespoon chili powder
Salt to taste

Soak beans for several hours or overnight. Drain; place in a heavy pot and cover with boiling water. Add oil, garlic, onions, and ham hock. Bring to a very slow boil and simmer until soft, about 2–3 hours, adding a little boiling water if needed. Beans must be watched and stirred occasionally as they tend to burn.

Add remaining ingredients and simmer another ½ hour or so.

This is a native Californian's recipe, going back several generations. It is delicious served with a barbecue dinner or Mexican dishes.

YIELD: 8–10 SERVINGS

Private Collection:
Recipes from The Junior League of Palo Alto
THE JUNIOR LEAGUE OF PALO ALTO, CALIFORNIA

· ·

Mexican-Style Black Beans

2 pounds dried black beans
2 pounds pork loin, cubed
1 large onion, diced
1 4-ounce can chopped green chilies
Salt
Chopped coriander or parsley

Soak beans in water overnight. Drain; cover with cold water. Bring to boil and simmer for 1 hour, or until still a bit firm. Add meat, onion, chopped chilies, and salt and cook for 1 hour or longer, or until beans are tender, adding a little water from time to time as needed to keep beans from sticking.

Serve sprinkled with coriander or parsley.

YIELD: 6 SERVINGS

THE JUNIOR LEAGUE OF TUCSON, ARIZONA

· ·

Feijoada

2 cups dried black beans
1 16-ounce can tomatoes
1 16-ounce can tomato sauce
1 large onion, chopped
1 clove garlic, minced
1 bay leaf
1 4-ounce can chopped green chilies
1 pound chorizo sausage
1 large ham bone with at least 3 cups of meat left on it

Bring beans to a boil and boil for 2 minutes in 6 cups unsalted water. Remove from heat and let stand 1 hour. Drain; add tomatoes and tomato sauce. Add onion, garlic, bay leaf, and green chilies. Cut chorizo into ½-inch slices and add. Submerge ham bone in beans and bring to a boil; reduce heat to simmer and cook at least 6 hours or longer.

Before serving, cut ham away from bone into bite-size pieces and return to beans.

Serve over cooked long-grain rice with crusty rolls and a tossed salad.

YIELD: 8–10 SERVINGS

THE JUNIOR LEAGUE OF BAKERSFIELD, CALIFORNIA

· · · · · · · · · · · · · · · · · · ·

Mamacita's Pinto Beans

3 cups dried pinto beans, washed and cleaned
½ cup oil
4 cloves garlic, chopped
½ teaspoon pepper
2 tablespoons powdered red chili
½ pound salt pork, diced
1 medium onion, quartered
1 tablespoon sugar

Soak beans in water to cover in refrigerator overnight. Drain; cover generously with fresh water and add all other ingredients. Boil for 1½ hours, skimming top occasionally and adding more water as needed to keep beans moist. Mash beans slightly and cook for another 30 minutes.

The beans may be served at this point or simmered all day for fullest flavor, adding water when necessary. Add salt just before serving.

Freezes well.

YIELD: 6 SERVINGS

Gourmet Olé
THE JUNIOR LEAGUE OF ALBUQUERQUE, NEW MEXICO

· ·

Vegetarian Lasagne

1 8-ounce package lasagne noodles
2 10-ounce packages chopped spinach
2 cups sliced fresh mushrooms
1 cup grated carrot
½ cup chopped onion
1 tablespoon oil
2 8-ounce cans tomato sauce
1 6-ounce can tomato paste
½ cup chopped black olives
1½ teaspoons oregano
2 cups cottage cheese, drained
1 pound Monterey Jack cheese, shredded
Parmesan cheese

Cook noodles in boiling unsalted water for 8–10 minutes or until tender; drain and set aside. Cook spinach according to package directions and drain well.

In a saucepan cook mushrooms, carrot, and onion in oil until tender. Stir in tomato sauce, tomato paste, olives, and oregano.

Recipe continues . . .

In greased 9 x 13-inch baking dish, layer half the noodles, cottage cheese, spinach, Jack cheese, and sauce mixture; repeat the layers, reserving about ½ cup cheese for the top. Sprinkle with Parmesan cheese.

Bake at 375° for 30 minutes. Let stand for 10 minutes before serving. Freezes well.

YIELD: 8 SERVINGS

THE JUNIOR LEAGUE OF BOISE, IDAHO

· ·

Pasta Molto Facile

¼ pound butter (no substitute)
4 cups quartered fresh mushrooms (1 pound)
1 clove garlic, minced
2¼ cups chopped fresh parsley
12 ounces thin, narrow noodles
1 pint sour cream
½ cup freshly grated Parmesan or Romano cheese plus
¼ cup freshly grated Parmesan cheese

In a large skillet slowly melt the butter (do not brown) and cook mushrooms over low heat until just done, about 5 minutes. Add garlic and cook an additional minute. Add 2 cups parsley and cook for another 2 minutes.

Cook noodles during above procedure. Drain and rinse briefly in very hot water. Return to pan in which they were boiled. Pour mushroom mixture over noodles, toss lightly, add the sour cream and the ½ cup cheese, and toss lightly again.

Place on platter, surround with the remaining parsley, and sprinkle with the ¼ cup Parmesan. Serve very hot.

YIELD: 6 SERVINGS

The California Heritage Cookbook
THE JUNIOR LEAGUE OF PASADENA, CALIFORNIA

· ·

New World Fettucine

12 ounces green fettucine

SAUCE:
3 tablespoons olive oil or butter
1 large onion, finely chopped
1 large green pepper, chopped
3 cloves garlic, chopped
2 tablespoons oregano
2 cups thinly sliced mushrooms
8 large, very ripe tomatoes, chopped
1 cup chopped parsley
1 tablespoon sugar
1 8-ounce can tomato purée
1 cup red wine
Grated Parmesan cheese

Place fettucine in 8-quart pot of boiling salted water and cook until it is al dente. Drain and set aside.

Heat 2 tablespoons of the oil or butter in large pot and in it sauté the onion, pepper, garlic, and oregano until onion is transparent. Add mushrooms and continue frying until mushrooms are tender. Add tomatoes and cook until very soft. Add parsley and sugar. Mix with a wooden spoon. Add tomato purée and wine. Mix everything together well. Bring to a boil; lower heat and simmer 1 hour, uncovered.

Place fettucine in clean pot with remaining oil or butter. Cook, stirring, until fettucine is heated through. Empty out onto serving plate, cover with sauce and sprinkle with grated Parmesan cheese.

YIELD: 6–8 SERVINGS

Que Sabroso!
THE JUNIOR LEAGUE OF MEXICO CITY, MEXICO

Arizona Beef Casserole

¾ pound ground round
¾ pound ground pork
Butter
1 teaspoon salt
2 large onions, chopped
1 clove garlic, minced
1 8-ounce package medium noodles
1 8-ounce can tomato sauce
1 12-ounce can Mexican-style corn
1 teaspoon chili powder
Salt to taste
4–5 tablespoons red wine
8 ounces sharp cheddar cheese, shredded

Brown meat in butter in skillet. Remove meat from skillet and sprinkle with salt. Brown onions and garlic lightly in skillet.

Cook noodles in salted water according to package directions. Drain.

Combine meat, onions, garlic, noodles, and next five ingredients lightly and spoon into buttered 5-quart casserole. Cover with cheese. Bake, uncovered, in 350° oven for 30 minutes.

If prepared early in the day, and more moisture is needed, add tomato sauce or wine.

YIELD: 10 SERVINGS

Something New Under the Sun
THE JUNIOR LEAGUE OF PHOENIX, ARIZONA

Vermicelli Carbinara

5 eggs
1 cup grated Parmesan cheese
3 tablespoons freshly chopped parsley
Freshly ground black pepper to taste
12 slices bacon
1 small onion, finely chopped
1 pound vermicelli
Additional grated Parmesan cheese

Combine eggs, 1 cup cheese, parsley, and pepper. Mix thoroughly with whisk or beater. Sauté bacon and onion until bacon is crisp and onion transparent. Pour off the drippings and crumble the bacon.

Cook vermicelli according to the package directions. Lift a portion of the cooked vermicelli from the water with a slotted spoon, letting the water run off, then drop it into the egg and cheese mixture and stir. The hot pasta will cook the eggs. Repeat this process until all of the vermicelli has been added. Add the bacon and onions; mix well.

Serve with additional grated cheese.

YIELD: 6 SERVINGS

THE JUNIOR LEAGUE OF LONG BEACH, CALIFORNIA

. . . .

Tagliarini with Clam Sauce

12 ounces tagliarini* or thin noodles
1 cup butter
1 bunch green onions, chopped
1 8-ounce can minced clams, drained, reserving broth
¼ teaspoon arrowroot
Reserved clam broth
Salt and white pepper to taste

Recipe continues . . .

Prepare tagliarini according to package directions.

Melt butter in frying pan. Gently sauté green onions for 2–3 minutes, or until softened. Add clams and sauté another minute just to heat through.

Stir arrowroot into 2 tablespoons reserved clam broth to make a paste, then stir into remaining broth and add to sautéed mixture. With a whisk, stir until thickened. Add salt and white pepper to taste.

To serve, heap tagliarini on warmed plates and pour sauce over.

YIELD: 3–4 MAIN-DISH SERVINGS; 6 SIDE-DISH SERVINGS

* Tagliarini is a thin Italian noodle that is at its very best served in a delicate sauce like this.

Private Collection:
Recipes from The Junior League of Palo Alto
THE JUNIOR LEAGUE OF PALO ALTO, CALIFORNIA

Calamari Sauce for Pasta

2 medium onions, chopped
5 tablespoons olive oil
2 cloves garlic, minced
3 cups white wine
1 cup tomato purée
½ cup chopped fresh parsley
1 teaspoon oregano
Salt and freshly ground pepper to taste
4 pounds small calamari (squid), cleaned and sliced crosswise into rings
1 pound mushrooms, sliced

In a heavy skillet sauté onions in olive oil until golden. Add the garlic and wine and boil for 3 minutes to let the alcohol evaporate. Add tomato purée, parsley, oregano, salt, and pepper. Add calamari, cover, and cook over medium heat for about 45 minutes, stirring frequently. Add the mushrooms about 5 minutes before serving.

Serve over freshly cooked pasta.

YIELD: 12 SERVINGS

San Francisco à la Carte
THE JUNIOR LEAGUE OF SAN FRANCISCO, CALIFORNIA

Noodles Amandine

1 12-ounce package fine noodles
½ cup butter
½ cup grated Parmesan cheese
1 cup sour cream
½ teaspoon basil
Salt and pepper to taste
1 cup toasted slivered almonds

Cook noodles in boiling water according to package directions. Drain and rinse with boiling water. Empty into a bowl, add the butter, Parmesan cheese, sour cream, basil, and salt and pepper to taste. Blend with a fork, lifting and turning until well mixed.

Turn mixture into a greased casserole dish and sprinkle almonds on top. Cover and heat in a 350° oven for 20–30 minutes.

YIELD: 6–8 SERVINGS

THE JUNIOR LEAGUE OF VANCOUVER, BRITISH COLUMBIA

Pasta Primavera

1 cup sliced zucchini
1½ cups broccoli flowerets or sliced green beans
1¼ cups snow peas
1 cup baby peas
6 stalks asparagus, sliced
1 pound spaghetti
12 cherry tomatoes, halved
3 tablespoons olive oil
2 teaspoons minced garlic
Salt and freshly ground pepper to taste
¼ cup chopped Italian parsley
⅓ cup pine nuts
10 large mushrooms, sliced
⅓ cup butter
½ cup freshly grated Parmesan cheese
1 cup heavy cream
⅓ cup chopped fresh basil
⅓ cup chicken consommé
Cherry tomatoes for garnish

Blanch zucchini, broccoli, snow peas, baby peas, mushrooms, and asparagus in boiling salted water for 1–2 minutes, or until just crisp-tender. Drain and refresh under cold water. Set aside. This can be done ahead of time.

Cook pasta in lots of boiling salted water until al dente, about 8–11 minutes. Drain and rinse with hot water.

While pasta is cooking, sauté tomatoes in 1 tablespoon of oil with 1 teaspoon garlic, the salt, pepper, and parsley. Set aside.

In another pan sauté pine nuts in remaining oil until brown and add mushrooms. Add remaining garlic and all vegetables. Simmer for a few minutes, or until vegetables are hot.

In a pan large enough for pasta and vegetables, melt butter. Add cheese, cream, and basil. Stir to blend and melt cheese. Add pasta and toss to coat with sauce. If sauce gets too thick, thin with a little chicken consommé. Add about one-third of vegetables and toss again.

Divide pasta into broad soup plates and top with remaining vegetables.

Garnish with cherry tomatoes. Season to taste with salt, pepper, and more grated Parmesan cheese if desired.

YIELD: 6 SERVINGS

A Taste of Oregon
THE JUNIOR LEAGUE OF EUGENE, OREGON

· · · · · · · · · · · · · · · · · · · ·

Rigattoni in Mushroom Sauce

1 tablespoon olive oil
½ pound mushrooms, sliced
½ cup chopped onion
1 cup water
1 6-ounce can tomato paste
1 28-ounce can tomatoes
2 tablespoons minced parsley
1 clove garlic, minced
1¼ teaspoons salt
¼ teaspoon pepper
¼ teaspoon basil
½ teaspoon oregano
12 ounces mozzarella cheese, shredded
12 ounces Swiss cheese, shredded
½ cup grated Parmesan cheese
1 pound rigattoni noodles, cooked*

Heat oil in saucepan and in it sauté mushrooms and onion until lightly browned. Stir in water, tomato paste, tomatoes, parsley, garlic, salt, pepper,

* To cook rigattoni, empty noodles into 2 quarts of rapidly boiling water, and add 2 teaspoons salt and 1 teaspoon oil. Boil until tender but firm, about 8–10 minutes. Drain and rinse with cold water.

Recipe continues . . .

basil, and oregano. Simmer over low heat for 1½ hours. Taste and adjust seasonings.

Mix together cheeses. Insert a heaping tablespoon of cheese into each cooked rigattoni. Arrange in a greased baking dish and cover with the sauce. Bake in a 300° oven for 1 hour.

YIELD: 8 SERVINGS

THE JUNIOR LEAGUE OF VANCOUVER, BRITISH COLUMBIA

• •

Spaghetti Pie

6 ounces spaghetti
3 tablespoons butter
2 eggs
⅓ cup grated Parmesan cheese
1½ pounds ground beef
½ cup chopped onion
½ cup chopped green pepper
1 4-ounce can chopped mushrooms
1 8-ounce can tomatoes, chopped
1 6-ounce can tomato paste
1½ teaspoons oregano
¾ teaspoon basil
¼ teaspoon salt
2 cloves fresh garlic, minced
1 cup cottage cheese, well drained (8 ounces)
1 cup shredded mozzarella cheese

Cook spaghetti until just tender—do not overcook. Drain. Stir butter, eggs, and Parmesan cheese into spaghetti. Make spaghetti mixture into a "crust" and press into a buttered 10-inch pie plate.

In skillet, cook ground beef, onion, and green pepper until meat is done. Drain off excess fat. Stir in mushrooms, tomatoes, tomato paste, oregano, basil, salt, and garlic. Simmer for 30 minutes.

Spread cottage cheese over bottom of spaghetti "crust." Fill pie with meat-tomato mixture. Cover with foil and bake in a 350° oven for 45 minutes. Uncover. Top with shredded mozzarella cheese. Bake an additional 7–8 minutes, or until cheese has melted.

Serve with garlic bread and a tossed salad.

YIELD: 6–8 SERVINGS

Gourmet Olé
THE JUNIOR LEAGUE OF ALBUQUERQUE, NEW MEXICO

· ·

Spaghetti Toss

1 10-ounce package frozen chopped broccoli
1 onion, chopped
1 clove garlic, minced
2 tablespoons butter or cooking oil
8 ounces pepperoni, thinly sliced
⅓ pound mushrooms, sliced
1 pound spaghetti
Grated Parmesan cheese

Parboil broccoli in ½ cup water for 3–5 minutes. Drain.

In medium skillet, sauté onion and garlic in butter or oil until tender but not brown. Add pepperoni and mushrooms and cook over medium heat 5 minutes more. Add broccoli and mix.

Meanwhile, cook spaghetti according to package directions; drain.

Toss spaghetti with other ingredients, including Parmesan cheese, and serve.

YIELD: 6 SERVINGS

THE JUNIOR LEAGUE OF SAN JOSE, CALIFORNIA

· ·

Peek's Spaghetti Sauce

2 pounds ground round
3 cups chopped onion
3 cloves garlic, minced
1 tablespoon salt
2 8-ounce cans tomato sauce
2 16-ounce cans whole tomatoes
1 6-ounce can tomato paste
1 tablespoon Worcestershire sauce
1 tablespoon red wine vinegar
1 teaspoon Tabasco
1 teaspoon basil
1 teaspoon rosemary
1 teaspoon marjoram
1 tablespoon oregano
1 tablespoon chili powder
1 tablespoon paprika
1 tablespoon sugar
1 teaspoon pepper
3 bay leaves
3 cups minced green pepper
1 cup sliced fresh mushrooms
1 cup fresh minced parsley

Brown meat, onion, and garlic with salt in large, heavy frying pan, stirring frequently. Set aside.

Combine remaining ingredients in large, heavy kettle; add meat and bring to a boil. Reduce heat and simmer slowly for 5–6 hours.

May be frozen in tightly covered containers.

YIELD: 4 QUARTS

THE JUNIOR LEAGUE OF OAKLAND-EAST BAY, CALIFORNIA

Linguine with Tomatoes and Zucchini

⅓ cup butter
⅓ cup chopped onion
1 green pepper, seeded and cut into strips
4 ounces linguine, cooked and drained
2–3 cups sliced zucchini
4 medium tomatoes, peeled, seeded, and cut into strips
¼ cup chopped parsley
½ cup shredded Gruyère or other Swiss cheese
½ cup freshly grated Parmesan cheese

Melt butter in a skillet and sauté onion for about 5 minutes. Add green pepper and cook a few minutes more. Combine with remaining ingredients, reserving a few tablespoons Parmesan cheese for top. Place in buttered 2-quart casserole and top with cheese.

Bake covered at 350° for 30–40 minutes, or until cheese is bubbling. Do not overcook.

YIELD: 6 SERVINGS

Colorado Cache
THE JUNIOR LEAGUE OF DENVER, COLORADO

. . . .

Easy Baked Lasagna

3 pounds ground beef
1–2 cloves garlic, minced
1 tablespoon parsley
3 cups marinara sauce
1 12-ounce can tomato paste
1 teaspoon salt and a dash of pepper
2 tablespoons oregano
8 ounces lasagna noodles
1 pint cottage cheese, drained
8 ounces mozzarella cheese, sliced

Recipe continues . . .

In large skillet or saucepan brown meat with garlic and parsley. Add marinara sauce, tomato paste, salt, pepper, and oregano. Bring to a boil and simmer for 1–1½ hours. Sauce will thicken.

Cook lasagna noodles according to package directions. Drain well. Crisscross noodles on bottom of shallow 9 x 13-inch pan. Spread half the cottage cheese in a layer over the noodles. Cover with half the sauce. Repeat: layer of noodles, cottage cheese, remaining meat sauce. Top with mozzarella cheese slices. Bake for 1 hour at 250–300°.

May be frozen but should be thawed before baking.

YIELD: 6 SERVINGS

THE JUNIOR LEAGUE OF BUTTE, MONTANA

Ricotta Dumplings

4 eggs
1 pound ricotta cheese
1 cup Parmesan cheese
1 cup bread crumbs
1 10-ounce package frozen spinach
Salt and pepper to taste
⅛ teaspoon garlic powder
1 cup flour
Tomato sauce

Mix all ingredients except flour and sauce. Form into small balls and roll in flour to coat thoroughly. Drop balls into boiling salted water. When they rise to the top of the water, they are finished cooking.

Transfer cheese balls to a baking dish. Cover with tomato sauce. Bake at 350° for 40 minutes. Serve warm.

YIELD: 20 APPETIZER SERVINGS

THE JUNIOR LEAGUE OF SAN JOSE, CALIFORNIA

Strozzapreti
(*Gnocchi Verdi*)

2 10-ounce packages frozen chopped spinach
1 pound ricotta cheese
3 eggs, beaten
¼ teaspoon ground nutmeg
Pinch salt
1 teaspoon ground pepper
2 cups grated Parmesan cheese
¾ cup flour
½ cup melted butter

Cook spinach according to package directions. Don't overcook. Drain and cool. Squeeze out moisture by hand. Chop again.

Drain ricotta cheese if necessary and empty into a mixing bowl with the spinach, eggs, nutmeg, salt, pepper, and 1½ cups of the Parmesan cheese. Mix well and chill.

Put flour on wax paper and lightly dust the hands. Form spinach mixture into walnut-size balls, then roll in flour and gently shape into 1 x 2-inch rolls. Place on wax paper. You should have about 48 spinach rolls.

Drop 8–10 rolls at a time into briskly boiling water and cook until they rise to the top, about 2–3 minutes. Remove with slotted spoon and turn into a shallow buttered ovenproof dish. Sprinkle with a little butter and some of the reserved ½ cup Parmesan cheese. Keep warm in a very low oven. Continue cooking spinach dumplings and sprinkling with butter and cheese until all are done. Serve at once.

These can be made ahead and warmed in oven before serving.

YIELD: 8 SERVINGS

THE JUNIOR LEAGUE OF SAN JOSE, CALIFORNIA

Pirohi

A Ukrainian potato-cheese dumpling served with melted butter and sour cream.

DOUGH:
2 cups flour
1 teaspoon salt
½ teaspoon baking powder
2 tablespoons oil
¾ cup cold water

FILLING:
1 onion, chopped
3 tablespoons butter
2 cups hot mashed potatoes
1 cup dry cottage cheese
1½ teaspoons salt
1 egg
¼ teaspoon pepper

Mix dough ingredients together and work with hands until dough is smooth. Let stand while making filling.

To make filling, sauté onion in butter, then mix together potatoes, cottage cheese, salt, egg, pepper, and onion. Put aside.

Roll dough out to about ¼-inch thickness and cut into rounds using a jar top or cup. Place a heaping teaspoon of filling on each round of dough. Fold over and press edges together well, pinching edges to seal.

Drop filled balls into boiling salted water. Cook about 10 minutes, or until the balls rise to the surface. Lift out, drain, and place in a lightly buttered casserole. Keep in warm oven until ready to serve.

Serve with melted butter and sour cream.

May be frozen.

YIELD: ABOUT 2 DOZEN PIROHI

THE JUNIOR LEAGUE OF EDMONTON, ALBERTA

Crepes and Enchiladas

Tetrazzini Crepes

12 crepes
2 whole chicken breasts (1½ pounds)
5 ounces fresh mushrooms
6 tablespoons margarine
⅓ cup flour
¾ cup light cream or half and half
⅓ cup dry sherry
1 cup shredded, sharp natural cheddar cheese (4 ounces)
2 tablespoons chopped, pitted ripe olives
2 tablespoons grated Parmesan cheese

BATTER FOR 12 CREPES:
1½ cups milk
2 eggs
¼ teaspoon salt
1 cup flour
1 teaspoon baking powder
2 tablespoons margarine

Make crepes: Beat together or whirl in blender the first five batter ingredients. Melt margarine in a 7-inch crepe pan and stir into batter. Refrigerate batter for 1 hour before baking crepes.

To bake crepes, pour a scant ¼ cup batter into pan and tilt to coat bottom. Bake about 1 minute over medium heat, or until golden. Turn and bake for 30 seconds. Crepes may be made ahead, stacked, wrapped in foil and refrigerated a day or so, or frozen.

Make filling and sauce: In a saucepan cover chicken with salted water. Cover saucepan and simmer until chicken is tender, about 30 minutes. Reserve 1¼ cup broth for sauce. Remove skin and bones from chicken and dice meat (about 2 cups diced chicken).

In small skillet, brown mushrooms in 3 tablespoons of margarine. Set aside.

In a saucepan, melt remaining margarine; stir in flour. Gradually stir in the reserved chicken broth and the cream. Cook and stir until sauce is thickened and bubbly. Stir in the dry sherry and cheddar cheese and stir until cheese is melted.

To chicken, add mushrooms, olives, and 1 cup of the cheese sauce. Spoon about 3 tablespoons of chicken filling on each crepe. Roll like jelly rolls and arrange side by side in a buttered 9 x 13-inch baking dish; pour the remaining cheese sauce over. Sprinkle with Parmesan cheese. Bake at 375° for about 20 minutes.

YIELD: 6 SERVINGS

THE JUNIOR LEAGUE OF RIVERSIDE, CALIFORNIA

· · · · · · · · · · · · · · · · ·

California Crepes Fruit de la Mer

12 tablespoons butter (1½ sticks)
12 tablespoons flour
2 cups half and half
2 cups heavy cream
1 cup sherry
2 cups Parmesan cheese
½ teaspoon salt
¼ teaspoon pepper
5 4-ounce cans mushrooms
5 cups cooked diced shrimp
40 crepes
1 20-ounce can pineapple chunks, drained
2 11-ounce cans mandarin orange segments, drained

Melt butter in a large casserole. Add flour and blend until smooth. Slowly add half and half and the cream, stirring constantly until sauce is smooth and thick. Add sherry, 1½ cups Parmesan cheese, salt, and pepper. Set aside 1½ cups sauce. To the remainder of the sauce add mushrooms and shrimp.

Use your favorite crepe recipe. Fill each crepe with approximately ½

Recipe continues . . .

cup shrimp mixture. Secure with a wooden pick. Arrange crepes on baking sheets. Spread tops with remaining sauce. Sprinkle with remaining ½ cup cheese. Refrigerate if made ahead.

Cook 20 minutes at 350°. Remove wooden picks. Garnish with pineapple and orange segments.

YIELD: 20 SERVINGS

THE JUNIOR LEAGUE OF RIVERSIDE, CALIFORNIA

Chili Relleno Crepes

BATTER FOR 6 CREPES:
4 eggs
3 tablespoons confectioner's sugar
½ cup sifted flour
½ cup half and half

FILLING:
1 7-ounce can green chilies
1 pound Monterey Jack cheese, cut into strips
1 pound sharp cheddar cheese, shredded

SAUCE:
1 15-ounce can tomato sauce
¼ teaspoon garlic powder
Dash chili powder
Dash marjoram

Beat eggs well. Add sugar, Beat in flour and half and half alternately, a little at a time. Grease crepe pan lightly with butter. Over low heat make crepes (see page 340), using about ¼ batter at a time. Cook until bubbles form on top; turn to brown other side.

Wash and seed chilies; drain. On each crepe place a chili, a strip of Jack cheese, and some shredded cheddar. Roll crepe and place seam side down in a 9 x 12-inch pan.

Combine sauce ingredients and heat to simmering. Cover crepes in pan with remaining cheddar cheese and pour sauce over. Bake in 350° oven for 30 minutes, or until heated through and all cheese is melted.

YIELD: 6 SERVINGS

THE JUNIOR LEAGUE OF SANTA BARBARA, CALIFORNIA

· · · · · · · · · · · · · · · · · ·

Italian Cannellone

BATTER FOR 12 CREPES:
6 eggs at room temperature
1½ cups water
1½ cups flour
¼ teaspoon salt

Beat 6 eggs until frothy. Add remaining batter ingredients. Combine until thoroughly mixed. Place ¼ cup batter in hot frying pan. Cook on one side for 1 minute; turn and cook until done. When cooked, stack one on top of the other and cover with a cloth until ready to use.

CHEESE FILLING:
2 eggs
2 pounds ricotta cheese
8 ounces mozzarella cheese, shredded
⅓ cup grated Parmesan cheese
1 teaspoon salt
¼ teaspoon pepper
¼ teaspoon nutmeg

SAUCE TOPPING:
1 1-pound jar spaghetti sauce
Sliced mozzarella chese
Grated Parmesan cheese

Recipe continues . . .

To make filling, combine filling ingredients and beat until fluffy.

Put small amount of spaghetti sauce on the bottom of a glass baking pan. Put a heaping spoonful of cheese filling on each crepe and roll. Place seam side down in baking pan. Cover with remaining spaghetti sauce, then with mozzarella cheese. Sprinkle with Parmesan cheese. Bake at 325° for 20–30 minutes.

YIELD: 12 SERVINGS

THE JUNIOR LEAGUE OF SPOKANE, WASHINGTON

. . . .

Mushroom Crepes

12 crepes
4 tablespoons butter
1½ pounds mushrooms, sliced
2 tablespoons flour
½ cup heavy cream
12 thin slices cooked ham
1 cup light cream
1 cup shredded Swiss, Gruyère, or Danish Samsoe cheese
Parsley

Prepare crepes. Melt 3 tablespoons butter over medium heat until bubbly. Add mushrooms and sauté until just lightly browned. Sprinkle with 1 tablespoon of flour and stir. Add cream and cook over medium heat until mixture is thickened and liquid is reduced to about ⅓ cup, about 8 minutes. Set aside.

Place a piece of ham on each crepe and then spoon on about ¼ cup of the mushroom filling. Roll and arrange seam side down in a buttered 9 x 12-inch dish.

In a small saucepan heat remaining 1 tablespoon butter. Stir in the remaining 1 tablespoon flour and cook until mixture is bubbly. Gradually stir in the light cream. Cook, stirring, over medium heat until sauce is thickened. Pour the sauce over the crepes. Sprinkle with cheese. Bake, uncovered, at 400° for 15 minutes. Sprinkle chopped parsley on top before serving.

YIELD: 6 SERVINGS

A Taste of Oregon
THE JUNIOR LEAGUE OF EUGENE, OREGON

. . . .

Crepes Clinton

FILLING:
4 tablespoons butter
2 onions, chopped
½ pound fresh mushrooms, sliced
½ 10-ounce package frozen chopped spinach, thawed and well drained
2 cups coarsely chopped cooked chicken or turkey
6 tablespoons sour cream
2 tablespoons sherry
Salt to taste

Melt butter in a large skillet. Add onions and sauté until onions are soft. Add mushrooms and sauté for a few minutes. Remove from heat. Add spinach, chicken, sour cream, sherry, and salt. Stir until well blended. This mixture may be made ahead and refrigerated.

SAUCE:
6 tablespoons butter
6 tablespoons flour
½ cup sherry
2 cups chicken stock
1 cup milk
¾ cup freshly grated Parmesan cheese
½ cup shredded Swiss or Gruyère cheese
Salt to taste

Recipe continues . . .

Melt butter and remove from heat. Add flour and stir until smooth. Stir in sherry, stock, and milk. Return pan to the heat and cook, stirring constantly, until mixture is thick and at a full boil. Reduce heat and simmer. Add the cheeses and salt. Stir over low heat until cheese is melted. Remove pan from heat and cover with a piece of wax paper so that a skin does not form. The sauce may be frozen.

8–12 crepes (see page 340). To assemble crepes, fill the crepes with the warmed filling; roll and place side by side in a baking dish. Spoon some of the sauce over the crepes and bake at 350° for 15 minutes. Reheat the rest of the sauce over low heat and serve separately.

YIELD: 4–6 SERVINGS

Colorado Cache
THE JUNIOR LEAGUE OF DENVER, COLORADO

· ·

Puget Sound Salmon Crepes

¼ cup peanut oil
¼ cup flour
¾ teaspoon salt
⅛ teaspoon white pepper
1 medium onion, minced
1 cup heavy cream
1 cup whole milk
2 tablespoons sherry
2 egg yolks
1 pound cooked salmon, boned and flaked
12 crepes (see page 340)

In a heavy saucepan, combine oil, flour, salt, and pepper and blend until smooth. Add onion and cook for 2 minutes, stirring constantly until mixture is thick and bubbly. Remove from heat. Gradually blend in cream, milk, and sherry. *Set aside 1 cup of this sauce.*

Slowly blend remaining sauce into the egg yolks. Stir vigorously over moderate heat until mixture bubbles. Remove from heat and stir in the salmon.

Fill the crepes with the salmon mixture and fold up. Arrange them in a greased casserole and cover with the reserved sauce. Bake at 375° for about 20 minutes, or until heated through.

YIELD: 4–6 SERVINGS

THE JUNIOR LEAGUE OF TACOMA, WASHINGTON

Cheese and Bean Enchiladas

2 pounds ground round
1 large onion, chopped
1 1-pound 13-ounce can refried beans
1 teaspoon salt
2 cloves garlic, minced
1 cup sliced olives
12 corn tortillas
Oil for frying
1 10-ounce can mild enchilada sauce
½ 10-ounce can hot enchilada sauce
2 cups shredded sharp cheddar cheese
2 cups shredded Monterey Jack cheese
8 ounces sour cream

Sauté beef with onions. Stir in beans, salt, garlic, and ½ cup olives. Heat until bubbly.

Fry tortillas in a little hot oil until soft. Drain and dry on paper towels. Pour half of each enchilada sauce in a baking pan. Fill tortillas with meat and bean filling and roll. Place seam side down in pan on top of sauce.

Recipe continues . . .

Pour the other half of each can sauce over rolls. Sprinkle cheeses over top and bake, uncovered, at 350° for 15 minutes.

Spoon sour cream on top and sprinkle with remaining olives.

YIELD: 6 SERVINGS (2 ENCHILADAS EACH)

THE JUNIOR LEAGUE OF SPOKANE, WASHINGTON

· ·

Ham-Cheese Enchiladas

12 ham slices
1 pound Monterey Jack cheese, cut into ½-inch strips
1 4-ounce can green chilies, cut into ⅛-inch strips
12 small flour tortillas

SAUCE:
½ cup flour
¼ pound butter
1 quart milk
¾ pound cheddar cheese, diced
1 teaspoon prepared mustard
1 teaspoon salt
Dash seasoning salt
½ onion, grated

Place a ham slice, some Jack cheese, and chili strips on each tortilla and roll tighly. Arrange seam side down, side by side in greased baking dish.

In saucepan blend flour and butter. Gradually stir in milk and cook, stirring, until sauce is smooth and thick. Add cheese and seasonings. Add onion. May be made ahead and frozen or refrigerated.

Pour sauce over the tortillas, covering them thoroughly. Bake at 350° for 45 minutes.

YIELD: 12 SERVINGS (1 ENCHILADA EACH)

THE JUNIOR LEAGUE OF LONG BEACH, CALIFORNIA

· ·

Creamy Cheese Enchiladas

6 flour tortillas
3 cups shredded Monterey Jack cheese
6 tablespoons chopped green onions

SAUCE:
¼ cup butter
¼ cup flour
2 cups chicken broth
1 cup sour cream
1 4-ounce can green chilies, seeded and chopped

Fill each tortilla with ½ cup cheese and 1 tablespoon green onion. Roll each individually and place in a shallow 8-inch square baking dish.

Melt butter in saucepan over medium heat. Add flour, stirring constantly. Stir in chicken broth to make a thick sauce. Remove from heat and add sour cream and green chilies. Stir until smooth.

Pour sauce over tortillas. Bake at 350° for 20 minutes.

YIELD: 6 SERVINGS (1 ENCHILADA EACH)

A Taste of Oregon
THE JUNIOR LEAGUE OF EUGENE, OREGON

Enchilada Veronica

2 cups chopped onion
½ cup butter
½ cup flour
1 teaspoon salt
4 cups milk
1 4-ounce can chopped California green chilies
2 cups cooked, diced chicken
2 8-ounce cans seedless grapes, drained, or 2 cups fresh seedless grapes
2 cups shredded Monterey Jack cheese
½ pound fresh mushrooms, sliced and sautéed
12 corn tortillas
½ cup toasted slivered almonds

Make white sauce: Sauté onion in butter until onion is tender. Add flour, salt, and milk to make a medium-thick sauce. Add the green chilies and set aside.

In a separate large bowl toss together the chicken, grapes, cheese, and mushrooms.

Warm the tortillas. Cold tortillas tend to crack when rolled, so flip each tortilla back and forth in a greased, hot frying pan over low heat until they are warm and pliable.

Place a spoonful of chicken mixture across the center of each warm tortilla. Roll tortillas around the filling and place seam side down in two lightly greased 7 x 11-inch baking dishes.

After all the tortillas are filled and rolled, pour sauce over enchiladas. Bake at 350° for 25–30 minutes, or until heated through. Sprinkle toasted almonds over top during last 5 minutes of baking.

YIELD: 12 SERVINGS (1 ENCHILADA EACH)

THE JUNIOR LEAGUE OF SAN DIEGO, CALIFORNIA

Delarna's Beef Enchiladas

2 pounds ground beef
1½ sticks butter
3–4 tablespoons flour
4–5 cups water
2 tablespoons chili powder mixed in 1 cup water
1 teaspoon salt, or more to taste
12 tortillas
Cooking oil
4 cups shredded mild cheddar cheese
Shredded lettuce and taco sauce

Brown ground beef. While meat is cooking, melt butter in a saucepan. Stir in flour to make a paste. Add water and cook, stirring, until gravy thickens. Add chili powder mixed with water and salt. Taste and adjust salt and chili powder if you want it hotter.

Heat tortillas, one at a time, in frying pan with a little oil until just warm or soft enough to roll. Spoon ¼ cup gravy over each flat tortilla. Top with about 2 tablespoons beef and sprinkle with about 2 tablespoons of the cheese. Roll and place seam side down in a 9 x 13-inch pan. Continue this process until all 12 tortillas are in the pan. Pour the rest of the gravy over the enchiladas and sprinkle with remainder of cheese. Bake in preheated 300° oven, for about 5 minutes, or until cheese is melted.

Serve hot with lettuce and taco sauce.

YIELD: 12 SERVINGS (1 ENCHILADA EACH)

THE JUNIOR LEAGUE OF OGDEN, UTAH

Cheese Enchiladas

16 corn tortillas
Oil
1 pound longhorn cheese, shredded
1 4-ounce can minced olives
1 bunch green onions, chopped

SAUCE:
4 cloves garlic, minced
⅓ cup oil
2 tablespoons flour
2 tablespoons chili powder
1 19-ounce can enchilada sauce
2 8-ounce cans tomato sauce
1 teaspoon salt
1 cup water

Fry tortillas for a second in hot oil just until soft. Mix cheese, olives, and chopped green onions. Put approximately 1 heaping tablespoon of this mixture on each tortilla. Roll and place seam side down in large baking pan.

Make sauce: Sauté garlic in oil, add flour and chili powder and mix well. Add enchilada sauce and tomato sauce, salt, and water. Let simmer 1 hour. Can be made in quantities and frozen.

Cover enchiladas with sauce, sprinkle with remaining grated cheese mixture, and bake at 400° for 20–30 minutes, or until sauce is bubbling.

YIELD: 8 SERVINGS

THE JUNIOR LEAGUE OF BAKERSFIELD, CALIFORNIA

Enchiladas de Zucchini

3 tablespoons butter
3 tablespoons oil
12 corn tortillas
1 yellow onion, minced
2 tablespoons butter
1 pound ground beef
4 cups grated unpeeled zucchini
¾ cup chopped ripe olives
1 teaspoon garlic powder (optional)
Salt and pepper to taste
2 cups shredded Monterey Jack cheese
2 10-ounce cans enchilada sauce
1–1½ cups shredded cheddar cheese

Over medium heat, melt 3 tablespoons each butter and oil in a 10–12-inch skillet. Fry the tortillas, one or two at a time, for approximately 5 seconds each, turning once. Remove with a spatula as soon as they become limp and drain well on paper towels.

Sauté onion in 2 tablespoons butter until transparent. Add ground beef and cook until all pink is gone. Drain off fat. Add zucchini, olives, salt and pepper, and garlic powder if desired. Sauté entire mixture 5 more minutes, stirring from time to time.

To form enchiladas, place a fried tortilla on a plate. Heap a rounded ¼ cup of zucchini mixture in center of tortilla and top with a heaping tablespoon of Monterey Jack cheese. Roll tortilla and place seam side down in a shallow baking dish, preferably 8¾ x 13½ inches. When all tortillas are filled, pour enchilada sauce over top and sprinkle with cheddar cheese. Bake, uncovered, at 350° for 15 minutes. (If enchiladas have been refrigerated, bake for 30 minutes.)

Recipe continues . . .

Serve with a tossed salad and, for an extra touch, pass a bowl of sour cream.

YIELD: 6 SERVINGS (2 ENCHILADAS EACH)

Private Collection:
Recipes from The Junior League of Palo Alto
THE JUNIOR LEAGUE OF PALO ALTO, CALIFORNIA

· · · · · · · · · · · · · ·

Chicken Enchiladas

24 tortillas
1 cup hot oil
4 large chicken breasts, cooked and shredded

SAUCE:
1 6-ounce can tomato purée
1 medium onion, quartered
1 clove garlic
2 green jalapeño peppers, fresh or canned
Salt to taste

GARNISH:
2 cups shredded lettuce
2 cups shredded Monterey Jack cheese
1 cup chopped green or Bermuda onion

Quickly dip each tortilla in the hot oil to soften. Do not fry till crisp! Put about 2 tablespoons shredded chicken on each tortilla and roll. Arrange seam side down in a shallow ovenproof baking dish.

Blend all sauce ingredients until smooth. Pour the sauce over the enchiladas and bake at 375° for 20–25 minutes.

Serve with suggested garnishes.

YIELD: 8 SERVINGS (3 ENCHILADAS EACH)

Que Sabroso!
THE JUNIOR LEAGUE OF MEXICO CITY, MEXICO

· ·

Chicken Enchiladas with Pinata Topping

2 cups diced cooked chicken or turkey
2 cups shredded cheddar cheese
1 2¼-ounce can sliced ripe olives, drained
8 corn tortillas

SAUCE:
½ cup minced onion
1 clove garlic, minced
2 tablespoons oil
1 10½-ounce can chicken broth
1 10½-ounce soup can water
1½ tablespoons chili powder
¼ cup flour
½ cup canned red chili sauce

Combine chicken, 1½ cups cheese, and olives. Set aside.

Soften tortillas in a skillet in a little hot oil.

Make sauce: Sauté onion and garlic in oil; add broth and water. Mix chili powder, flour, and chili sauce into a paste; mix into broth mixture.

Grease a 7 x 12-inch baking pan. Dip each tortilla in sauce, then form enchilada by rolling tortilla around some of the chicken mixture. Place

Recipe continues . . .

seam side down in baking dish. Bake at 350° for 25 minutes, or until hot. Garnish with remaining cheese and return to oven to melt cheese.

Serve with Pinata Topping.

YIELD: 4 SERVINGS (2 ENCHILADAS EACH)

PINATA TOPPING:
1 pint sour cream
1½ teaspoons seasoned salt
½ teaspoon chili powder
Salt and pepper to taste
1 cup diced ripe avocado
1 cup diced, peeled, fresh tomatoes, drained of juice
2 tablespoons minced green onion and tops

Combine thoroughly the sour cream and the spices. Fold in remaining ingredients. Serve as topping for enchiladas or as a dip for tortilla chips.

THE JUNIOR LEAGUE OF SACRAMENTO, CALIFORNIA

· ·

Turkey Enchiladas

2 4-ounce cans green chilies
1 large clove garlic, minced
2 tablespoons salad oil
1 1-pound 12-ounce can tomatoes
2 cups chopped onion
2 teaspoons salt
½ teaspoon oregano
3 cups shredded cooked turkey
2 cups sour cream
½ pound shredded cheddar cheese (2 cups)
⅓ cup salad oil
12 corn tortillas

Rinse seeds from chilies and chop. Sauté with garlic in 2 tablespoons oil.

Combine tomatoes with onion, 1 teaspoon salt, and oregano. Simmer, uncovered, until thick, about 30 minutes. Set aside.

Combine turkey, sour cream, cheese, and remaining salt, or salt to taste.

Heat oil and dip tortillas, one at a time, in hot oil just until they become limp. Fill them with the turkey mixture, roll, and arrange side by side, seam side down, in a large shallow baking dish. Pour sauce over and bake at 350° for 35 minutes, or until heated through.

This can be refrigerated and made ahead.

YIELD: 6 SERVINGS (2 ENCHILADAS EACH)

Something New Under the Sun
THE JUNIOR LEAGUE OF PHOENIX, ARIZONA

Vegetables

Artichokes with Dipping Sauce

1 medium onion, minced
1 carrot, minced
1 garlic clove, minced
4 sprigs parsley, minced
6 tablespoons oil
½ teaspoon rosemary
¾ cup white wine
6 artichokes
½ cup mayonnaise

Put the minced vegetables into a large saucepan with the oil, rosemary, and the wine. Set the artichokes on top of the mixture, cover the pan, and cook over low heat 45–50 minutes, or until the artichokes are done.

Remove the artichokes and stir the mayonnaise into the sauce remaining in the saucepan. Serve the sauce with the artichokes.

YIELD: 6 SERVINGS

THE JUNIOR LEAGUE OF SANTA BARBARA, CALIFORNIA

· · · · · · · · · · · · · · · ·

Artichoke-Cheese Casserole

2 10-ounce packages frozen artichoke hearts
8 ounces cream cheese
⅔ cup softened butter
¼ cup chopped chives
Salt and pepper to taste
1 cup heavy cream
½ cup Parmesan cheese

Cook artichoke hearts until barely tender. Layer in buttered baking dish.

Blend cream cheese, butter, chopped chives, salt, and pepper. Add enough cream to make a spreadable mixture. Spread over artichokes.

Sprinkle Parmesan cheese liberally over the top. Bake 20–30 minutes at 350°, or until brown.

Can be made ahead of time and baked just before serving.

YIELD: 4 SERVINGS

THE JUNIOR LEAGUE OF BAKERSFIELD, CALIFORNIA

· · · · · · · · · · · · · · · · · · · ·

Artichoke and Spinach Surprise

4 6-ounce jars marinated artichoke hearts
3 10-ounce packages frozen chopped spinach, thawed
2 8-ounce packages cream cheese, softened
5 tablespoons softened butter
¾ cup milk
½ cup grated Parmesan cheese
½ cup salted sunflower seeds (optional)

Drain the artichoke hearts well and arrange in the bottom of a buttered 9 x 13-inch baking dish. Cover artichoke hearts with thawed spinach.

Cream together the softened cream cheese and butter. Gradually add the milk, stirring until mixture is creamy. Pour over the artichokes and spinach. Top with Parmesan cheese and sunflower seeds if desired. Cover and refrigerate for 24 hours.

Bake for 30–45 minutes at 350°.

YIELD: 12 SERVINGS

THE JUNIOR LEAGUE OF SACRAMENTO, CALIFORNIA

· · · · · · · · · · · · · · · · · · · ·

Spinach-Artichoke Bake

2 10-ounce packages frozen chopped spinach
½ pound fresh mushrooms
6 tablespoons butter
1 tablespoon flour
½ cup milk
½ teaspoon salt
⅛ teaspoon garlic powder
1 20-ounce can artichoke hearts, drained
1 cup sour cream
1 cup mayonnaise
¼ cup lemon juice

Cook spinach as directed; drain. Reserve a few whole mushrooms for garnish; slice remaining mushrooms. Sauté sliced mushrooms in 4 tablespoons of the butter.

Melt remaining butter in saucepan; blend in flour. Gradually stir in milk and cook, stirring, until sauce is thickened. Add seasonings. Stir in sliced mushrooms and spinach.

Arrange artichokes in baking dish; pour spinach mixture over artichokes. Blend sour cream, mayonnaise, and lemon juice; stir over low heat until smooth and hot, and pour over spinach mixture. Garnish with reserved mushrooms and bake at 375° for 15 minutes.

YIELD: 6–8 SERVINGS

THE JUNIOR LEAGUE OF BILLINGS, MONTANA

Broccoli Soufflé

1 10-ounce package frozen broccoli
3 tablespoons butter
3 tablespoons flour
1 teaspoon salt
1 cup milk
⅛ teaspoon nutmeg
1 teaspoon lemon juice
4 egg yolks, beaten
4–6 egg whites

Cook broccoli. Drain. Melt butter; stir in flour and salt and cook until bubbly. Gradually stir in milk and cook, stirring, until thick. Stir in nutmeg, lemon juice, and broccoli. Cool slightly, then beat in egg yolks.

When broccoli mixture is cool, beat egg whites until stiff and fold into mixture. Turn into buttered 1½-quart casserole and bake in a preheated 325° oven for 1 hour.

YIELD: 6 SERVINGS

THE JUNIOR LEAGUE OF BILLINGS, MONTANA

· · · · · · · · · · · · · · · · · · ·

Brussels Sprouts and Chestnuts

3 10-ounce packages frozen Brussels sprouts
¼ cup butter
¼ cup flour
1 cup chicken broth
1 cup half and half
1 cup shredded Swiss cheese
1 11-ounce can whole water chestnuts, drained and sliced
Salt and pepper to taste
4 slices crisply fried bacon, crumbled

Recipe continues . . .

Cook Brussels sprouts in boiling salted water until barely tender. Drain well.

In a deep frying pan, melt butter and stir in flour. Gradually stir in chicken broth and half and half. Cook over low heat, stirring constantly, until mixture bubbles and thickens. Add cheese. Stir until it melts. Remove sauce from heat. Fold in Brussels sprouts and chestnut slices. Reheat, adding salt and pepper to taste.

Spoon mixture into serving dish. Top with crumbled bacon.

YIELD: 10 SERVINGS

THE JUNIOR LEAGUE OF GREAT FALLS, MONTANA

Cabbage Soy

1 small head cabbage
¼ pound bacon, cut in 1-inch pieces
¼ teaspoon salt
1 teaspoon soy sauce
1 chicken bouillon cube dissolved in ½ cup water
½ teaspoon sugar

Cut cabbage in 1-inch pieces. Cook bacon in heavy frying pan until crisp and brown. Add cabbage; sauté 3 minutes.

Add remaining ingredients, cover, and cook 5 minutes more.

YIELD: 4 SERVINGS

No Regrets
THE JUNIOR LEAGUE OF PORTLAND, OREGON

Ukrainian Cabbage Rolls

These are so different from the "giant" sausage ones—lovely with all kinds of meat dishes, they are served in Ukrainian homes as a side dish, something extra.

1 head cabbage
2 cups rice
1 small onion, minced
3 tablespoons cooking oil
3–4 slices bacon, minced
Salt and pepper to taste
1–2 teaspoons chopped fresh dill
4 cups hot chicken broth
1–2 teaspoons butter
½ cup sour cream

Wash and core cabbage. Place cabbage in a large bowl; pour boiling water over it. Cover and after a few minutes remove softened leaves one by one. It may be necessary to add more boiling water as the leaves are removed because the cabbage leaves should be soft enough to roll. Cut heavy vein from leaves and cut into 3–4-inch rectangles. Set aside.

Wash rice and partially cook in 2–2½ cups boiling water for 5–10 minutes. Rice will not be totally cooked. Drain, empty into a large bowl, and set aside. Sauté onion in oil, add minced bacon, and sauté gently until bacon is crisp. Add to rice, mix well, and season with salt, pepper, and dill.

To assemble cabbage rolls, place 1 teaspoon rice mixture on each leaf rectangle and roll like a tiny package in such a way that rice will not fall out. Rolls should be neat looking and small (thumb-size).

Place cabbage rolls in layers in a greased 12-cup casserole. Add hot chicken broth and dot with butter. Cover and bake in a 325° oven for 1½–2 hours, or until broth is absorbed.

Before serving, spread sour cream on top of the rolls.

YIELD: 8–12 SERVINGS

THE JUNIOR LEAGUE OF EDMONTON, ALBERTA

·   ·   ·   ·   ·   ·   ·   ·   ·   ·   ·

Caponata

Caponata is an interesting variation of ratatouille. It keeps beautifully, travels well, and is best served at room temperature or only slightly warm.

1 cup olive oil
1 1½-pound eggplant, peeled and cut into 1-inch cubes
2 large green peppers, cut into 1-inch pieces
2 large onions, diced
2 cloves garlic, minced
1 28-ounce can solid-pack tomatoes, undrained
⅓ cup red wine vinegar
2 tablespoons sugar
2 tablespoons capers
2 tablespoons tomato paste
2 teaspoons salt
½ cup chopped fresh parsley
½ cup rinsed, thickly sliced pimento-stuffed green olives
½ teaspoon freshly ground pepper
2 teaspoons crumbled dried basil
½ cup pine nuts, sautéed in olive oil

In a large, heavy saucepan combine 1 cup olive oil, eggplant, green peppers, onions, garlic, and tomatoes and cook for about 20–30 minutes, or until vegetables are just tender. Add wine vinegar, sugar, capers, tomato paste, salt, parsley, green olives, pepper, and basil. Cover and simmer for 15 minutes.

Add pine nuts and serve warm (not hot), at room temperature, or cold. May be refrigerated for as long as 3 weeks.

YIELD: 10–12 SERVINGS

San Francisco à la Carte
THE JUNIOR LEAGUE OF SAN FRANCISCO, CALIFORNIA

Celery au Gratin

2 tablespoons butter
2 tablespoons flour
1 cup chicken stock
¼ cup light cream
Salt and pepper to taste
2 cups cut celery, parboiled
¼ cup blanched chopped almonds
¾ cup shredded cheddar cheese
¾ cup buttered toasted bread crumbs

Make cream sauce of butter, flour, stock, and cream. Add salt and pepper to taste. Add celery and chopped almonds.

Bake in buttered casserole topped with cheese and crumbs at 350° until cheese melts and ingredients are heated through.

YIELD: 4–6 SERVINGS

Epicure
THE JUNIOR LEAGUE OF NEWPORT HARBOR, CALIFORNIA

· · · · · · · · · · · · · · · · · ·

Corn Azteca

3 medium onions, finely chopped
3 tablespoons butter or margarine
3 cups fresh corn (4 large ears) or 2 10-ounce packages frozen corn
¼ cup water
1 cup sour cream (½ pint)
1 cup shredded Monterey Jack cheese
½–1 4-ounce can diced green chilies
¾ teaspoon salt
¼ teaspoon pepper
Pimentos

Recipe continues . . .

Cook onions in butter until soft. Add corn and water. Cover tightly and cook over moderate heat for 5 minutes, stirring once. Remove cover and, over high heat, boil away most of the liquid. Stir in sour cream, cheese, chilies, salt, and pepper. Heat through, but do not boil.

Use pimentos to garnish.

YIELD: 8 SERVINGS

THE JUNIOR LEAGUE OF SAN DIEGO, CALIFORNIA

Sweet Sour Cucumbers

5 large cucumbers
2 generous tablespoons butter
2 large tablespoons flour
¼ cup vinegar
3–4 tablespoons brown sugar
Salt and pepper to taste

Peel cucumbers and slice lengthwise; scoop out seeds. Cut in 1½-inch pieces. Cook in salted water; drain well in a colander, reserving 1¼ cup liquid.

In top of double saucepan over direct heat, brown butter, blend in flour, cucumber liquid, and vinegar, then stir in the brown sugar and salt and pepper.

Set saucepan over boiling water, add cucumbers, cover, and let stand for ½ hour before serving, stirring occasionally.

YIELD: 6–8 SERVINGS

THE JUNIOR LEAGUE OF OAKLAND-EAST BAY, CALIFORNIA

Lemon Green Beans

½ cup sliced onion
2 tablespoons butter
2 tablespoons flour
1 teaspoon salt
¼ teaspoon pepper
½ teaspoon grated lemon peel
1 tablespoon chopped parsley
1 cup sour cream
5 cups cooked, drained, French-style green beans
3 tablespoons shredded cheddar cheese
2 tablespoons melted butter
½ cup dry bread crumbs

Sauté the onion in the butter until soft. Stir in flour, salt, pepper, lemon peel, and parsley. Blend in sour cream, stirring until smooth. Add the beans and turn into a medium-size casserole. Top with cheese. Combine melted butter and crumbs and sprinkle over the beans. Bake in a 350° oven until the cheese melts and the crumbs are brown.

YIELD: 4 SERVINGS

THE JUNIOR LEAGUE OF VANCOUVER, BRITISH COLUMBIA

Eggplant-Tomato Casserole

1 medium eggplant
Salt
3 medium tomatoes
1 large onion
8 tablespoons olive oil
Fine dry bread crumbs
½ pound sharp cheddar cheese or ¼ pound each
Monterey Jack and cheddar, shredded

Recipe continues . . .

Peel the eggplant. Slice it into ⅛–¼-inch slices. Salt the slices and let stand at least 1 hour to draw the water. At the end of the hour, pat the slices dry. Slice the tomatoes and the onion.

In a heavy skillet, heat 1 tablespoon of the oil. Sauté the onion slices until limp. Set onion aside.

In the same skillet, heat more oil and sauté the eggplant slices until brown. Use the olive oil accordingly until all the eggplant slices are cooked. Set eggplant aside.

Grease a 1½-quart casserole. Sprinkle with the bread crumbs. Layer the onion, eggplant, and tomatoes until all are used. Sprinkle cheese on top. At this point you may wrap and freeze.

Bake in a 325° oven for 35–40 minutes, or until bubbly and the cheese is gooey.

YIELD: 4–6 SERVINGS

THE JUNIOR LEAGUE OF SAN DIEGO, CALIFORNIA

. . . .

Eggplant Rolls

2 eggplants, thinly sliced lengthwise
Oil
1½ cups ricotta cheese
½ cup grated Romano cheese
1 egg
1 tablespoon chopped fresh basil or 1 teaspoon dried basil
1 garlic clove, minced
¼ teaspoon oregano
¼ teaspoon nutmeg
Salt and pepper

TOMATO SAUCE:
2 8-ounce cans tomato sauce
1 6-ounce can tomato paste
½ teaspoon sugar

Remove purple skin from eggplant slices and brush with oil. Broil for 4–5 minutes, or until browned. Turn the slices, brush again with oil, and broil another 4 minutes. Cool.

In a bowl combine ricotta, half the Romano, egg, and seasonings. Spread some of the mixture on each of the cooled eggplant slices and roll like a small jelly roll. Arrange them in one layer, seam side down, in a greased baking dish.

In a bowl combine ingredients for sauce; pour over the rolls, top with remaining Romano cheese, and bake in a 350° oven for 20 minutes.

YIELD: 4 SERVINGS

THE JUNIOR LEAGUE OF SANTA BARBARA, CALIFORNIA

· · · · · · · · · · · · · · · · · ·

Braised Leeks with Cheese

8 large leeks
8 slices bacon
1 cup water
Salt and pepper to taste
Dash ground thyme
2 tablespoons butter
2 tablespoons flour
1 cup milk
1 egg yolk
½ cup heavy cream
2 tablespoons shredded Swiss cheese

Using white and light-green parts, cut leeks into 2-inch pieces and then into fourths lengthwise (about 6 cups). Rinse thoroughly in a bowl of water, then lift out of water, instead of draining, to avoid sand.

Cut bacon into 2-inch pieces and brown in frying pan. Drain drippings. Add leeks, water, salt, pepper, and thyme. Cover tightly and cook until leeks are tender and water has evaporated, about 20–25 minutes.

Recipe continues . . .

Melt butter in saucepan and stir in flour with a whisk until smooth. Add milk, stirring and cooking until it comes to a boil. Cook 5 minutes. Stir egg yolk and cream together and mix into white sauce.

Combine sauce and leeks. Pour into shallow oven dish, sprinkle with cheese, and bake at 375° for 20 minutes, or until golden.

YIELD: 6 SERVINGS

Private Collection:
Recipes from The Junior League of Palo Alto
THE JUNIOR LEAGUE OF PALO ALTO, CALIFORNIA

Swiss Mushroom Bake

1 pound fresh mushrooms, sliced
1 tablespoon butter
⅓ cup sour cream
1 tablespoon flour
Salt and pepper
½ cup shredded Swiss cheese
¼ cup finely chopped parsley

Sauté mushrooms in butter; cover and cook for 2 minutes. Blend sour cream with flour; add salt and pepper to taste and stir into mushrooms, cooking until mixture boils.

Put mixture in a shallow 1-quart casserole and sprinkle with Swiss cheese and parsley. Bake at 425° for 10 minutes.

Good with barbecued steak, roast beef and a green vegetable.

YIELD: 4–6 SERVINGS

THE JUNIOR LEAGUE OF SAN DIEGO, CALIFORNIA

Scalloped Mushrooms

3 pounds fresh mushrooms, chopped
½ cup butter
1 cup heavy cream
1 teaspoon salt
½ teaspoon pepper
⅛ teaspoon cayenne
3 cups shredded, soft Monterey Jack cheese

In large frying pan sauté mushrooms over medium heat in butter for about 5 minutes. Add cream and continue to cook until liquid is almost gone, stirring when needed. Season with salt, pepper, and cayenne.

Spoon mixture into a shallow casserole and cover with shredded cheese. Bake at 400° until cheese is melted and lightly browned, about 10 minutes.

YIELD: 8 SERVINGS

THE JUNIOR LEAGUE OF BOISE, IDAHO

· · · · · · · · · · · · · · · · · · ·

Glazed Onions

36 small white onions, peeled
⅓ cup melted butter
1 cup whole blanched almonds
1 tablespoon brown sugar
1 teaspoon salt
Pinch each cayenne, ground cloves, and nutmeg

Put onions in large flat casserole. Pour butter over them, add remaining ingredients, and toss gently until coated.

Bake, covered, at 350° for 1 hour, or until onions are richly glazed and fork-tender. If onions seem stubborn about cooking, you may add a

Recipe continues . . .

little wine or chicken broth to the pan to encourage steaming, though they're prettier if you don't.

YIELD: 6–8 SERVINGS

Epicure
THE JUNIOR LEAGUE OF NEWPORT HARBOR, CALIFORNIA

· · · · · · · · · · · · · · · · · ·

Onions Agrodolce

24 small white onions
3 tablespoons olive oil
3 tablespoons sherry
3 tablespoons vinegar
2 tablespoons brown sugar
⅛ teaspoon salt
Dash cayenne

Brown onions in hot oil. Add sherry, vinegar, and sugar. Simmer for 20 minutes, or until onions are tender.

Add salt and cayenne. Serve immediately.

YIELD: 4 SERVINGS

Heritage Cookbook
THE JUNIOR LEAGUE OF SALT LAKE CITY, UTAH

· · · · · · · · · · · · · · · · · ·

Stuffed Baked Onions

4 large onions
2 tablespoons butter
4 slices bacon, crisply fried and crumbled
8 tablespoons cheese spread

Remove center from onions. Steam outside shells for 4 minutes.

Dice removed centers and sauté in butter until limp. Add bacon bits and stuff onions with the mixture. Top each onion with 2 tablespoons cheese spread.

Bake for 20 minutes at 350°.

YIELD: 4 SERVINGS

THE JUNIOR LEAGUE OF BUTTE, MONTANA

Green Pepper Sauté

4 large green peppers, seeded and cut into lengthwise strips
2–3 tablespoons olive oil
1–2 teaspoons garlic salt
1 teaspoon freshly ground pepper

Sauté green pepper strips in fairly hot olive oil just until limp but still crunchy 5–10 minutes. Sprinkle with garlic salt and freshly ground pepper. May use some red peppers for color without changing taste.

Excellent with beef, roast leg of lamb or spareribs; pretty with veal piccata.

YIELD: 6 SERVINGS

Epicure
THE JUNIOR LEAGUE OF NEWPORT HARBOR, CALIFORNIA

Sheepherder Potatoes

8 slices bacon, cut into small pieces
2 medium onions, chopped
4 medium potatoes, peeled and sliced crosswise ¼ inch thick
Salt and pepper to taste

Recipe continues . . .

Fry bacon until not quite crisp. Add chopped onions and cook until onion is limp. Pour off all but about 2 tablespoons of bacon drippings.

Tear a piece of aluminum foil large enough to hold and cover the potatoes. Center the potatoes on the foil and pour bacon mixture over top. Season to taste with salt and pepper and mix lightly, taking care not to pierce the foil. Seal the foil so that steam will not escape—that is how the potatoes cook—try to leave some air space between the potatoes and the foil.

Slide the aluminum "bag" onto a cookie sheet and bake at 300° for 1½ hours.

YIELD: 4 SERVINGS

THE JUNIOR LEAGUE OF BOISE, IDAHO

· · · · · · · · · · · · · · · · ·

Potatoes Dauphinois

2 cups milk
½ cup butter
½ teaspoon salt
¼ teaspoon white pepper
3 pounds baking potatoes (4 large)
6 cloves garlic, peeled
1 cup heavy cream
1 cup shredded Swiss cheese

Combine milk, butter, salt, and pepper in a large saucepan. Slowly bring to a boil.

Peel potatoes. Rinse without soaking; dry thoroughly. Slice fairly thinly, letting slices drop into the hot milk.

Put wooden picks in garlic for easy removal later. Blend garlic and cream into milk. Slowly return to a boil and simmer 15 minutes, or until potatoes are half done. Remove garlic.

Pour potatoes with liquid into buttered 1½- or 2-quart baking dish. Sprinkle with cheese. Bake at 325° for 10–15 minutes.

YIELD: 6 SERVINGS

Heritage Cookbook
THE JUNIOR LEAGUE OF SALT LAKE CITY, UTAH

Poppy Seed Sour Cream Potatoes

6 large potatoes
1 cup shredded sharp cheddar cheese
1 pint sour cream
½ cup half and half
Salt and pepper to taste
¼ cup poppy seeds
1 bunch green onions, tops included, chopped

Boil potatoes until tender. Refrigerate until cold, then peel and grate, using large side of grater.

Combine with the remaining ingredients and place in lightly buttered casserole. Bake at 350° for 20–25 minutes covered, then uncover and bake 10 additional minutes.

YIELD: 8 SERVINGS

No Regrets
THE JUNIOR LEAGUE OF PORTLAND, OREGON

Gourmet Potatoes

6–7 medium-size red potatoes
⅓ cup minced green onion including tops
¼ cup margarine
2 cups shredded cheddar cheese
1½ cups sour cream
1 teaspoon salt
Pepper to taste

Boil potatoes in skins; cool, peel, and grate.

In a saucepan sauté onion in margarine. Add cheese and cook until cheese melts. Remove from heat and add sour cream, salt, and pepper.

Fold this mixture into potatoes and empty into a buttered 2-quart casserole dish. Bake at 325° for 30 minutes.

YIELD: 6 SERVINGS

THE JUNIOR LEAGUE OF SANTA BARBARA, CALIFORNIA

Potatoes, Onions, Mushrooms au Gratin

5 pounds potatoes, boiled and chilled
½ cup butter
1 pound mushrooms, sliced
¾ cup flour
1 quart milk
1 cup half and half
1 10½-ounce can condensed beef consommé
1 pound sharp cheddar cheese, shredded
1 tablespoon salt
¼ teaspoon pepper
1 teaspoon Worcestershire sauce
2 15-ounce cans small white onions, drained

Cut chilled potatoes into ½-inch cubes.

Heat butter in a large saucepan and in it sauté the mushrooms until lightly browned. Stir in the flour. Add the milk, half and half, and consommé, stirring until blended. Add the cheese, salt, pepper, and Worcestershire sauce. Cook, stirring, until smooth and thickened. Remove from heat.

Add the potatoes and onions, mixing carefully. Spoon the mixture into a 4-quart casserole. This may be done ahead at this point and refrigerated covered.

Bake at 350° for about 1 hour, or until golden on top and bubbly.

YIELD: 12 SERVINGS

No Regrets
THE JUNIOR LEAGUE OF PORTLAND, OREGON

· · · · · · · · · · · · · · · · · ·

Baked Ratatouille

2 large onions, sliced
2 large cloves garlic, minced
1 medium eggplant, cut in ½-inch cubes
6 medium zucchini, thickly sliced
2 green peppers, seeded and cut in chunks
4 large tomatoes, cut in chunks
2 teaspoons salt
1 teaspoon basil
¼ cup minced parsley
4 tablespoons olive oil

Layer the onions, garlic, eggplant, zucchini, peppers, and tomatoes in a 5–6-quart casserole. Sprinkle a little of the salt, basil, and parsley between each layer. Sprinkle with olive oil. Cover and bake at 350° for 3 hours. Baste the top occasionally with some of the liquid. If it becomes soupy, uncover during the last hour of cooking to let the juices cook down.

Recipe continues . . .

Mix gently after removing from the oven. Add salt to taste. This may be served hot, cold, or reheated and is good to serve as a buffet dish for a crowd.

YIELD: 12 SERVINGS

THE JUNIOR LEAGUE OF BAKERSFIELD, CALIFORNIA

Serbian Spinach

1 quart small-curd cottage cheese
⅛ pound butter, cubed
¼ pound mild cheddar cheese, cubed
3 eggs, beaten
1 10-ounce package frozen chopped spinach, thawed and drained
¼ teaspoon salt
3 tablespoons flour

Combine all ingredients except flour. Stir with large spoon until well mixed. Add flour and mix in the same manner until well blended.

Butter the sides and bottom of a flat baking dish. Spoon mixture into baking dish and bake in a 350° oven for 1 hour, or until brown spots appear on the surface.

This is an excellent dish for company as it can be made and baked the day before, then reheated at 300° until it warms through. It goes well with most main dishes.

YIELD: 8 SERVINGS

THE JUNIOR LEAGUE OF GREAT FALLS, MONTANA

Spinach alla Firenze

1 10-ounce package frozen chopped spinach
¼ cup chopped onion
3 tablespoons butter
1 clove garlic, minced
2 tablespoons flour
1 cup milk
¼ teaspoon salt
¼ teaspoon nutmeg
1 hard-cooked egg, chopped
2 tablespoons grated Parmesan cheese
3 slices bacon, diced and crisply cooked
Grated Parmesan cheese

Cook spinach just until separated—do not overcook. Drain thoroughly.

Sauté onion in butter until soft; add garlic. Blend in flour; add milk. Bring to a boil, stirring occasionally. Remove from heat. Add seasoning, egg, the 2 tablespoons cheese, and bacon to sauce.

Combine spinach and sauce mixture. Turn into 1-quart casserole and sprinkle with additional Parmesan cheese. May be prepared ahead to this point and refrigerated.

Bake at 325° for 15–30 minutes, or until bubbly around edges.

This recipe is easily doubled.

YIELD: 3–4 SERVINGS

No Regrets
THE JUNIOR LEAGUE OF PORTLAND, OREGON

Broccoli-Stuffed Tomato

6 tomatoes
Salt and pepper to taste
1 cup finely chopped onion
¾ stick butter, melted
2 10-ounce packages frozen chopped broccoli
¾ cup crushed, dry bread stuffing mix
2 eggs, lightly beaten
4 tablespoons grated Parmesan cheese

Cut tomatoes in half crosswise. Trim a thin slice from top and bottom so halves will sit flat on work surface. Hollow out juicy seed part of tomato and sprinkle with salt and pepper. Turn tomato halves upside down on paper towel to drain off excess liquid.

In Dutch oven, sauté the onion in butter for about 5 minutes. Add broccoli. Heat and break apart as it cooks until broccoli is tender and water is almost evaporated. Remove from heat and stir in stuffing mix and eggs. Season with salt and pepper to taste.

Put 2 spoonfuls of broccoli mixture in each tomato half. Sprinkle with Parmesan cheese. Bake, uncovered, in 350° oven for about 15 minutes, or until heated through.

YIELD: 12 SERVINGS

THE JUNIOR LEAGUE OF RIVERSIDE, CALIFORNIA

Tomatoes with Mushrooms

8 firm but ripe tomatoes
¼ pound butter
1¼ pound mushrooms, sliced
1 cup sour cream
1 tablespoon flour
3 ounces Roquefort or blue cheese
¼ teaspoon mixed herbs
1 teaspoon chopped parsley
2 tablespoons sherry
Salt and pepper to taste
Sesame seeds

Cut slice from top one-third of tomatoes. Scoop out soft part and set shell upside down to drain.

Melt butter and sauté mushrooms until moisture is evaporated. Over low heat stir in sour cream and flour. Stir in cheese and herbs, parsley, and sherry.

Stuff tomatoes loosely with mushroom mixture and sprinkle with sesame seeds. Bake at 375° for 15 minutes. Serve immediately.

YIELD: 8 SERVINGS

THE JUNIOR LEAGUE OF BOISE, IDAHO

Sacramento-Style Stuffed Tomatoes

8 medium-size firm but ripe tomatoes
1½ cups sour cream
1½ teaspoons salt
½ teaspoon white pepper
1½ teaspoons sugar
1½ tablespoons flour
½ teaspoon ground cumin
4 tablespoons chopped green onion
3–4 tablespoons diced green chilies
1 cup shredded extra-sharp cheddar cheese

Cut ¼ inch off the core end of each tomato. Squeeze gently to remove seeds and scoop out a small indentation in the center.

In a small bowl, combine the sour cream, salt, pepper, sugar, flour, cumin, green onion, and green chilies. Stir until well blended. Spoon a little of the mixture into each of the tomatoes. Sprinkle cheese over the top.

Bake in a 450° oven for 10 minutes. Tomatoes should be at room temperature before baking. They can also be prepared early in the day.

A great accompaniment for a barbecued summer meal.

YIELD: 8 STUFFED TOMATOES

THE JUNIOR LEAGUE OF SACRAMENTO, CALIFORNIA

· · · · · · · · · · · · · · · · ·

Baked Tomatoes in Cream

6–8 medium tomatoes
Sugar
¼ pound butter
2 cups heavy cream
2 tablespoons chopped chives (or more)
1½ teaspoons salt

Peel tomatoes and cut a cone-shaped hole about 1 inch deep in the stem end of each. Place tomatoes in baking dish and fill holes with sugar. Place a lump of butter on each tomato.

Add approximately ¼ inch warm water to baking dish. Bake at 350° for 20 minutes, or until tomatoes are tender. Do not bake too long or tomatoes will not hold shape. In the meantime, warm the cream, chives, and salt.

To serve, place tomatoes in individual sauce bowls and spoon equal amounts of cream mixture and tomato broth from baking dish over the tomatoes. Correct seasoning of sauce before serving. Depending upon juiciness of tomatoes, sometimes more cream than broth is needed.

YIELD: 6–8 SERVINGS

Private Collection:
Recipes from The Junior League of Palo Alto
THE JUNIOR LEAGUE OF PALO ALTO, CALIFORNIA

· · · · · · · · · · · · · · · · · · ·

Fresh Corn, Tomato, Zucchini Pot

4 ears fresh corn
5 medium tomatoes, unpeeled
6–7 small zucchini
2 medium onions
2 cloves garlic, minced
Salt and pepper to taste
½ cup butter

Using a very sharp knife, cut the corn from the cob into a large earthenware casserole.

Wash the tomatoes and zucchini and pat dry. Slice the core ends from the tomatoes and discard, then slice the tomatoes into ¼-inch slices. Trim ¼ inch off each end of the zucchini and discard, then slice the zucchini

Recipe continues . . .

lengthwise into four pieces. Add the tomatoes and zucchini to the casserole as well as the onions, sliced and separated into thin rings. Add the garlic, salt, and pepper and mix the vegetables together carefully. Dot with butter, cover, and bake in a preheated 325° oven for 45 minutes. Add no extra liquid.

This combination of vegetables is especially nice when served with barbecued turkey or barbecued butterfly leg of lamb.

YIELD: 6 SERVINGS

The California Heritage Cookbook
THE JUNIOR LEAGUE OF PASADENA, CALIFORNIA

Chinese Vegetables and Cashews

2 tablespoons salad oil
1 medium onion, sliced ¼ inch thick
2 cups sliced mushrooms
2 cups diagonally sliced celery
2 red or green peppers, cut into chunks
1 5-ounce can water chestnuts, drained
½ cup chicken broth
2 tablespoons cornstarch
1¼ teaspoons salt
2 tablespoons water
2 tablespoons soy sauce
16 ounces canned or fresh bean sprouts, well drained
2 cups cashews

Heat oil in a large skillet or wok. Add onion, mushrooms, celery, peppers, and water chestnuts; cook over high heat, stirring quickly and frequently, until vegetables are well coated with oil. Add chicken broth; cover and cook 5 minutes.

Meanwhile, mix cornstarch, salt, water, and soy sauce until smooth. Stir into vegetable mixture. Cook, stirring quickly, until mixture boils and thickens. Stir in bean sprouts and cashews. Cook until heated through. Serve at once.

YIELD: 8 SERVINGS

THE JUNIOR LEAGUE OF VANCOUVER, BRITISH COLUMBIA

Mixed Vegetables on the Grill

½ pound fresh green beans, cut in 1-inch pieces
1 medium onion, thinly sliced and separated into rings
½ green pepper, cut in strips
¼ pound mushrooms, sliced
2 medium tomatoes, sliced
⅓ cup butter or margarine
2 teaspoons horseradish mustard
1 tablespoon brown sugar
1½ teaspoons salt
¼ teaspoon pepper

Put vegetables on two large layers of heavy-duty aluminum foil and toss together lightly. Cream butter or margarine, horseradish mustard, sugar, salt, and pepper together and dot the mixture over the vegetables. Wrap loosely, sealing the foil with double folds.

Cook directly on hot coals for 30–40 minutes, or on the grill 3 inches from the hot coals for 1 hour, or until vegetables are just tender, turning the package halfway through cooking.

YIELD: 4 SERVINGS

THE JUNIOR LEAGUE OF SEATTLE, WASHINGTON

Cheese and Vegetables

2 tablespoons vegetable oil
1 large dry onion, thinly sliced
1 medium green pepper, diced
½ pound fresh mushrooms, quartered
1 pound zucchini, cut in 1-inch chunks
1 small clove garlic, minced
¾ teaspoon salt
Freshly ground pepper
½ teaspoon crushed oregano leaves
12 ounces mozzarella cheese, thinly sliced

Heat oil in a large skillet and in it sauté onion slices over medium heat until soft, approximately 5 minutes. Stir in green pepper, mushrooms, zucchini, garlic, salt, pepper, and oregano. Stir-fry until vegetables are tender but still crisp.

Arrange cheese evenly on vegetables. Cover. Remove from heat and let stand for 5 minutes, or until cheese is melted. Serve immediately.

Excellent when served with steak.

YIELD: 6 SERVINGS

THE JUNIOR LEAGUE OF GREAT FALLS, MONTANA

Layered Vegetable Casserole

1 large eggplant, peeled and sliced
½ cup flour mixed with ½ teaspoon salt and ⅛ teaspoon pepper
½ cup oil
½ cup chopped parsley
1 teaspoon dried thyme
Salt and pepper
4 tomatoes, peeled and sliced
1 large onion, finely chopped
1 large green pepper, finely chopped
12 ounces mozzarella cheese, sliced
1½ cups half and half
3 eggs
2 egg yolks
Dash nutmeg

Dip eggplant slices in seasoned flour and fry in part of the oil, adding more as needed, until eggplant is brown and soft. Transfer slices to a greased 8½ x 13½-inch baking dish and season with some of parsley, thyme, salt, and pepper. Cover with a layer of tomatoes and season with more of the parsley, thyme, salt, and pepper. Sprinkle with some of the chopped onion and green pepper. Add a layer of mozzarella cheese. Repeat layers of eggplant, tomato, and cheese, sprinkling each with remaining herbs, spices, and chopped vegetables until all are used.

Beat half and half with whole eggs and yolks. Season with salt, pepper, and nutmeg. Pour over vegetables and bake in a 375° oven for 25 minutes.

YIELD: 8 SERVINGS

THE JUNIOR LEAGUE OF SANTA BARBARA, CALIFORNIA

Yam Casserole

4 large yams
5 tablespoons butter or margarine
½ teaspoon salt
¼ teaspoon pepper
2 tablespoons brown sugar
2 eggs
2 tablespoons white wine or sherry
½ teaspoon cinnamon

Bake yams, wrapped in foil, at 450° for about 1 hour, or until done. Discard skins. Mash yams with 4 tablespoons of the butter. Add salt, pepper, sugar, eggs, and wine. Beat until fluffy.

Pour into buttered casserole and sprinkle with cinnamon. Dot with remaining 1 tablespoon butter. Bake in 350° oven for 30 minutes.

YIELD: 6 SERVINGS

THE JUNIOR LEAGUE OF CALGARY, ALBERTA

. . . .

Shredded Zucchini

1 small onion, chopped
1 tablespoon oil
4 medium zucchini, scrubbed well but not peeled
½ teaspoon salt
¼ teaspoon pepper
1 bay leaf
1 tablespoon chopped parsley

Lightly brown the onion in the oil.

Shred the zucchini on a grater, using the coarsest side. Add to the onion in the pan, stirring to mix in onion and coat with oil. Add salt, pepper, and bay leaf. Cover tightly, reduce heat, and simmer for 6–8 minutes. Stir once or twice. Add a teaspoon of water if it starts to stick.

Serve sprinkled with parsley.

YIELD: 4 SERVINGS

THE JUNIOR LEAGUE OF LOS ANGELES, CALIFORNIA

Zucchini Susannah

3–4 medium zucchini
2 tablespoons cooking oil
1 tablespoon flour
3–4 tablespoons milk
½ teaspoon salt
½ teaspoon pepper
Dash nutmeg
½ cup shredded Swiss cheese
½ cup grated Parmesan cheese

Shred zucchini on large grater. Put oil in skillet. Add zucchini and cook 10 minutes, stirring gently. Add flour and stir. Add milk to make a thin sauce. Add salt, pepper, and nutmeg.

Combine Swiss and Parmesan cheese. Add 5 heaping tablespoons of cheese mixture to zucchini. Stir thoroughly. Empty into casserole. Top with remaining cheese mixture. Bake at 350° until bubbly.

YIELD: 6–8 SERVINGS

THE JUNIOR LEAGUE OF CALGARY, ALBERTA

Zucchini Boats

4 medium zucchini
3 large tomatoes
1 small clove garlic, minced
¼ teaspoon crushed oregano
¼ cup freshly grated Parmesan cheese
½ cup shredded cheddar cheese
6 slices bacon, crisply fried and crumbled

Wash zucchini and cut in half lengthwise. Parboil until tender but not too soft. Discard the seeds, and drain.

Peel and seed the tomatoes, then dice and drain them. Add garlic, oregano, and cheeses and mix well. Fill the zucchini boats with this mixture. Top with crumbled bacon and broil until the cheese is bubbly.

This dish may be prepared well ahead and popped into the oven at the last minute.

YIELD: 4–8 SERVINGS

THE JUNIOR LEAGUE OF TACOMA, WASHINGTON

. . . .

Zucchini Slippers

4 zucchini
2 eggs, well beaten
1½ cups shredded sharp cheddar cheese
1 cup small-curd cottage cheese
2 tablespoons parsley
Salt and pepper to taste

Cut off and discard ends of zucchini, scrub well, and cook whole in boiling salted water for 10 minutes. Remove squash from water and cut in half lengthwise. Scoop out center seeds and drain well.

Mix together eggs, cheeses, parsley, salt, and pepper. Arrange squash "slippers" in ovenware dish and fill with cheese mixture. Bake, uncovered, at 350° for 15 minutes. Increase oven temperature to 450° and bake for 5 minutes longer, or until browned.

YIELD: 8 SERVINGS

Epicure
THE JUNIOR LEAGUE OF BILLINGS, MONTANA

· · · · · · · · · · · · · · · · · · · ·

Zucchini au Gratin

1½ pounds zucchini
½ pint sour cream
2 tablespoons butter
2 tablespoons grated Parmesan cheese
1 teaspoon salt
½ teaspoon pepper
2 egg yolks, well beaten
1 tablespoon chopped chives
Buttered bread crumbs
Grated Parmesan cheese

Slice zucchini and cook until barely tender.

Drain and empty into baking dish. Mix sour cream, butter, Parmesan cheese, salt, and pepper in saucepan and cook, stirring, over low heat until cheese is melted. Remove from heat and add egg yolks and chopped chives. Pour mixture over zucchini; cover with bread crumbs and plenty of grated cheese. Brown at 350° for 30 minutes.

Can be made well in advance, refrigerated, and put into the oven in time to brown before serving.

YIELD: 6 SERVINGS

Epicure
THE JUNIOR LEAGUE OF NEWPORT HARBOR, CALIFORNIA

· · · · · · · · · · · · · · · · · · · ·

Salads

Antipasto Salad

1 stalk celery
¼ pound fresh green beans
2 carrots
1 small head cauliflower
1 green pepper
1 small eggplant
1 cup olive oil
1 bay leaf
¼ pound small fresh mushrooms
1 3½-ounce jar cocktail onions, drained
12 pitted green olives
12 pitted ripe olives
1 cup tomato catsup
1 cup red wine vinegar
4 tablespoons sugar
1 tablespoon dry mustard
Salt and pepper to taste

Cut the celery into ½-inch pieces. Trim and break the green beans into small pieces. Scrape the carrots and cut into ½-inch pieces. Trim the cauliflower and break into small buds. Remove seeds from the pepper and cut into thin strips. Cut the unpeeled eggplant into small cubes.

Heat the olive oil in a large, heavy skillet. Add the bay leaf and all the vegetables except the mushrooms, cocktail onions, and olives. Cook the vegetables over medium heat until tender but still slightly crisp.

Add the mushrooms, cocktail onions, and olives to the vegetables. Stir in the catsup, vinegar, sugar, mustard, salt, and pepper and cook for another 5 minutes.

Cool and then chill before serving. It is important to observe the *under-cooking rule* when preparing this dish.

YIELD: 10–12 SERVINGS

THE JUNIOR LEAGUE OF SAN JOSE, CALIFORNIA

Italian Garbanzo Salad

1 15½-ounce can garbanzo beans, drained
1 large green pepper, sliced
1 medium onion, sliced and separated into rings
1 4-ounce jar pimento, sliced
1 medium cauliflower, separated into flowerets
1 cup Italian dressing
Salt and pepper to taste

Combine all ingredients; marinate in the dressing for 1 hour or more. Serve chilled.

YIELD: 8 SERVINGS

THE JUNIOR LEAGUE OF TACOMA, WASHINGTON

.   .   .   .

Avocado and Orange Salad

1 avocado, sliced
1 cucumber, peeled and sliced
1 head butter lettuce, torn into pieces
2 tablespoons sliced green onion
1 11-ounce can Mandarin oranges, drained

DRESSING:
½ cup oil
¼ cup orange juice
2 tablespoons sugar
2 tablespoons red wine vinegar
1 tablespoon lemon juice
½ teaspoon grated orange peel
¼ teaspoon salt

Recipe continues . . .

In a salad bowl combine the avocado, cucumber, lettuce, sliced onion, and the oranges.

Mix all the dressing ingredients and pour dressing over the salad just before serving.

YIELD: 4 SERVINGS

THE JUNIOR LEAGUE OF SANTA BARBARA, CALIFORNIA

Green Beans Vinaigrette

3 pounds fresh green beans
1 tablespoon grated onion
1¼ teaspoons salt
½–¾ teaspoon freshly ground pepper
1 tablespoon Dijon mustard
3 tablespoons wine vinegar
12 tablespoons olive oil
½ teaspoon lemon juice

Steam the green beans 10–15 minutes. They should be barely cooked and crispy-tender. Rinse in cold water and chill.

Combine all remaining ingredients except olive oil and lemon juice. Gradually whisk in the olive oil and lemon juice. Pour dressing over beans and marinate in refrigerator until ready to serve.

YIELD: 12 SERVINGS

THE JUNIOR LEAGUE OF LOS ANGELES, CALIFORNIA

Summer Slaw

1 cabbage
1 white onion
½ cup sugar
½ cup cider vinegar
1 teaspoon dry mustard
1 teaspoon salt
1 teaspoon pepper
1 teaspoon celery seed
½ cup oil
8 cherry tomatoes

Core and shred cabbage; slice onion and combine with cabbage in salad bowl. Bring sugar, vinegar, mustard, salt, pepper, and celery seed to a boil, stirring until sugar is dissolved. Remove from heat. Add oil.

Pour mixture over cabbage and onion. Refrigerate 4 hours or overnight.

Serve with cherry tomatoes.

YIELD: 8 SERVINGS

THE JUNIOR LEAGUE OF BUTTE, MONTANA

Jim's Caesar Salad

1 large clove garlic
1 2-ounce can anchovy fillets
2 eggs
3 tablespoons salad oil (preferably olive oil)
3 tablespoons vinegar
1 lemon
½ teaspoon salt
½ teaspoon pepper
1½ teaspoons sugar
2 heads romaine lettuce
1 cup croutons
⅓ cup Parmesan cheese, grated

In salad bowl, preferably wooden, crush garlic and mix to a paste with the anchovies. Add eggs to paste; mix well. Blend salad oil, vinegar, juice of lemon, salt, pepper, and sugar into anchovy paste. Chill until serving time.

Tear romaine into bite-size pieces, patting dry with paper towels. Chill. Add romaine to dressing and toss until well coated.

Add Parmesan and croutons. Toss and serve.

YIELD: 6 SERVINGS

THE JUNIOR LEAGUE OF SAN JOSE, CALIFORNIA

Luncheon Chicken Salad

8 cups cooked, boned, skinned, and diced chicken
2 6½-ounce cans water chestnuts, cut into bite-size pieces
2 pounds seedless grapes (5 cups)
2 cups sliced celery
1 17-ounce can pineapple chunks, drained
1 tablespoon curry powder
2 tablespoons soy sauce
1¾ cups mayonnaise
1 cup slivered almonds

Mix all ingredients except mayonnaise and nuts and refrigerate for 3 hours. Fold in mayonnaise and nuts before serving.

YIELD: 12 SERVINGS

THE JUNIOR LEAGUE OF RIVERSIDE, CALIFORNIA

· ·

Curried Chicken Salad

1 large chicken, cooked, boned, skinned, diced, and chilled
1 cup mayonnaise
2 tablespoons heavy cream
2 teaspoons lemon juice
1 teaspoon curry powder
2 teaspoons soy sauce
1 cup halved seedless grapes
1–2 cups fresh, diced pineapple or 1 pound 4-ounce can
unsweetened pineapple chunks, drained
1 8-ounce can water chestnuts, drained and sliced
½–1 cup chopped celery
½ cup slivered almonds (optional)

Recipe continues . . .

Mix chicken with mayonnaise, cream, lemon juice, curry, and soy sauce and chill for 2 hours. Add remaining ingredients and chill for at least 1 hour.

Serve attractively on lettuce leaves.

YIELD: 4–6 SERVINGS

THE JUNIOR LEAGUE OF SANTA BARBARA, CALIFORNIA

Chicken Salad with Yogurt

2½ cups diced cooked chicken
1 cup plain yogurt
1 teaspoon curry powder
1 teaspoon salt
1 tablespoon lemon juice
2 stalks celery, diced
1 14-ounce can pineapple tidbits, drained

Combine ingredients. Blend together well. Chill.

Serve on salad greens.

YIELD: 4–6 SERVINGS

Something New Under the Sun
THE JUNIOR LEAGUE OF PHOENIX, ARIZONA

Green Chili Salad

4 tomatoes, cut in wedges
1 3½-ounce can whole green chilies, drained and sliced
¼ pound fresh mushrooms, sliced
16 pitted black olives
2 tablespoons minced green onion
1 lemon, thinly sliced
4 tablespoons olive oil
3 tablespoons wine vinegar
¼ teaspoon salt
¼ teaspoon pepper
¼ teaspoon oregano
¼ teaspoon cumin

Toss together tomatoes, chilies, mushrooms, olives, green onion, and lemon. Mix remaining ingredients, then pour over vegetables and refrigerate for 3 hours.

At serving time remove lemon. Serve on beds of lettuce.

YIELD: 8 SERVINGS

Gourmet Olé
THE JUNIOR LEAGUE OF ALBUQUERQUE, NEW MEXICO

· ·

Beth's Chinese Tossed Salad

1 head romaine
1 1-pound can bean sprouts, drained, or 2 cups fresh bean sprouts
1 15-ounce can water chestnuts, sliced
5 slices bacon, crisply fried and crumbled
2 hard-boiled eggs
Salt and pepper

Recipe continues . . .

DRESSING:
1 cup salad oil
½ cup sugar
⅓ cup catsup
¼ cup vinegar
2 tablespoons grated onion
2 teaspoons Worcestershire sauce

Combine all salad ingredients in bowl. Add salt and pepper to taste.

Combine dressing ingredients in blender or shake well in screw-top jar until well mixed. Add to salad, tossing lightly.

YIELD: 6–8 SERVINGS

THE JUNIOR LEAGUE OF TACOMA, WASHINGTON

· · · · · · · · · · · · · · · · · ·

Chinese Salad

4 6-ounce cans water chestnuts, sliced
2 6-ounce cans bamboo shoots, sliced
1 head chinese cabbage, sliced
1 cup diced, cooked shrimp
½ cup slivered almonds
2 cups Thompson seedless grapes
Juice of 1 lime
2 tablespoons soy sauce
2 teaspoons prepared mustard
1 tablespoon honey
1 cup mayonnaise

In a large bowl mix water chestnuts, bamboo shoots, sliced cabbage, shrimp, almonds, and grapes. Chill well.

In a blender mix lime juice, soy sauce, mustard, honey, and mayonnaise. Set aside so flavor blends.

Just before serving, toss salad with dressing.

YIELD: 12 SERVINGS

THE JUNIOR LEAGUE OF OAKLAND-EAST BAY, CALIFORNIA

"Brown Derby" Cobb Salad

½ head lettuce
½ bunch watercress
1 small bunch chicory
½ head romaine
2 tablespoons minced chives
2 medium tomatoes
2 chicken breasts, cooked and boned
6 slices bacon, fried and drained
1 avocado
3 hard-boiled eggs
½ cup Roquefort cheese, crumbled
Special French Dressing

Finely chop lettuce, watercress, chicory, and romaine and combine in wide, shallow bowl. Add chives.

Peel, seed, and dice tomatoes. Dice chicken, bacon, avocado, and eggs. Arrange tomatoes, chicken, bacon, avocado and eggs over greens. Sprinkle with cheese. Chill.

Toss at table with ½ cup Special French Dressing.

Recipe continues . . .

SPECIAL FRENCH DRESSING:
¼ cup water
¼ cup red wine vinegar
¼ teaspoon sugar
1½ teaspoons lemon juice
½ teaspoon salt
½ teaspoon pepper
½ teaspoon Worcestershire sauce
¾ teaspoon English mustard
½ clove garlic
¼ cup olive oil
¾ cup oil

Combine ingredients and chill.

YIELD: 6 SERVINGS

Something New Under the Sun
THE JUNIOR LEAGUE OF PHOENIX, ARIZONA

. . . .

Japanese Cucumber Slices

Slice a Japanese cucumber very thinly. Do not peel. (English cucumber can be used.) Sprinkle the slices generously with salt and toss so that all slices are salted. Set aside for ½ hour.

Rinse cucumber slices several times in cold water. Dry the slices on a tea towel so they are free of water. Put slices in a bowl and cover with the sauce. Cover bowl and refrigerate for about 2 hours before serving.

SAUCE:
¼ cup white vinegar
1 teaspoon superfine granulated sugar
1 teaspoon Japanese soy sauce
¼ teaspoon Japanese seasoning salt

Mix all ingredients together and stir until the sugar and seasoning salt are dissolved.

YIELD: 2 SERVINGS

THE JUNIOR LEAGUE OF SEATTLE, WASHINGTON

Cucumbers in Dill

4 cucumbers
1 cup boiling water
¾ cup sour cream
¼ cup lemon juice
3 tablespoons minced fresh dill
1½ teaspoons salt
⅛ teaspoon pepper
1 teaspoon sugar

Peel the cucumbers and slice very thinly. Pour boiling water over them and let stand for 5 minutes. Drain and plunge into ice water. Drain again.

Mix together sour cream, lemon juice, dill, salt, pepper, and sugar. Pour over the cucumbers, tossing until well mixed. Chill 30 minutes before serving.

YIELD: 6–8 SERVINGS

THE JUNIOR LEAGUE OF RIVERSIDE, CALIFORNIA

Cucumber Mold

1 3-ounce package lime-flavored gelatin
¾ cup hot water
¾ cup drained, shredded or ground unpeeled cucumbers
¼ cup finely sliced green onion
1 cup large-curd cottage cheese
1 cup mayonnaise
1 teaspoon horseradish
¼ teaspoon salt

Dissolve gelatin in hot water. Chill until partially set. Combine remaining ingredients and stir into gelatin mixture. Chill until set.

YIELD: 6–8 SERVINGS

THE JUNIOR LEAGUE OF OGDEN, UTAH

Crab Salad

¾ cup mayonnaise
¼ teaspoon garlic salt
Juice of ½ lime
3 teaspoons Dijon mustard
1 teaspoon Worcestershire sauce
½ teaspoon dried tarragon leaves
8 dashes Angostura bitters
1 tablespoon brandy
Lettuce leaves for garnish
1 pound fresh crabmeat, chilled

Mix all ingredients except lettuce leaves and crabmeat. Chill.

Garnish individual salad plates with lettuce leaves. Gently fold crabmeat into sauce mixture and arrange on top of lettuce.

YIELD: 4 SERVINGS

San Francisco à la Carte
THE JUNIOR LEAGUE OF SAN FRANCISCO, CALIFORNIA

· ·

Farmers' Market Salad

DRESSING:
1 cup mayonnaise
¼ cup chopped parsley
¼ cup vinegar
¼ cup crumbled blue cheese
½ cup sour cream
2 tablespoons chopped green onion
1 tablespoon lemon juice
1 clove garlic, minced
Salt to taste
Freshly ground pepper to taste

SALAD:
1 head romaine
1 head iceberg lettuce
4 hard-boiled eggs, cut in wedges
3 tomatoes, cut into sections
1 16-ounce can peas, drained, or 2 cups fresh peas

Recipe continues . . .

Combine all dressing ingredients. Refrigerate.

Shred romaine and iceberg lettuce. Toss with tomatoes and eggs. Add peas and dressing. Toss again.

YIELD: 10 SERVINGS

Heritage Cookbook
THE JUNIOR LEAGUE OF SALT LAKE CITY, UTAH

· ·

Sour Cream Fruit Salad

1 8-ounce can Mandarin oranges, drained
1 cup shredded coconut
1 cup pineapple chunks
1 cup tiny marshmallows
1 cup sour cream

Combine all ingredients. Let stand in refrigerator for at least 8 hours.

YIELD: 8 SERVINGS

THE JUNIOR LEAGUE OF BUTTE, MONTANA

· · · · · · · · · · · · · · · · · ·

Gazpacho Salad

2 medium cucumbers, peeled and sliced
2 teaspoons salt
⅔ cup olive oil
⅓ cup wine vinegar
1 clove garlic, minced
1 teaspoon dried basil
1 teaspoon dried tarragon
1 teaspoon salt
½ teaspoon ground pepper
10 mushrooms, sliced
4 green onions, sliced
3 large tomatoes, peeled and cut in wedges
1 green pepper, sliced
½ pound shredded Swiss cheese
4 hard-boiled eggs, peeled and sliced

Sprinkle cucumbers with salt and let stand 30 minutes.

Combine oil, vinegar, garlic, basil, tarragon, salt, and pepper in a bowl. Add mushrooms and green onions.

Drain cucumbers and pat dry, then combine with the tomatoes and green pepper, mixing gently. In a large bowl, put a layer of the mixed vegetables, then the dressing with the mushrooms and onions, and keep alternating. Cover bowl and refrigerate for 4 hours.

Just before serving, add cheese and eggs; toss.

YIELD: 8 SERVINGS

Gourmet Olé
THE JUNIOR LEAGUE OF ALBUQUERQUE, NEW MEXICO

Greek Country Salad

4 large tomatoes
2 medium cucumbers
½ cup crumbled feta cheese
½ cup sliced pitted black olives
3 tablespoons olive oil
½ teaspoon salt
Freshly ground pepper to taste
½ teaspoon crumbled oregano

Peel and slice tomatoes and cucumbers. Arrange slices in a shallow salad bowl. Sprinkle with cheese and olives. Blend olive oil, salt, pepper, oregano; pour over salad.

If you know where to buy feta cheese and salty dried black olives, the salad can be authentic; but it will be just as good if easily available blue cheese and American ripe olives are used.

YIELD: 8 SERVINGS

Private Collection:
Recipes from The Junior League of Palo Alto
THE JUNIOR LEAGUE OF PALO ALTO, CALIFORNIA

Guacamole Salad

½–1 cup mashed avocado
2 tablespoons lemon juice
½ cup sour cream
½ cup salad oil
1 clove garlic
½ teaspoon sugar
½ tablespoon chili powder
¼ teaspoon salt
Few dashes Tabasco
½ head each romaine and iceberg lettuce
½ cup sliced pitted black olives
½ cup shredded cheddar cheese
¼ cup chopped green onions, including green tops
1 cup corn chips
1 1-pound can albacore tuna, drained
2 tomatoes, cut in wedges, for garnish

Put first nine ingredients in blender; blend, then chill. Arrange remaining ingredients in salad bowl and toss gently with dressing.

YIELD: 8 SERVINGS

THE JUNIOR LEAGUE OF LOS ANGELES, CALIFORNIA

Hearts of Palm and Olive Salad

⅓ cup salad oil
2 tablespoons lemon juice
1 teaspoon sugar
½ teaspoon salt
½ teaspoon aromatic bitter
¼ teaspoon paprika
2 tablespoons chopped green stuffed olives
1 tablespoon chopped onion
1 tablespoon chopped celery
1 14-ounce can hearts of palm, drained and sliced
6 cups torn greens
Sliced fresh mushrooms (optional)
Sliced marinated artichoke hearts (optional)

Combine first nine ingredients. Shake well and chill.

At serving time toss with the hearts of palm and greens. Mushrooms and artichoke hearts may be added if desired.

YIELD: 6 SERVINGS

Something New Under the Sun
THE JUNIOR LEAGUE OF PHOENIX, ARIZONA

* * * * * * * * * * * * * * *

Mandarin Salad

¼ head iceberg lettuce, torn in pieces
¼ head romaine, torn in pieces
1 cup chopped celery
2 green onions and tops, thinly sliced
¼ cup sliced almonds
1 tablespoon plus 1 teaspoon sugar
1 11-ounce can Mandarin oranges, drained

Prepare both types of lettuce and put in a plastic bag with the celery and onions. Refrigerate until ready to serve.

Cook almonds with the sugar over low heat, stirring constantly, until sugar melts and almonds are coated, about 5–10 minutes. Cool almonds and split. Five minutes before serving, pour dressing into bag of greens; add Mandarin oranges and almonds. Close bag and shake. Empty into serving bowl and serve.

Salad and dressing can be made early in the day and refrigerated. Almonds can be prepared ahead, cooled, and stored at room temperature.

YIELD: 4–6 SERVINGS

DRESSING:
½ teaspoon salt
Dash pepper
2 tablespoons sugar
2 tablespoons vinegar
¼ cup salad oil
Dash red pepper sauce
1 tablespoon minced parsley

Shake ingredients in tightly covered jar. Refrigerate.

YIELD: 4–6 SERVINGS

THE JUNIOR LEAGUE OF RIVERSIDE, CALIFORNIA

Mexican Chef Salad

1 8½-ounce can pitted ripe olives, sliced
2 cups shredded lettuce
1 16-ounce can kidney beans, drained
2 tomatoes, chopped and drained
1 tablespoon canned chopped green chilies
1 large avocado, diced
½ cup sour cream
2 tablespoons Italian dressing
1 teaspoon instant minced onion
¾ teaspoon chili powder
½ teaspoon salt
⅛ teaspoon pepper
½ cup shredded cheddar cheese
½ cup coarsely crushed corn chips

Combine olives, lettuce, beans, tomatoes, and chilies. Chill thoroughly. Blend avocado, sour cream, dressing, and seasonings; chill.

Toss greens with dressing; top with cheese and chips.

YIELD: 6 SERVINGS

Gourmet Olé
THE JUNIOR LEAGUE OF ALBUQUERQUE, NEW MEXICO

Salad Niçoise

2 16-ounce cans whole new potatoes, drained and thickly sliced
1 16-ounce can cut green beans, drained
1 14-ounce can water-packed artichoke hearts, drained and halved
1 large onion, thinly sliced
3 cups Garlic Dressing
Salad greens, torn into chunks
3 6½-ounce cans water-packed tuna, drained and flaked
1 pint cherry tomatoes, halved
1 4½-ounce can sliced black olives, drained
6 hard-boiled eggs, quartered
½ cup canned or bottled red peppers, cut in strips
1 large green pepper, cut into thin rings
2 2-ounce cans anchovies rolled with capers, drained
¼ cup chopped fresh parsley
Salt and freshly ground black pepper

Combine potatoes, beans, artichoke hearts, and onion in a bowl. Pour dressing over them. Refrigerate for a minimum of 3 hours, turning occasionally.

Line a very large salad bowl, preferably one with sloping sides, with salad greens, covering both the bottom and sides. Mound tuna in center of the bottom of bowl.

Drain refrigerated vegetables as well as possible, reserving the dressing. Arrange vegetables on top of greens. Arrange tomatoes on top of vegetables and tuna. Arrange olive slices in same manner, then the eggs, the red peppers, the green pepper rings, and, last, the anchovies. Sprinkle with parsley. Sprinkle with small amount of salt and freshly ground black pepper. Pour dressing over all. Do not toss.

Must be served by reaching deep into salad at sides and middle in order to get some of every ingredient.

Salad can be arranged in bowl at last possible minute before guests arrive. Do not pour dressing on until ready to serve. Should be refrigerated until ready to serve.

Recipe continues . . .

GARLIC DRESSING:
2 cups olive oil
½ cup tarragon vinegar
¼ cup fresh lemon juice
2 medium cloves garlic, minced
1 tablespoon dry mustard
1 teaspoon salt and pepper

Combine all ingredients in covered jar. Shake well before using. Refrigerate.

YIELD: 12 MAIN-DISH SERVINGS

THE JUNIOR LEAGUE OF GREAT FALLS, MONTANA

· ·

Crunchy Pea Salad

1 10-ounce package petite frozen peas (if unavailable, substitute
same amount of any small frozen peas)
1 cup diced celery
¼ cup diced green onion, including top
1 cup salted cashew nuts or macadamia nuts, broken into small pieces
¼ cup crisply fried bacon bits
1 cup sour cream
¼ cup Garden Cafe dressing
½ teaspoon salt

Combine all ingredients. Chill. Serve on lettuce leaf.
Crunchy Pea Salad is good served as a main dish for lunch or served with other salads for a buffet dinner.

YIELD: 10 SERVINGS

GARDEN CAFE DRESSING:

⅔ tablespoon fresh lemon juice
1 cup red wine vinegar
1¼ teaspoons salt
1 teaspoon finely ground pepper
1 tablespoon Worcestershire sauce
1 teaspoon Dijon mustard
1 clove garlic, minced
1 teaspoon sugar
3 cups corn oil

Combine all ingredients and mix well. Store in refrigerator.
Dressing is good on tossed salads, crisp lettuce, and vegetables as well.

YIELD: 1 QUART

THE JUNIOR LEAGUE OF GREAT FALLS, MONTANA

· ·

Ensalada de Naranja
(Orange Salad)

1 large head Boston lettuce
2 large oranges, peeled and thickly sliced
1 cucumber, thinly sliced
1 small sweet onion, thinly sliced
1 green pepper, thinly sliced
3 tablespoons olive oil
1 tablespoons wine vinegar
1½ teaspoons salt

Arrange clean, crisp lettuce leaves in salad bowl. Between the greens and standing on edge, set thick slices of peeled oranges with thin slices of un-

Recipe continues . . .

peeled cucumber in between. Strew thin slices of onion and green pepper on top and season with mixture of oil, vinegar, and salt.

Good complement to Mexican food.

YIELD: 6 SERVINGS

From an Adobe Oven . . . to a Microwave Range
THE JUNIOR LEAGUE OF PUEBLO, COLORADO

Palace Court Salad with Green Goddess Dressing

This original San Francisco tempter comes from the Garden Court of the Palace Hotel.

1 pound fresh crabmeat or small shrimp, cooked and shelled
2 cups diced celery
1 tablespoon minced onion
½–1 cup mayonnaise
2 large tomatoes, thickly sliced
6 large artichoke bottoms, cooked
1 head iceberg lettuce, shredded
3 hard-boiled eggs, finely chopped

In a bowl combine the crab or shrimp, celery, and onion. Add just enough mayonnaise to bind the ingredients together. Set aside.

On each plate place a thick slice of tomato, put an artichoke bottom on it, then the crab or shrimp mixture. Circle each mound with some shredded lettuce and garnish with chopped egg. Serve Green Goddess Dressing on the side.

YIELD: 6 SERVINGS

GREEN GODDESS DRESSING:
1¾ cups mayonnaise
¼ cup sour cream
6–8 anchovy filets, mashed
3 tablespoons minced fresh tarragon leaves
2 tablespoons minced fresh chives
1 tablespoon chopped fresh parsley
¼ cup tarragon vinegar
1 clove garlic, minced

Combine all ingredients in a jar and shake well to mix thoroughly. Let stand for at least 1 hour to allow the flavors to blend.

Can be stored in the refrigerator for several days.

YIELD: ABOUT 2½ CUPS

San Francisco à la Carte
THE JUNIOR LEAGUE OF SAN FRANCISCO, CALIFORNIA

· · · · · · · · · · · · · · · · · · · ·

Papaya and Crab

3 fresh ripe papayas, halved
1 pound King crabmeat cut into chunks
1 fresh lime

For each serving, top half a ripe papaya with crab chunks. Garnish with fresh lime slices. Serve with Curry Sauce.

YIELD: 6 SERVINGS

Recipe continues . . .

CURRY SAUCE:
1 cup mayonnaise
¼ teaspoon ground ginger
1 teaspoon curry powder
1 clove garlic, minced
1 teaspoon honey
1 tablespoon lime juice

Combine all ingredients and mix well. Chill for at least 1 hour.

THE JUNIOR LEAGUE OF SANTA BARBARA, CALIFORNIA

· · · · · · · · · · · · · · · · ·

Frozen Pineapple Salad

8 ounces cream cheese
¼ cup sugar
¼ cup brown sugar
2 cups plain yogurt
1 15¼-ounce can crushed pineapple, well drained
2 tablespoons chopped walnuts
2 tablespoons red and green candied cherries

In a small mixing bowl, beat together cream cheese and sugars. Stir in yogurt and drained pineapple. Spoon into 10 paper cups in muffin pans. Combine walnuts and cherries; spoon a little on top of each cup.

Cover, freeze until firm. Let stand 10 minutes before serving.

YIELD: 10 SERVINGS

THE JUNIOR LEAGUE OF SPOKANE, WASHINGTON

· · · · · · · · · · · · · · ·

Chilled Curried Rice Salad

1 tablespoon olive oil
1 teaspoon curry
1 13¾-ounce can chicken broth
1 cup chopped celery
1 cup raw converted rice
½ cup water
½ cup toasted slivered almonds
⅔ cup raisins
⅓ cup mayonnaise
⅔ cup or more coconut
6 tomatoes, halved or cut into wedges
Parsley for garnish

In a saucepan heat the oil. Add the curry and heat gently for 1 minute. Add broth, celery, rice, and water. Heat to boiling. Lower heat, cover, and simmer for 20–25 minutes, or until liquid is absorbed.

Chill 6 hours or more. Stir in almonds, raisins, mayonnaise, and coconut.

Serve in tomato halves or with tomato wedges garnished with parsley. A great summer salad. Good for picnics.

YIELD: 6–8 SERVINGS

THE JUNIOR LEAGUE OF LOS ANGELES, CALIFORNIA

Salad by Committee

3 6-ounce jars marinated artichoke hearts, diced (reserve juice)
1 pound fresh mushrooms, thinly sliced
2 pounds cooked chicken or turkey breast meat, diced
2 pounds cooked ham, diced
2 pounds cheddar cheese, shredded
2 pounds bacon, fried and crumbled
12 hard-boiled eggs, grated
3–4 ripe avocados, diced
1 7¾-ounce can pitted ripe olives, thinly sliced
2 bunches radishes, thinly sliced
2 bunches green onions, thinly sliced
1½ pints cherry tomatoes, halved
5–6 heads of lettuce, preferably mixed greens, torn into bite-size pieces

DRESSING:
1 cup salad oil
⅓ cup wine vinegar
Reserved artichoke juice from 3 6-ounce jars
½ teaspoon dry mustard
½ teaspoon garlic powder
1 teaspoon sugar
½ teaspoon salad herbs
Salt and pepper to taste

Make dressing first: Mix oil, vinegar, artichoke juice and seasonings. Marinate artichoke hearts and mushrooms in dressing 3–4 hours.

When ready to serve, mix all remaining ingredients together in a very large wooden bowl. Toss with dressing, mushrooms, and artichoke hearts. Each member of the "Committee" brings part of the ingredients.

YIELD: 16 SERVINGS

Colorado Cache
THE JUNIOR LEAGUE OF DENVER, COLORADO

· · · · · · · · · · · · · · ·

Supper Salad

½ cup chopped green onion
¾ cup chopped celery
½ cup sour cream
¼ cup mayonnaise
2 tablespoons fresh lemon juice
1 tablespoon chopped parsley
1 teaspoon prepared horseradish
1 tablespoon prepared mustard
1 teaspoon salt
¼ teaspoon dried oregano leaves
⅛ teaspoon ground pepper
1 pound fresh mushrooms, thinly sliced
1 pound cooked turkey, lamb or roast beef, cut into julienne strips
Salad greens
Orange slices or cherry tomatoes for garnish

Mix all ingredients except mushrooms, meat, and salad greens and garnish in large salad bowl. This part of the recipe can be done ahead.

One to 3 hours before serving, toss mushrooms and meat with dressing in the bowl. Refrigerate for flavors to blend.

Serve on fresh salad greens and garnish with orange slices or cherry tomatoes.

YIELD: 6 SERVINGS

THE JUNIOR LEAGUE OF SANTA BARBARA, CALIFORNIA

Seven-Layer Salad

1½ heads iceberg lettuce
½ cup chopped celery
½ cup chopped green pepper
½ cup chopped red onion
1 10-ounce package frozen peas, thawed
1 pint mayonnaise
2 tablespoons sugar
6 ounces shredded cheddar cheese
8 slices bacon, crisply cooked and crumbled

Tear lettuce in small pieces into a large salad bowl (a glass bowl shows off layers). Add, in layers: celery, green pepper, onion, and peas. Cover with mayonnaise; sprinkle sugar evenly over mayonnaise. Top with cheese, then bacon. Cover with plastic wrap.

Refrigerate 8 hours before serving.

YIELD: 12 SERVINGS

THE JUNIOR LEAGUE OF RIVERSIDE, CALIFORNIA

· · · · · · · · · · · · · · · · · · · ·

Shrimp Avocado Vinaigrette

1 pound cooked shrimp
3 avocados
2 teaspoons dry mustard
½ teaspoon salt
¼ teaspoon black pepper
⅓ cup olive oil
3 tablespoons wine vinegar
1 onion, chopped
1 clove garlic, minced

Shell and devein shrimp; cut into small pieces. Cut the avocados in half and scoop out the meat. Reserve the avocado shells and cut the meat into cubes. Combine with the shrimp.

Mix the mustard, salt, pepper, and oil; stir until well blended. Add the vinegar, onion, and garlic; beat well.

Pour sauce over the shrimp and avocado meat, fill the shells with this mixture.

YIELD: 6 SERVINGS

No Regrets
THE JUNIOR LEAGUE OF PORTLAND, OREGON

· · · · · · · · · · · · · · · · ·

Molded Shrimp Salad

3 envelopes unflavored gelatin
¾ cup cold water
2½ cups tomato juice
1 6-ounce snappy cocktail sauce
¼ cup vinegar
3 tablespoons lemon juice
1½ teaspoons basil
1 teaspoon salt
1 teaspoon sugar
⅛ teaspoon onion powder
⅛ teaspoon black pepper
½ teaspoon Worcestershire sauce
1 cup chopped celery
½ cup chopped green pepper
1 4-ounce can pitted ripe olives
1 avocado, diced
½ cup chopped cucumber
1 cup fresh shrimp, cooked

Recipe continues . . .

Soften gelatin in cold water. Bring 1 cup tomato juice to a boil and stir in gelatin until dissolved. Add remaining tomato juice, cocktail sauce, vinegar, lemon juice, basil, salt, sugar, onion powder, pepper, and Worcestershire sauce. Refrigerate until beginning to thicken, then stir in celery, green pepper, olives, avocado, cucumber, and shrimp.

Pour into a 6-cup mold. Refrigerate overnight.

Unmold on chilled serving platter.

YIELD: 8 SERVINGS

THE JUNIOR LEAGUE OF SAN JOSE, CALIFORNIA

Korean Spinach Salad

1½ pounds fresh spinach
8 ounces fresh or canned bean sprouts
1 8½-ounce can water chestnuts, drained and sliced
5 slices bacon
⅔ cup salad oil
⅓ cup sugar
⅓ cup catsup
⅓ cup white wine vinegar
⅓ cup finely chopped green onion
2 teaspoons Worcestershire sauce
Salt and pepper
2 hard-boiled eggs, sliced

Trim and discard spinach stems. Rinse leaves and pat dry. Tear into bite-size pieces. Combine spinach, sprouts, and water chestnuts. Fry bacon until crisp; drain and crumble into salad. Cover and refrigerate.

In jar combine oil, sugar, catsup, vinegar, onion, and Worcestershire sauce. Stir and chill.

Just before serving, pour over dressing and toss. Sprinkle with salt and pepper and garnish with egg slices.

YIELD: 8 SERVINGS

A Taste of Oregon
THE JUNIOR LEAGUE OF EUGENE, OREGON

· · · · · · · · · · · · · · · ·

Tabbouleh

½ cup bulgur wheat
3 medium tomatoes, finely chopped
1 cup finely chopped parsley
1 cup finely chopped onion
⅓ cup fresh lemon juice
2 teaspoons salt
⅓ cup salad oil
2 tablespoons finely chopped mint (optional)
Freshly ground pepper

Pour 2 cups boiling water over the wheat; let sit 10 minutes, and pour off excess liquid. Add tomatoes, parsley, and onions. Mix lemon juice, salt, oil, mint, and ground pepper and pour over wheat mixture. Refrigerate until ready to use.

YIELD: 6 SERVINGS

A Taste of Oregon
THE JUNIOR LEAGUE OF EUGENE, OREGON

· · · · · · · · · ·

Marinated Tijuana Tomatoes

1½ cups oil
1 cup vinegar
¼ cup sugar
1 clove garlic, minced
1 7-ounce can green chili salsa
6 green onions, including part of tops, chopped
3–4 tomatoes, finely chopped
1 4-ounce can chopped green chilies
½ teaspoon oregano
Dash celery seed
Salt and pepper
6 tomatoes, quartered
1 2-ounce can anchovy filets

Combine all ingredients except the 6 tomatoes and anchovy filets. Chill. This is your "salsa."

Two hours before serving, quarter the 6 tomatoes; add to the salsa marinade. Toss gently. Chill.

Serve in lettuce cups. Top with a crisscross of anchovy filets.

YIELD: 6 SERVINGS

Epicure
THE JUNIOR LEAGUE OF NEWPORT HARBOR, CALIFORNIA

· ·

Tomato-Bean Salad

½ cup sour cream
¼ cup Italian salad dressing
1 16-ounce can cut green beans, drained
2 medium tomatoes, peeled, chopped, and drained
¼ cup finely chopped onion

Thoroughly combine sour cream and Italian dressing. Add beans, tomatoes, and onion. Mix well. Chill 2–3 hours, or until ready to serve.

If desired, garnish with additional tomato wedges. Serve on bed of lettuce leaves.

YIELD: 3 CUPS SALAD

THE JUNIOR LEAGUE OF SAN JOSE, CALIFORNIA

. . . .

Tortilla Salad

2 pounds ground beef
½ teaspoon salt
¼ teaspoon pepper
1 15¼-ounce can red kidney beans, drained

Brown ground beef. Add salt, pepper, and kidney beans. Spoon over individual servings of the following salad.

SALAD:
1 envelope cheese and garlic dressing
1 head lettuce, chopped or broken into pieces
1 avocado, sliced
3 medium tomatoes, sliced in bite-size pieces
1 large package tortilla chips
1 purple onion, sliced
½ pound Monterey Jack or cheddar cheese, shredded
1 head romaine, torn into bite-size chunks
1 cup sliced black olives

Prepare cheese and garlic dressing according to package instructions. Combine all salad ingredients and pour dressing over.

YIELD: 5–6 SERVINGS

THE JUNIOR LEAGUE OF OGDEN, UTAH

. . . .

Vermicelli Salad

1 12-ounce package vermicelli
6 hard-cooked eggs, chopped
6 stalks celery, chopped
6 medium sweet pickles, chopped
¼ yellow onion, chopped
Salt to taste
1½ cups mayonnaise
1 cup cooked shrimp or crabmeat, chilled
Paprika

Break dry vermicelli in half and cook as directed on package. Drain and run under cold running water to prevent sticking. When noodles cool, add eggs, celery, pickles, onion, salt, and mayonnaise. Mix well and refrigerate. Before serving add seafood and toss lightly. Sprinkle with paprika.

YIELD: 10–12 SERVINGS

THE JUNIOR LEAGUE OF BOISE, IDAHO

Zucchini Salad

1 small clove garlic, minced
1 teaspoon ground pepper
1 teaspoon Dijon mustard
2 tablespoons tarragon vinegar
6 tablespoons oil
1½ cups thinly sliced zucchini
1 cup cherry tomatoes, halved
6 cups torn romaine and butter lettuce

Combine garlic, pepper, mustard, vinegar, and oil in salad bowl. Beat until blended. Add zucchini and tomatoes and let marinate in refrigerator.

At serving time, add lettuce; toss and serve.

YIELD: 6 SERVINGS

THE JUNIOR LEAGUE OF LONG BEACH, CALIFORNIA

Pancakes, Breads, and Coffee Cakes

Sour Cream Pancakes

¾ cup sifted all-purpose flour
½ teaspoon salt
1 teaspoon sugar
¼ teaspoon baking soda
4 eggs, well beaten
1 cup cottage cheese
1 cup sour cream

Return sifted flour to sifter and add salt, sugar, and baking soda.

Beat eggs until pale and frothy. With wire whisk, beat in cottage cheese and sour cream, then add flour mixture until just mixed.

Heat well-oiled griddle until a few drops of water evaporates immediately. Ladle batter onto griddle to make 5-inch pancakes. Turn when quite brown on the underside. Cook until equally brown on other side. Be careful not to have griddle too hot or insides of cakes will not cook.

YIELD: 4 SERVINGS

Private Collection:
Recipes from The Junior League of Palo Alto
THE JUNIOR LEAGUE OF PALO ALTO, CALIFORNIA

· · · · · · · · · · · · · ·

Apple Pancake

6 eggs
1 cup milk
⅔ cup flour
½ teaspoon salt
2–3 tablespoons butter or margarine
3 apples, peeled and sliced
1 tablespoon lemon juice
½ cup sugar
½ teaspoon cinnamon

In advance blend eggs, milk, flour, and salt in blender. Set aside for 1–2 hours.

Preheat oven to 375°. Put butter or margarine in a shallow metal pan. Place in oven until shortening is melted.

Pour in batter. Top with the sliced apples. Bake at 375° for 10–15 minutes, or until the batter puffs and sets.

Sprinkle lemon juice, sugar, and cinnamon over the surface. Serve at once.

YIELD: 6 SERVINGS

THE JUNIOR LEAGUE OF SEATTLE, WASHINGTON

Fresh Strawberry Puff Pancake

¼ cup butter
3 eggs
1½ cups milk
½ cup sugar
¾ cup unsifted all-purpose flour
¼ teaspoon salt
3 cups strawberries, halved
Sour cream
Brown sugar

Put butter in a 9-inch ovenproof frying pan or other baking dish. Place dish in a 425° oven until butter melts and bubbles, about 10 minutes.

Meanwhile beat together the eggs, milk, 6 tablespoons of the sugar, flour, and salt until smooth. Remove pan from oven and immediately pour mixture all at once into the hot pan. Return pan to oven and bake at 425° for 30 minutes, or until edges are puffed and browned.

Combine strawberries with remaining 2 tablespoons of sugar. When pancake is done remove from oven and immediately spoon strawberries into the center. Cut into wedges and pass sour cream and brown sugar.

YIELD: 4 SERVINGS

No Regrets
THE JUNIOR LEAGUE OF PORTLAND, OREGON

Yorkshire Pudding

1 cup flour
2 eggs
½ cup milk
½ cup water
Salt to taste

Combine all ingredients and beat with electric beater until surface bubbles, about 2 minutes.

Melt enough fat from roasting pan to cover bottom of square cake pan. Add batter and bake at 350° for 1 hour or 450° for 30 minutes.

YIELD: 6–8 SERVINGS

THE JUNIOR LEAGUE OF CALGARY, ALBERTA

Whipped Cream Biscuits

2 cups cake flour
3 teaspoons baking powder
1 teaspoon salt
1 cup heavy cream, whipped

Mix dry ingredients and fold into whipped cream. Pat out softly in rectangular pan. Cut in squares. Bake at 450° until lightly browned.

YIELD: 12 SERVINGS

THE JUNIOR LEAGUE OF GREAT FALLS, MONTANA

Fizzles

2 cups sifted flour
¼ cup sugar
1 teaspoon baking soda
¼ teaspoon salt
½ cup shortening
⅞ cup buttermilk

Sift flour before measuring. Resift with the other dry ingredients. Cut in the shortening. Add buttermilk and mix lightly with a fork. Drop onto an ungreased baking sheet and bake at 400° for 8–10 minutes.

YIELD: 16 LARGE BISCUITS

THE JUNIOR LEAGUE OF TACOMA, WASHINGTON

Fried Buttermilk Scones

2 envelopes active dry yeast
¼ cup warm water
1 quart warm buttermilk
2 eggs
2 tablespoons sugar
2 tablespoons vegetable oil
1 tablespoon baking powder
1½ teaspoons salt
½ teaspoon baking soda
About 8 cups flour

HONEY BUTTER:
1 cup butter
1¼ cups honey
1 egg yolk

One day in advance soften yeast in warm water. Let stand 5 minutes. Mix warm buttermilk, eggs, sugar, vegetable oil, baking powder, salt, baking soda, 4 cups flour, and yeast. Beat until smooth. Add remaining flour to make a soft dough. Cover. Let rise until double in bulk. Punch down. Cover and refrigerate overnight.

Just before frying, roll out on a floured surface. Cut into 2½ x 3½-inch rectangles and fry in hot (365°) fat until golden brown on one side. Flip over. Brown other side. Drain on paper towel.

Make Honey Butter by combining butter, honey, and egg yolk. Beat with electric mixer for 10 minutes. Serve with scones.

YIELD: 4–5 DOZEN SCONES

Heritage Cookbook
THE JUNIOR LEAGUE OF SALT LAKE CITY, UTAH

Mrs. Hewitt's Scones

4 cups flour
½ cup sugar
1 teaspoon salt
4 teaspoons baking powder
1 cup lard or shortening
2 eggs
1 cup or more milk
1 cup raisins

Mix together flour, sugar, salt, and baking powder; cut in lard until mixture looks like coarse meal. Beat eggs and combine with milk. Make a hole in dry ingredients and add egg and milk combination. Add raisins. Stir with a fork until all dry ingredients are moistened. Dough should be soft.

Gather dough into a ball and roll out to ¼-inch thickness on floured board. Cut with 2½-inch cookie cutter, place on ungreased baking sheets, and bake at 425° for about 10 minutes.

YIELD: ABOUT 24 SCONES

THE JUNIOR LEAGUE OF CALGARY, ALBERTA

Mexican Spoon Bread

1 1-pound can creamed corn
¾ cup milk
⅓ cup oil
2 eggs
1 cup yellow corn meal
½ teaspoon baking soda
1 teaspoon salt
1 4-ounce can chopped green chilies
2 cups shredded longhorn or medium-sharp cheddar cheese

Recipe continues . . .

Combine first seven ingredients. Pour half of mixture into buttered 1½-quart casserole. Sprinkle chilies and 1 cup of the shredded cheese evenly over top. Spoon remaining mixture over, and top with remaining cup cheese.

Bake in 400° oven for 45 minutes.

YIELD: 4–6 SERVINGS

Something New Under the Sun
THE JUNIOR LEAGUE OF PHOENIX, ARIZONA

Cottage Crescents

½ pound butter
1 cup cottage cheese
2 cups flour
¼ cup melted butter
¾ cup brown sugar
¾ cup ground nuts
Cinnamon to taste

Soften and cream together butter and cottage cheese. Add flour. Roll out ⅛ inch thick in a 15 x 20-inch rectangle. Spread with melted butter and sprinkle with brown sugar, nuts, and cinnamon. Cut into 2½-inch squares, then into triangles. Roll each triangle like a crescent roll.

Bake in 350° oven for 20 minutes on lightly greased cookie sheet.

YIELD: 5 DOZEN CRESCENTS

Something New Under the Sun
THE JUNIOR LEAGUE OF PHOENIX, ARIZONA

Cheese Puff Ring Gougère

1 cup milk
¼ cup butter
½ teaspoon salt
Dash pepper
1 cup unsifted all-purpose flour
4 eggs
1 cup shredded Swiss cheese

Heat milk and butter in a 2-quart saucepan; add salt and pepper. Bring to a full boil and add flour all at once, stirring over medium heat about 2 minutes, or until mixture leaves the side of the pan and forms a ball.

Remove pan from heat and beat in eggs by hand, one at a time, until mixture is smooth and well blended. Beat in ½ cup of cheese.

Using a large spoon, make seven equal mounds of dough in a circle on a greased baking sheet, using about three-quarters of the dough. Each ball of dough should just touch the next one.

Using remaining dough, place a small mound of dough on the top of each large one.

Sprinkle remaining ½ cup cheese over all.

Bake on center rack at 375° for 55 minutes, or until puffs are lightly browned and crisp.

Delicious accompanying soup or a luncheon salad.

YIELD: 6 SERVINGS

Private Collection:
Recipes from The Junior League of Palo Alto
THE JUNIOR LEAGUE OF PALO ALTO, CALIFORNIA

Hungarian Butter Horns

4 cups flour
½ teaspoon salt
1 cake yeast or 1 envelope active dry yeast
1½ cups butter
3 egg yolks, beaten (reserve whites for filling)
½ cup sour cream
1 teaspoon vanilla
Confectioners' sugar

FILLING:
3 egg whites
1 cup sugar
1 cup finely ground nuts
1 teaspoon vanilla

Sift flour and salt into mixing bowl, add crumbled yeast or yeast powder, and cut in butter until mixture looks like meal. Add beaten yolks, sour cream, and vanilla. Mix well to a smooth dough. Wrap in wax paper and chill until filling is made.

To make filling, beat 3 egg whites until stiff, beat in sugar gradually, then fold in the nuts and vanilla. Set aside.

Dredge a pastry board with sugar. Divide chilled dough into eight parts. Roll out each part in a circle about the size of a pie plate and cut into eight wedges. Spread 1 teaspoon of filling on each wedge and roll from wide end of triangle to the tip. Line a baking sheet with greased brown paper. Arrange the horns on the paper and bake in a preheated 400° oven for 15–18 minutes.

YIELD: 64 HORNS

Gourmet Olé
THE JUNIOR LEAGUE OF ALBUQUERQUE, NEW MEXICO

Sour Cream Kringle

1 cup softened margarine
2 cups flour
1 cup sour cream
1⅓ cups brown sugar
1 cup chopped pecans
Sugar

Mix the margarine, flour, and sour cream together and chill overnight.

Divide dough into four equal parts. Roll each part into a 6 x 12-inch rectangle on a heavily floured board. On each, sprinkle ⅓ cup brown sugar and ¼ cup pecans down the middle lengthwise. Fold edges over each other and seal ends on each of the four kringles. Turn over and place on two baking sheets.

Sprinkle with sugar; bake 30 minutes at 350°.

YIELD: 4 KRINGLES

THE JUNIOR LEAGUE OF RIVERSIDE, CALIFORNIA

· · · · · · · · · · · · · · · · · · ·

Irish Soda Bread

3 cups flour
½ cup sugar
3 teaspoons baking powder
1 teaspoon baking soda
½ teaspoon salt
1 cup raisins
1 egg
2 teaspoons melted shortening
1¾ cups buttermilk

Recipe continues . . .

Sift together dry ingredients. Add raisins.

Combine egg, shortening and buttermilk and stir into dry ingredients. Transfer dough to an oiled 5 x 9-inch loaf pan and bake at 350° for 1 hour. (At high altitude, add 2 tablespoons more flour and bake at 375°.)

YIELD: 1 5 x 9-INCH LOAF

THE JUNIOR LEAGUE OF BUTTE, MONTANA

Pioneer Whole Wheat Bread

1 yeast cake or envelope active dry yeast
¼ cup warm water
2 cups milk
¼ cup honey
2 tablespoons vegetable oil
¾ teaspoon salt
4 cups whole wheat flour

Soften yeast in ¼ cup warm water for 10 minutes.

Scald 2 cups milk. Cool. Mix milk, honey, vegetable oil and salt. Stir in dissolved yeast and whole wheat flour. Mix well. Knead until easy to handle. Let rise 15 minutes. Put into two small greased loaf pans and let rise 15 minutes.

Bake at 350° for 45 minutes.

YIELD: 2 LOAVES

Heritage Cookbook
THE JUNIOR LEAGUE OF SALT LAKE CITY, UTAH

Dilly Bread

1 envelope active dry yeast
¼ cup lukewarm water
1 cup cottage cheese
2 tablespoons sugar
1 teaspoon salt
1 tablespoon minced onion
¼ teaspoon baking soda
1½ tablespoons melted butter
1 egg, beaten
2 rounded teaspoons dill weed
2½ cups all-purpose flour

Soften yeast in warm water.

Heat cottage cheese to lukewarm. Do not get it too hot. Add yeast, sugar, salt, onion, soda, butter, egg, and dill weed to the warmed cottage cheese. Mix the cottage cheese mixture into the flour to form a stiff dough.

Turn onto a floured board. Knead until satiny. Place in a greased bowl and cover. Let dough rise until double in bulk. Punch dough down and form into two loaves.

Place in 5 x 9-inch loaf pans and let rise again until double. Bake in 350° oven for 30 minutes.

For a soft crust butter tops of hot loaves.

YIELD: 2 LOAVES

THE JUNIOR LEAGUE OF OAKLAND-EAST BAY, CALIFORNIA

. . . .

Beer Bread

3 cups self-rising flour
3 tablespoons sugar
1 12-ounce can beer
1 stick butter, melted

Recipe continues . . .

Lightly mix together the first three ingredients. Batter will be lumpy. Pour into greased 4 x 8-inch loaf pan. Pour one-third of the melted butter over mixture. Bake at 375° for 40 minutes, then pour one-third more of melted butter on top of bread. Continue baking for 10 more minutes; pour last third of butter on bread and bake 10 minutes longer.

YIELD: 6–8 SERVINGS

THE JUNIOR LEAGUE OF BAKERSFIELD, CALIFORNIA

Banana Bread

1 cup sugar
½ cup softened butter
3 ripe bananas, mashed
2 eggs, well beaten
1¼ cups cake flour
½ teaspoon salt
1 teaspoon baking soda

Cream together sugar and butter. Add bananas and eggs. Sift the cake flour, salt, and baking soda together three times. Blend together the banana mixture and the flour mixture. Do not overmix.

Bake in greased and floured loaf pan at 350° for 45–50 minutes.

YIELD: 1 LOAF

THE JUNIOR LEAGUE OF LOS ANGELES, CALIFORNIA

Lemon Tea Bread

1 cup softened butter
2 cups sugar
4 eggs, beaten
1 cup milk
3 cups sifted flour
2 teaspoons baking powder
1 teaspoon salt
Grated rind of 2 lemons
1 cup nuts

GLAZE:
1 cup sugar
1 cup lemon juice

Cream butter and sugar. Beat in eggs; gradually stir in milk. Combine dry ingredients and stir into egg mixture. Add lemon rind and stir until mixture is well blended. Stir in nuts.

Pour batter into two well-greased loaf pans. Bake at 325° for 1 hour.

Combine sugar and lemon juice. Remove baked bread from oven and, while still in the pans, pour the sugar and lemon juice mixture over them. Cool slightly and remove loaves from pans.

A marvelous way to use those California lemons. Freezes well and is delightful to serve with tea or even as dessert.

YIELD: 2 LOAVES

THE JUNIOR LEAGUE OF SACRAMENTO, CALIFORNIA

Sour Cream Coffee Cake

1 cup sour cream
1 teaspoon baking soda
½ cup soft butter
1 cup white sugar
2 eggs, well beaten
1 teaspoon vanilla
1¾ cups flour
2 teaspoons baking powder
½ teaspoon salt
⅓ cup brown sugar
½ teaspoon cinnamon
¼ cup chopped walnuts or pecans

Combine sour cream and soda and set aside.

Cream the butter and sugar. Add the eggs and vanilla. Beat well. Add flour, baking powder, and salt, then stir in the sour cream mixture.

Combine the sugar, cinnamon and chopped nuts. Spread half the batter in a greased bundt or angel food cake pan. Sprinkle half of the sugar and cinnamon mixture on the batter and pour remaining batter on the top. Sprinkle remaining topping over the cake. Bake in a 350° oven for 40–50 minutes. Let cool in the pan before removing.

YIELD: 8–10 SERVINGS

THE JUNIOR LEAGUE OF VANCOUVER, BRITISH COLUMBIA

Ever-Ready Muffins

2 cups boiling water
2 cups 100% bran
1 cup shortening
3 cups sugar
4 eggs, beaten
1 quart buttermilk
5 cups flour
1 teaspoon salt
5 teaspoons baking soda
4 cups bran buds

Use a large bowl to mix these muffins. Pour the boiling water over the bran and let soak. Cream shortening and sugar. Add beaten eggs, buttermilk, and the soaked bran. Sift dry ingredients together and stir into buttermilk mixture. Add bran buds. Stir until moistened.

Fill greased muffin cups two-thirds full and bake at 400° for about 15–18 minutes.

Fruit and nuts may be added if desired.

Recipe may be stored up to 6 weeks in the refrigerator if tightly covered.

YIELD: 6 DOZEN MUFFINS

THE JUNIOR LEAGUE OF TACOMA, WASHINGTON

Rhubarb Sticky Muffins

1 cup finely chopped rhubarb
¼ cup butter
½ cup firmly packed brown sugar
⅓ cup butter
⅓ cup sugar
1 egg
1½ cups flour
2 teaspoons baking powder
½ teaspoon salt
½ teaspoon nutmeg
½ cup milk

Combine rhubarb, ¼ cup butter, and brown sugar in a small bowl and mix with a fork until blended. Put in the bottom of twelve large greased muffin cups.

Beat ⅓ cup butter, sugar, and egg until fluffy. Sift flour, baking powder, salt, and nutmeg. Add to butter-sugar mixture alternately with milk. Stir just to blend. Spoon on top of rhubarb. Bake in a 350° oven for 20–25 minutes.

Invert pan on rack and let stand for a few minutes. Remove pan. Serve warm.

YIELD: 12 LARGE MUFFINS

THE JUNIOR LEAGUE OF VANCOUVER, BRITISH COLUMBIA

Sourdough Hotcakes

½ envelope active dry yeast
1½ tablespoons lukewarm water
2 cups buttermilk or sour milk
1 cup flour
2 cups flour
2 cups milk
½ cup sourdough starter (see Index)
2 eggs, beaten
3 tablespoons melted butter
3 tablespoons sugar
1½ teaspoons baking soda
1 teaspoon salt

In advance soften yeast in water. Add buttermilk and flour. Let stand at room temperature overnight. Next day, refrigerate for up to 3 weeks.

The night before the pancakes are to be made, mix flour, milk, and ½ cup starter. Let stand overnight in a draft-free place.

In the morning, thoroughly mix in eggs, melted butter, sugar, baking soda, and salt. Fry on a lightly greased griddle.

Leftover batter can be refrigerated and used the next day by adding a pinch of baking soda.

YIELD: 6 SERVINGS

Heritage Cookbook
THE JUNIOR LEAGUE OF SALT LAKE CITY, UTAH

Utah Strawberry Days Sourdough Waffles

¾ cup sourdough starter (see Index)
2 cups flour
1½ cups warm water
4 tablespoons sugar
¾ teaspoon baking soda
¾ teaspoon salt
2 egg whites
2 egg yolks, beaten
¼ cup vegetable oil
1 cup heavy cream
2 cups sliced fresh strawberries

One day in advance put sourdough starter in a large bowl. Gradually mix in flour. Thoroughly blend in warm water. Cover. Put in warm place (90°) overnight.

Next day, combine half the sugar, the baking soda, and salt. Set aside. Beat egg whites just until stiff peaks form. Set aside. Mix egg yolks and vegetable oil into sourdough starter. Stir in sugar mixture. Gently fold in egg whites. Bake in hot waffle iron 4–5 minutes, or until gold brown. While baking, whip heavy cream with remaining sugar.

To serve, put a scoop of whipped cream on each waffle. Top with fresh strawberries.

YIELD: 4 WAFFLES

Heritage Cookbook
THE JUNIOR LEAGUE OF SALT LAKE CITY, UTAH

Butterflake Rolls

2 cakes yeast or 2 envelopes active dry yeast
½ cup warm water
½ cup sugar
½ cup shortening
¼ cup warm water
3 eggs, beaten
4½ cups sifted flour
2 teaspoons salt
Melted butter

One day in advance, soften yeast in ½ cup warm water. Stir in 1 table-spoon of the sugar. Set aside for 10 minutes. In another bowl, combine shortening and remaining sugar. Stir in ¼ cup warm water, beaten eggs, and yeast. Stir in flour and salt. Cover and refrigerate overnight.

Divide dough in half. Roll out to a ¼-inch-thick rectangle. Brush with melted butter. Starting at wide side, roll like a jelly roll. Pinch seams to seal. Cut in 1½-inch slices. Dip in melted butter and put butter side up in buttered muffin tins. Let rise until double in bulk, about 1 hour.

Bake at 400° for 10 minutes, or until light brown.

YIELD: 30 ROLLS

Heritage Cookbook
THE JUNIOR LEAGUE OF SALT LAKE CITY, UTAH

Aunt Marcelle's Overnight Rolls

1 stick butter, melted
1 cup lukewarm milk
1 package active dry yeast
¼ cup warm water
¼ cup plus 1 tablespoon sugar
2 eggs
4 cups flour
1 teaspoon salt
Melted butter

Add butter to milk. Combine yeast with water and the 1 tablespoon sugar. Beat eggs and add to yeast mixture. Add remaining sugar. Mix. Add flour and salt. Beat with spoon until well mixed—mixture will be sticky. Cover bowl and let stand in refrigerator overnight.

Next day divide dough into four parts. Roll each into a 12-inch circle. Brush with melted butter. Cut into twelve pie-shape pieces. Roll from large end to point. Place point end down on greased pan. Let rise 4–5 hours. Bake 12 minutes at 375°.

YIELD: 48 ROLLS

THE JUNIOR LEAGUE OF OGDEN, UTAH

· · · · · · · · · · · · · · · · · · · ·

Three-Day Buns

1 envelope active dry yeast
½ cup water
1 cup flour
2 cups water
1 cup sugar
1 egg
1½ teaspoons salt
½ cup oil
6–7 cups flour

Day one: In a jar, combine yeast with ½ cup water. Place lid on jar for 6 hours. Then in a mixing bowl, combine 1 cup flour and 2 cups water and mix with the yeast mixture. Cover and leave until next day.

Day two: In a large bowl combine sugar, egg, salt, and oil. Add first day's mixture. Gradually work in 6–7 cups flour and let rise all day. Before retiring, punch down dough and shape into buns. Place buns on a well-greased pan. Let stand, uncovered, until morning.

Day three: Bake at 350° for about 20–25 minutes.

The dough is suitable for cinnamon or other sweet rolls.

YIELD: ABOUT 4 DOZEN BUNS

THE JUNIOR LEAGUE OF CALGARY, ALBERTA

*   *   *   *   *   *   *   *   *   *   *   *   *   *   *   *

Potato Rolls

1 envelope active dry yeast
½ cup lukewarm water
⅔ cup shortening
½ cup sugar
1 teaspoon salt
1 cup mashed potatoes
1 cup scalded milk
2 eggs, well beaten
6–7 cups flour

Dissolve yeast in lukewarm water. Add shortening, sugar, salt, and mashed potatoes to scalded milk. When cool, add yeast. Mix thoroughly. Add eggs. Stir in enough flour to make a stiff dough. Refrigerate for several hours or overnight.

When ready to make rolls, punch down. Roll one-quarter of the dough at a time into a rectangle on a floured surface and cut into strips. Tie each strip in a single knot, as a bow knot. Arrange on oiled baking sheets. Allow

Recipe continues . . .

about 2½ hours for rolls to rise. Bake in 400° oven for 10–12 minutes, or until golden brown.

This dough makes wonderful cinnamon rolls.

YIELD: 4–5 DOZEN ROLLS

A Taste of Oregon
THE JUNIOR LEAGUE OF EUGENE, OREGON

. . . .

French Honey Bread

2 envelopes active dry yeast
2½ cups very warm water
¾ tablespoon sugar
¾ tablespoon salt
2 tablespoons vegetable oil
2 tablespoons honey
7 cups flour

In large mixing bowl soften yeast in ½ cup of the warm water with the sugar for 5 minutes. Add remaining water, salt, oil, and honey. Gradually beat in the flour. Cover the bowl and let stand for 20 minutes. Punch down with oiled fist every 7 minutes five times.

Divide the dough in half and shape each half like French bread. Place loaves on oiled baking sheet and let rise for 30 minutes to 1 hour, or until double in size.

Bake in a preheated 400° oven for 25 minutes.

YIELD: 2 LOAVES

THE JUNIOR LEAGUE OF SEATTLE, WASHINGTON

. . . .

Italian Bread

2½ cups warm water
2 teaspoons sugar
2 envelopes active dry yeast
7¼ cups flour
3 teaspoons salt
Corn meal
1 egg white
1 tablespoon water

Measure water into a large mixing bowl and add sugar. Stir until sugar is dissolved. Sprinkle in yeast and let stand 10 minutes. Stir well. Beat in 3 cups flour and salt. Add enough remaining flour to make a stiff dough. Turn onto floured board, cover with bowl, and let stand 15 minutes.

Knead dough for 20 minutes using as much remaining flour as dough will take. Grease large bowl. Add dough and turn so top is greased. Cover with a damp cloth and set in a warm place. Let rise until double, about 1½ hours. Punch down and let rise again until double, about 1 hour. Punch down and divide into two parts.

Grease a large cookie sheet; sprinkle with corn meal. Shape dough in two large buns; put on cookie sheet. Score top with a knife at intervals of about 1 inch.

Beat egg white and water. Brush top and sides of loaves. Let rise until double, 1–1½ hours. Preheat oven to 375°. Put a pan of hot water on bottom of oven. Bake bread for 20 minutes, remove from oven, and brush with egg mixture again. Return to oven and bake for 20 minutes longer, or until it's gold and sounds hollow when tapped with knuckles. Cool on racks.

YIELD: 2 LARGE BUNS

THE JUNIOR LEAGUE OF BILLINGS, MONTANA

Sourdough Bread and Starter

STARTER:
1 envelope active dry yeast
2 cups warm water
2 cups unbleached flour

Empty yeast into a warm mixing bowl and stir in water. Stir until yeast is dissolved. Add flour and stir until well blended. Cover with plastic wrap and let stand at room temperature for about 48 hours. (When ready, the starter will be bubbly with a somewhat yellowish liquid on top.)

Store starter in the refrigerator in a jar with a loose-fitting lid. Every time part of the starter is removed to make bread, it must be replenished, and at least once a week mix into the sourdough starter, 1 cup flour, 1 cup milk, and ⅓ cup sugar.

SOURDOUGH BREAD:
1 envelope active dry yeast
¼ cup warm water
1 teaspoon sugar
1 egg
¼ cup vegetable oil
½ cup water
1 teaspoon salt
⅓ cup sugar
1 cup sourdough starter
3½ cups flour

Dissolve yeast in warm water, stirring in the 1 teaspoon sugar. Let this sit 15 minutes. Mix the egg, vegetable oil, water, salt, and ⅓ cup sugar in a large mixing bowl. Add the sourdough starter to the egg mixture along with the yeast mixture. With electric mixer thoroughly blend in 2 cups of the flour. Add remaining flour and mix with a wooden spoon. Turn onto floured board and knead 10–20 times. Add a bit more flour if still sticky.

Rub mixing bowl with oil. Put dough in bowl, turning it to make sure the top of the dough is oiled. Cover bowl with cloth and let rise 2 hours in a warm place.

After dough has risen to double in bulk, punch down, pour onto floured board, and knead again for 2 minutes. Divide into 2 balls and place in 2 well-greased loaf pans. Cover and let rise 2 more hours in a warm place.

Bake at 350° for 20–25 minutes.

YIELD: 3 CUPS OF STARTER AND 2 LOAVES

Colorado Cache
THE JUNIOR LEAGUE OF DENVER, COLORADO

. . . .

Cracked Wheat Bread

¾ cup cracked wheat
2¼ cups boiling water
1¾ tablespoons active dry yeast
½ cup warm water
½ teaspoon sugar
⅜ cup margarine
3 tablespoons packed brown sugar
3 tablespoons molasses
2¼ tablespoons salt
1½ cups milk
3 cups whole wheat flour
About 4 cups all-purpose flour

Cook the cracked wheat in the boiling water until softened, about 10 minutes. Soften the yeast in ½ cup warm water with ½ teaspoon sugar. Set aside until the yeast doubles in volume.

Stir margarine, brown sugar, molasses, salt, and milk into the cracked wheat mixture. When the cracked wheat mixture has cooled to 100° add the yeast mixture. Stir in flour 1 cup at a time until the dough is stiff enough to turn out on a floured board and knead. Knead for 10 minutes, or until

Recipe continues . . .

texture is smooth and elastic. It may still be a bit sticky. Put into a bowl in an oven which is not turned on. Also put a saucepan of hot water in the oven. Let the dough rise until it is doubled in bulk, about 2 hours.

Punch dough down, cut in two or three pieces, depending on size of loaf desired (two 9 x 5-inch loaf pans or three smaller sizes). Knead into even balls, let rest for 10 minutes, then flatten, roll lengthwise, and tuck ends under to shape loaves. Put into very well-greased bread pans, return to turned-off oven with more hot water in saucepan, and let rise until double, about 1 hour.

Bake in a 375° oven for 40 minutes, or until the bread sounds hollow when tapped. Remove from pans and cool on racks. Do not cut bread until completely cool.

YIELD: 2 LARGE LOAVES OR 3 SMALLER LOAVES

THE JUNIOR LEAGUE OF VANCOUVER, BRITISH COLUMBIA

· · · · · · · · · · · · · · · · · · ·

Babas

This is a Ukrainian Easter bread.

1 cup milk
⅓ cup flour
2 teaspoons sugar
½ cup lukewarm water
2 envelopes active dry yeast
10–12 egg yolks
3 whole eggs (1 for glaze)
1 teaspoon salt
¾ cup sugar
½–¾ cup melted butter
2 teaspoons vanilla
1 tablespoon grated lemon rind
1 cup or more raisins
4½–5 cups sifted flour

Bring the milk to a boil and remove from heat. Add the hot milk gradually to the flour and beat thoroughly until smooth and free of lumps. If necessary strain or press the mixture through a sieve. Cool to lukewarm.

Dissolve the 2 teaspoons sugar in the lukewarm water, sprinkle the yeast over it, and let stand until softened. Combine yeast with milk-flour mixture, beat well, cover, and let rise in a warm place until light and bubbly.

Beat the egg yolks and 2 whole eggs together with salt; add the ¾ cup sugar gradually and continue beating until light. Beat in the butter, vanilla, and lemon rind. Add raisins. Combine this mixture with the yeast sponge and mix well. Stir in enough flour to make a very soft dough and knead it in the bowl by working the dough over and over continually for about 10 minutes. Let rise until double in bulk, about 70–90 minutes.

Stir dough down and let stand for 30 minutes. Divide dough into large, oiled muffin tins. Brush surface with beaten egg and let rise again. When almost double in size bake at 350° for 15–20 minutes, or until lightly browned.

YIELD: 2 DOZEN BABAS

THE JUNIOR LEAGUE OF EDMONTON, ALBERTA

Caramelized Breakfast Rolls

2 cakes yeast or envelopes active dry yeast
2 teaspoons sugar
¼ cup warm water
2¼ cups milk
½ cup margarine
2 teaspoons salt
½ cup sugar
3 eggs, beaten
7½–8 cups flour
Softened margarine
Sugar
Cinnamon
2 cups brown sugar
½ pint heavy cream
Pinch salt

Crumble or sprinkle yeast into bowl, adding 2 tablespoons sugar and ¼ cup warm water. Stir and let work.

Scald milk and add margarine to melt. Cool to lukewarm, then add salt and ½ cup sugar; stir in beaten eggs. Add yeast mixture and flour, beating constantly. More flour may be needed. Turn onto floured board and knead until you're tired. Let dough rise in warm room until double in size, about 1½ hours. Punch down and let rise again until double in size, about 1 hour.

Cut dough in half. Roll out one half at a time on floured board into a 18 x 24-inch rectangle. Spread with margarine; sprinkle with sugar and cinnamon. Roll lengthwise and pinch dough together to form a "log." Cut log into 1-inch-wide slices.

Mix together the brown sugar, cream, and salt. Pour half the mixture into a 9 x 13-inch pan with greased sides. Place dough slices in the sugar mixture. Repeat with second half of dough and sugar mixture. Let dough rise to double. Then bake in 350° oven for 25 minutes, or until brown.

Turn out immediately onto wax paper set on top of newspaper. Scrape out and frost rolls with any remaining caramel in baking pans.

YIELD: 2 9 x 13-INCH PANS

THE JUNIOR LEAGUE OF BILLINGS, MONTANA

Desserts and Sweets

Raw Apple Cake

½ cup shortening
2 cups sugar
2 eggs, beaten
2 cups raw, peeled, grated apple
2 cups sifted flour
2 teaspoons baking soda
½ teaspoon salt
1 teaspoon cinnamon
1 teaspoon nutmeg
½ cup chopped nuts

RUM TOPPING:
½ cup butter
½ cup heavy cream
1 cup sugar
1 teaspoon vanilla
1 tablespoon rum

Cream the shortening and sugar together thoroughly. Add the remaining cake ingredients, mixing well. Pour into a 9 x 13-inch cake pan and bake at 350° for 35–40 minutes.

To make topping, heat the butter, cream, and sugar together until the sugar dissolves. Stir in the vanilla and rum.

Cut apple cake into squares and serve with hot Rum Topping.

YIELD: 12 SERVINGS

No Regrets
THE JUNIOR LEAGUE OF PORTLAND, OREGON

German Chocolate Cheesecake

1 package German chocolate cake mix
⅔ cup shredded coconut
⅓ cup soft butter
3 eggs
16 ounces cream cheese, softened
2 teaspoons vanilla
¾ cup sugar

Mix cake mix, coconut, butter, and 1 egg and put into bottom of a 9 x 12-inch ungreased pan. Beat cream cheese with remaining 2 eggs, the vanilla, and sugar until smooth. Spread over the cake mix in pan and bake at 350° for 20–25 minutes. Remove from oven and spread Sour Cream Frosting over top. Allow cake to cool. Refrigerate at least 8 hours before cutting.

YIELD: 15 SERVINGS

SOUR CREAM FROSTING:
¼ cup sugar
1 tablespoon vanilla
2 cups sour cream

Add sugar and vanilla to sour cream and stir until sugar is dissolved.

THE JUNIOR LEAGUE OF OGDEN, UTAH

Kootenai Cheesecake

¾ cup finely crushed graham cracker crumbs
3 tablespoons melted butter
2 tablespoons sugar
1 pint creamed small-curd cottage cheese
8 ounces cream cheese
1 cup sugar
2 tablespoons flour
3 eggs
½ pint heavy cream
¼ teaspoon salt
1 teaspoon vanilla

Mix together graham cracker crumbs, butter, and 2 tablespoons sugar. Pat into bottom and over seam of a spring-form pan. Bake at 350° for 8 minutes.

With a wooden spoon, force cottage cheese through a strainer. Cream the cream cheese, add the cottage cheese, and gradually beat in the 1 cup sugar mixed with flour. Add the eggs, one at a time, beating until smooth after each addition. Mix in cream, salt, vanilla and beat until blended. Turn into crumb-lined pan and bake at 325° for 1 hour or until knife inserted in center comes out clean.

May be served with a fresh fruit garnish, such as sliced peaches or strawberries.

YIELD: 6–8 SERVINGS

THE JUNIOR LEAGUE OF BOISE, IDAHO

Chocolate Mousse Cake

9 eggs, separated
⅔ cup sugar
3 4-ounce packages German chocolate
3 1-ounce squares unsweetened chocolate
2 tablespoons water
1½ teaspoons vanilla
4 cups heavy cream
3 dozen ladyfingers

Cream egg yolks and sugar. Melt German chocolate and unsweetened chocolate over hot water. Stir in the water and vanilla. Mixture will become thick. Beat into egg yolk and sugar mixture. Beat egg whites and fold in beaten egg whites; whip 1 cup of the cream and fold in.

Grease a 10-inch spring-form pan. Whip remaining cream until thick. Line the pan with ladyfingers on bottom and sides. Pour half the chocolate mixture into the pan and top with half the whipped cream. Make a layer of ladyfingers, pour remainder of chocolate mixture on top of ladyfingers, and add a final layer of the remaining whipped cream.

Chill in refrigerator for several hours—preferably overnight.

YIELD: 10–12 SERVINGS

THE JUNIOR LEAGUE OF SAN DIEGO, CALIFORNIA

Children's Favorite Devil's Food Cake

1 cup sugar
3 squares semisweet chocolate
2 egg yolks
¼ cup milk
1 tablespoon baking soda
1 cup sugar minus 2 tablespoons
¾ cup butter minus 1 teaspoon
2 egg yolks
2 cups sifted cake flour
1¼ cups plus 3 tablespoons milk
1 teaspoon vanilla
3 egg whites

In a saucepan combine 1 cup sugar, chocolate, 2 egg yolks, and ¼ cup milk. Cook over low heat, stirring constantly, until mixture is smooth. Remove from stove and stir in soda. Set aside to cool.

Cream 1 cup minus 2 tablespoons sugar, butter, and 2 egg yolks. Add alternately the sifted flour and milk. Add vanilla and custard mixture; mix well. Fold in egg whites beaten stiff but not dry. Pour into two 9 x 9-inch pans. Bake at 375° for 30 minutes.

Fill and frost with favorite frosting.

YIELD: 18 SERVINGS

From an Adobe Oven . . . to a Microwave Range
THE JUNIOR LEAGUE OF PUEBLO, COLORADO

· ·

Forgotten Cake

5 egg whites
¼ teaspoon salt
½ teaspoon cream of tartar
½ teaspoon vanilla
1½ cups sugar
1 pint heavy cream, whipped
1 pint peach yogurt*
6–8 peaches, sliced*

Preheat oven to 400°. Beat egg whites until foamy; add salt, cream of tartar, and vanilla and beat until stiff. Gradually add sugar, beating constantly, and beat 5 more minutes, or until stiff and dry. Spread in buttered 8 x 12-inch glass baking pan. Place in oven and turn off heat. Leave in oven 8 hours or overnight.

For the filling, mix whipped cream and yogurt. Cover meringue with sliced peaches; cover peaches with filling and add more peaches for decoration. Cover with plastic wrap and refrigerate for at least 8 hours.

* May use other fresh fruit in season; use that flavor of yogurt.

THE JUNIOR LEAGUE OF RIVERSIDE, CALIFORNIA

Creamy Italian Cake

½ cup butter
½ cup shortening
2 cups sugar
5 egg yolks
2 cups sifted flour
1 teaspoon baking soda
1 cup buttermilk
1 teaspoon vanilla
1 cup coconut
1 cup chopped walnuts
5 egg whites, stiffly beaten

CREAM CHEESE FILLING:
12 ounces cream cheese, softened
¼ cup butter
1 1-pound box confectioners' sugar
1 teaspoon vanilla
½ cup chopped walnuts

Cream butter and shortening with sugar until mixture is smooth. Add egg yolks and beat well. Combine the sifted flour with the soda and add to creamed mixture alternately with the buttermilk. Stir in vanilla, coconut, and walnuts. Fold in beaten egg whites. Pour into 3 8-inch pans lined with wax paper, greased, and lightly floured.

Bake at 350° for 25 minutes, or until layers test done. Cool before filling or frosting cake.

Beat cream cheese and butter until smooth. Add sugar to taste, approximately three-quarters of the box so that the filling will not be too sweet. Add vanilla and beat until smooth. Put layers together with filling and sprinkle top of cake with the nuts.

YIELD: 1 8-INCH 3-LAYER CAKE

THE JUNIOR LEAGUE OF TACOMA, WASHINGTON

Lemon-Sour Cream Pound Cake

3 cups sifted flour
¼ teaspoon baking soda
2 sticks butter, softened
3 cups sugar
6 eggs
1 cup sour cream
1 tablespoon lemon juice
1 teaspoon grated lemon rind

Resift flour twice with soda. Cream butter and add sugar slowly, beating constantly to cream well. Add eggs one at a time, beating well after each addition. Stir in the sour cream. Add flour mixture ½ cup at a time, beating constantly. Stir in the lemon juice and rind.

Turn batter into a well-greased 10-inch tube pan. Bake at 350° for 1½ hours.

YIELD: 12 SERVINGS

No Regrets
THE JUNIOR LEAGUE OF PORTLAND, OREGON

· · · · · · · · · · · · · · ·

Orange Cake

1 cup butter
1 cup sugar
3 eggs, separated
2 cups flour
1 teaspoon baking powder
1 teaspoon baking soda
1 cup sour cream
Grated rind from 1 orange

Recipe continues . . .

TOPPING:
½ cup sugar
¼ cup orange juice
⅓ cup orange liqueur

Cream butter; add sugar and 3 egg yolks which have been beaten until light.

Sift flour with the baking powder and baking soda. Add to butter mixture, alternately with the sour cream. Add the orange rind.

Beat egg whites until stiff but not dry. Fold into batter. Pour into greased tube pan and bake at 350° for 50 minutes.

Combine topping ingredients and stir until sugar is dissolved. Spoon topping over hot cake while it is still in the pan. Remove from pan when cool.

YIELD: 1 LOAF

THE JUNIOR LEAGUE OF CALGARY, ALBERTA

· · · · · · · · · · · · · ·

Lemon Grove Cake

1 cup softened butter
2 cups sugar
3 eggs, at room temperature
3 cups sifted flour
½ teaspoon baking soda
½ teaspoon salt
1 cup buttermilk
2 tablespoons packed grated lemon rind
2 tablespoons fresh lemon juice

In a very large bowl cream the 1 cup butter until light, slowly add the sugar, and continue beating until mixture is light and fluffy. Blend in eggs one at a time.

In another bowl sift together the flour, soda, and salt. Add the flour mixture alternately with the buttermilk to the creamed mixture, beginning and ending with the flour and beating after each addition. Mix in the 2 tablespoons rind and 2 tablespoons juice.

Pour the batter into a greased and lightly floured 10-inch tube pan or 12-cup bundt pan. Bake in a preheated 325° oven for 65–75 minutes, or until a toothpick inserted in the center comes out clean. Place the pan on a rack to cool for 10 minutes. Turn the cake out on a rack and spread with as much Lemon Icing as the cake can absorb (about a third to half of the icing). Allow cake to cool completely, then frost with remaining icing.

YIELD: 12 SERVINGS

LEMON ICING:
¼ cup softened butter
2 cups sifted confectioners' sugar
1½ tablespoons grated lemon rind
¼ cup fresh lemon juice

To prepare icing, in a mixing bowl blend together thoroughly the butter and confectioners' sugar. Mix in the rind and the juice, one tablespoon at a time, until the frosting is the desired spreading consistency. If the entire amount of lemon juice is used, the icing will be thin and possibly a little difficult to spread evenly; however, a very tangy frosting greatly enhances the flavor of the cake.

The frosting may be chilled for a few minutes to make it easier to spread.

YIELD: 12 SERVINGS

The California Heritage Cookbook
THE JUNIOR LEAGUE OF PASADENA, CALIFORNIA

Golden State Prune Cake

¾ cup melted butter
1 cup sugar
½ cup buttermilk
1 teaspoon baking soda dissolved in buttermilk
1½ cups flour
½ teaspoon salt
3 eggs, beaten
1 teaspoon vanilla
1 cup puréed cooked prunes

FROSTING:
1½ cups light cream
½ cup butter
2 cups confectioners' sugar
¾ square unsweetened chocolate
1 teaspoon vanilla

Mix butter and sugar together. Combine buttermilk and soda and stir into butter mixture alternately with the flour. Stir in salt, eggs, and vanilla. Fold in prunes.

Bake in two 9-inch cake pans at 375° for 20–25 minutes.

In heavy saucepan, combine cream, butter, and sugar. Cook to the soft-ball stage (238°). Remove from heat, add the chocolate and stir until chocolate is melted. Let set until cold and beat to right consistency. (If too runny add more confectioners' sugar.) Beat in vanilla.

YIELD: 1 9-INCH LAYER CAKE

THE JUNIOR LEAGUE OF SACRAMENTO, CALIFORNIA

Huckleberry Walnut Cream Cake

1½ cups heavy cream
2 teaspoons vanilla
3 eggs
1½ cups flour
1½ cups sugar
2 teaspoons baking powder
¼ teaspoon salt
1 cup finely chopped walnuts
1 cup huckleberries, drained

Beat cream with vanilla until stiff. Beat eggs until thick in another bowl. Fold eggs into cream. Fold in the sifted dry ingredients. Fold in walnuts and huckleberries. Pour into two greased and floured (9-inch) layer cake pans.

Bake 30 minutes in preheated oven at 350°. Cool 10 minutes. Remove from pans. Cool completely. Fill and frost with Lemon Frosting.

YIELD: 12 SERVINGS

LEMON FROSTING:
1 cup butter
3 cups confectioners' sugar
2 tablespoons lemon juice
1 teaspoon lemon juice
1 teaspoon vanilla
4 egg yolks

Beat butter, sugar, juice, and vanilla. Beat in egg yolks one at a time. Frosting should be fluffy. Spread between layers and on top of cake.

Refrigerate until serving.

THE JUNIOR LEAGUE OF GREAT FALLS, MONTANA

Carrot Cake

1 ¾ cup sugar
1 cup oil
4 eggs
2 cups flour
2 teaspoons baking powder
2 teaspoons cinnamon
1 teaspoon salt
2 cups shredded carrot
1 cup chopped nuts
Crushed pineapple

Cream sugar and oil. Add eggs, one at a time, beating well after each addition. Sift dry ingredients and gradually stir into egg mixture. Fold in carrot and nuts.

Grease and flour three 9-inch layer pans. Divide batter into prepared pans and bake for 20 minutes at 375°. Cool on cake racks.

When cool, put layers together with crushed pineapple and frost with Cream Cheese Frosting.

YIELD: 1 9-INCH 3-LAYER CAKE

CREAM CHEESE FROSTING:
1 8-ounce package cream cheese
1 1-pound box confectioners' sugar
½ stick butter, softened
2 teaspoons vanilla

Combine all ingredients and mix to a frothy consistency.

THE JUNIOR LEAGUE OF BILLINGS, MONTANA

· · · · · · · · · · · · · ·

Lemon Schaum Torte

5 egg whites
¼ teaspoon cream of tartar
¼ teaspoon salt
1½ cups fine sugar
1½ teaspoons vanilla
6 egg yolks
1 cup sugar
⅛ teaspoon salt
Juice of 2 lemons
2 teaspoons grated lemon rind
2 tablespoons butter
1 cup heavy cream, whipped

Beat egg whites until stiff; add cream of tartar and salt. Beat in the 1½ cups sugar, a little at a time. Stir in vanilla. Spread in well-greased 8 x 12-inch pan. Preheat oven to 425° for 20 minutes. Put pan in oven, *shut off heat* immediately; *do not open oven* for 10 hours or overnight.

For filling, beat egg yolks with 1 cup sugar, salt, lemon juice, lemon rind and butter. Cook over simmering water until very thick. Cool. Fold in whipped cream. Spread over torte. Refrigerate for 12 hours.

Can be frozen. Great to make ahead for bridge club.

YIELD: 15 SERVINGS

From an Adobe Oven . . . to a Microwave Range
THE JUNIOR LEAGUE OF PUEBLO, COLORADO

Hottenholler Whiskey Cake

½ cup butter
1 cup sugar
3 beaten eggs
1 cup flour
½ teaspoon baking powder
¼ teaspoon salt
½ teaspoon nutmeg
¼ cup milk
¼ teaspoon baking soda
½ cup molasses
1 pound seedless raisins
2 cups chopped pecans
¼ cup bourbon

Cream butter with sugar; add beaten eggs. Mix together flour, baking powder, salt, and nutmeg; add to butter mixture. Add milk. Next mix soda into molasses and add to batter. Stir in raisins, nuts, and whiskey. Pour into greased, floured loaf pan and bake for 2 hours at 275°.

Let cool a few minutes. Then turn out on cake rack to cool completely.

From an Adobe Oven . . . to a Microwave Range
THE JUNIOR LEAGUE OF PUEBLO, COLORADO

Apricot Jam Strudel

This is an excellent shortcut method of making "puff"-type pastry, and once you have made it you will want to substitute it in recipes calling for the more traditional method of making flaky, layered pastry.

½ *pound butter*
½ *teaspoon salt*
2 cups flour
1 cup sour cream
1¼ cups apricot jam (other flavors may be used but apricot is best)
1 cup shredded coconut
⅔ *cup chopped walnuts or almonds*
Confectioners' sugar

Mix butter, salt, and flour as you would for pie crust, cutting butter into dry ingredients until it forms fine crumbs. Mix in sour cream and refrigerate overnight.

Next morning remove and let stand until dough is room temperature. Cut dough in half and roll each piece into a rectangle 10 x 15 inches. Spread with jam, coconut, and nuts. Roll like a jelly roll and place on greased cookie sheet. Bake at 350° for 1 hour.

Remove from oven and let cool for 5–10 minutes. Cut in slices, sprinkle with sugar, and serve.

Nice for a morning coffee but rich enough for dessert.

YIELD: 18 PIECES

THE JUNIOR LEAGUE OF TACOMA, WASHINGTON

Soufflé Dessert Crepes

BATTER FOR 16 CREPES:
2 cups flour
1 teaspoon salt
2 eggs, beaten
3 cups milk
Butter

Recipe continues . . .

Sift flour into mixing bowl and add salt. Make a well in flour mixture and pour in eggs. Add milk gradually. Stir from center out. (This may also be done by putting all ingredients in a blender.)

Heat 6-inch crepe pan over medium heat, brush with butter, and pour in about 2 tablespoons of the batter. Swirl pan to coat bottom evenly. Turn crepe when edges are brown to lightly brown other side. Stack with wax paper between.

This recipe makes more than the 16 crepes needed, but they freeze well.

When needed, separate the crepes and place them underside up on wax paper. Spread about a tablespoon of Meringue Filling on one half of each crepe. Lightly fold crepes into quarters. Arrange crepes side by side in a greased 8 x 11-inch baking dish. Bake at 400° for about 10 minutes.

Serve at once, spooning a tablespoonful of Warm Lemon Sauce over each serving.

YIELD: 8 SERVINGS (2 CREPES EACH)

MERINGUE FILLING:
2 egg whites
½ cup sugar
2 teaspoons grated lemon peel

Beat egg whites until frothy. Gradually add the sugar, beating until stiff. Fold in the lemon peel.

WARM LEMON SAUCE:
¼ cup sugar
1 teaspoon cornstarch
½ cup water
2 egg yolks, beaten
Juice of 1 lemon
½ teaspoon lemon peel

Combine the sugar and cornstarch in top of double saucepan. Stir in water, egg yolks, lemon juice, and lemon peel. Cook over hot, not boiling water, stirring often until sauce is smooth and thickened. Keep warm over hot water.

THE JUNIOR LEAGUE OF SAN DIEGO, CALIFORNIA

· ·

Upside-Down Apple Pie

1 tablespoon butter

4 tablespoons brown sugar

8 pecan halves

Pastry for 2-crust pie

6 large baking apples, peeled and sliced

1 tablespoon lemon juice

1 cup sugar

1 teaspoon cinnamon

¼ teaspoon nutmeg

3 tablespoons flour

1 tablespoon butter

Line a 9-inch pie plate with aluminum foil, turning down foil on the edges. Rub bottom with butter and spread evenly with brown sugar. Arrange pecan halves on top in pinwheel design, flat side up. Top with half the pastry, trimming along the outside edge to fit.

In large bowl, combine sliced apples and lemon juice, stirring to coat. Add sugar, cinnamon, nutmeg, and flour. Empty into bottom crust. Dot with butter. Cover with top pastry; trim and flute. Do not prick. Turn up foil edges to catch the brown sugar syrup during baking.

Bake for 1¼ hours at 375°, or until juices are bubbling all around the pie and crust is browned. Remove from oven. Cool 10 minutes. Invert into another 9-inch pie plate. Immediately peel off foil.

Serve warm or chilled.

YIELD: 8 SERVINGS

THE JUNIOR LEAGUE OF SAN DIEGO, CALIFORNIA

· ·

Merry Berry Pie

3 ounces cream cheese
2 tablespoons milk
1 baked 9-inch pie shell
2 pints fresh strawberries
1 10-ounce box frozen strawberries, thawed
1 cup sugar
3 tablespoons cornstarch
⅓ cup water
1 cup heavy cream, whipped

Mix cream cheese with milk until smooth; spread over bottom of pie crust. Arrange washed and hulled fresh strawberries on cheese. Purée frozen berries in blender. Bring purée to a boil and stir in sugar until dissolved. Blend cornstarch with water and add to strawberry mixture. Cook over low heat, stirring occasionally, until thickened. Watch carefully to prevent scorching. Cool and pour over berries. Chill thoroughly.

Top with whipped cream, sweetened to taste, before serving.

YIELD: 6–8 SERVINGS

From an Adobe Oven . . . to a Microwave Range
THE JUNIOR LEAGUE OF PUEBLO, COLORADO

· ·

French Silk Pie

CRUST:
1¼ cups graham cracker crumbs
2 tablespoons sugar
¼ cup melted butter

FILLING:
¼ pound butter, softened
¾ cup sugar
2 teaspoons vanilla
2 squares unsweetened chocolate, melted
2 eggs

TOPPING:
Sweetened whipped cream
Chopped nuts
Grated semisweet chocolate

Combine cracker crumbs, sugar, and butter. Mix well and press into bottom and sides of pie plate. Bake at 400° for 8 minutes. Chill.

To prepare filling, cream butter, sugar, vanilla, and melted chocolate. Add eggs one at a time, beating for 5 minutes at high speed after each. This is important! Pour into crust and refrigerate overnight.

Before serving spread with whipped cream and sprinkle with nuts and chocolate.

YIELD: 6–8 SERVINGS

From an Adobe Oven . . . to a Microwave Range
THE JUNIOR LEAGUE OF PUEBLO, COLORADO

· · · · · · · · · · · · · · · · · · ·

Scrumptious Mocha Pie

CRUST:
18 chocolate cream-filled sandwich cookies
⅓ cup butter, melted

Recipe continues . . .

FILLING:
1 quart coffee ice cream
2 squares unsweetened chocolate
½ cup sugar
1 tablespoon butter
1 5½–6-ounce can evaporated milk or ¾ cup heavy cream

TOPPING:
1 ounce Kahlua liqueur
1 cup heavy cream, whipped
Sugar to taste
½ cup chopped nuts

Crush cookies to fine crumbs. Add melted butter. Mix well. Press around sides and bottom of 9-inch pan. Chill.

Fill pie shell with coffee ice cream. Freeze.

Melt chocolate over hot water and stir in sugar and butter. Slowly add evaporated milk or cream. Cook over hot water until smooth. Chill.

Spread chocolate mixture over top of ice cream.

Add Kahlua to whipped cream; sweeten with sugar to taste. Spread over pie and sprinkle top with chopped nuts. Freeze.

YIELD: 8 SERVINGS

No Regrets
THE JUNIOR LEAGUE OF PORTLAND, OREGON

· · · · · · · · · · · · · · · ·

Ice Cream Meringue Pie

1 pint chocolate ice cream, softened
1 baked 9-inch pastry shell, cooled
1 pint strawberry ice cream, softened

MERINGUE:
4 egg whites
½ teaspoon vanilla
¼ teaspoon cream of tartar
½ cup sugar

Spread chocolate ice cream in baked pie shell; cover with layer of straw-berry ice cream. Place in freezer.

To prepare meringue, beat egg whites with vanilla and cream of tartar. Gradually add sugar, beating until stiff and glossy. Spread over ice cream, carefully sealing to edge of pastry. Bake in 475° oven for 2–3 minutes, or until lightly browned. Freeze several hours or overnight.

To serve, cut in wedges and drizzle with Chocolate Sauce.

CHOCOLATE SAUCE:
4 squares unsweetened chocolate
¾ cup water
1 cup sugar
6 tablespoons butter
1 teaspoon vanilla

Heat chocolate and water in saucepan. Stir constantly over low heat until smooth. Stir in sugar; simmer for about 5 minutes, or until slightly thick-ened. Remove from heat. Stir in butter and vanilla.

YIELD: 6–8 SERVINGS

From an Adobe Oven . . . to a Microwave Range
THE JUNIOR LEAGUE OF PUEBLO, COLORADO

Jamaica Rum Pie

CRUST:

1 cup graham cracker crumbs
4 tablespoons melted butter
3 tablespoons sugar

FILLING:

1 tablespoon unflavored gelatin
½ cup water
3 eggs, separated
1 cup sugar
½ cup Jamaica rum
1 pint heavy cream
1 square unsweetened chocolate, grated

Mix crust ingredients and press onto bottom and sides of a 9-inch pie plate.

Soak gelatin in the water, then stir over low heat until thoroughly dissolved.

Beat egg whites until stiff. Beat in ⅓ cup of the sugar and one-third of the dissolved gelatin.

In another bowl beat egg yolks with ⅓ cup of the sugar, one-third of the gelatin, and the rum. Fold into the whipped egg whites.

Whip the cream until stiff with remaining ⅓ cup sugar and one-third of the gelatin and fold half into combined mixture. Pour into pie shell.

Top with the remaining whipped cream and sprinkle with grated chocolate.

Chill for 2 hours.

YIELD: 8 SERVINGS

THE JUNIOR LEAGUE OF TUCSON, ARIZONA

Pecan Pie

1 cup white corn syrup
½ cup sugar
3 eggs
1 cup broken pecans
1 teaspoon vanilla
Pinch salt
4 tablespoons melted butter
1 8-inch unbaked pastry shell

Mix all ingredients and pour into unbaked pie shell. Bake at 350° for about 45 minutes, or until firm.

YIELD: 1 8-INCH PIE

THE JUNIOR LEAGUE OF BILLINGS, MONTANA

· ·

Pike's Peak Spiked Apple Crisp

5 cups peeled, sliced apples (Pippin, Jonathan, or Winesap)
½ teaspoon cinnamon sugar
1 teaspoon grated lemon rind
1 teaspoon grated orange rind
1 jigger Grand Marnier
1 jigger Amaretto di Saronno
¾ cup granulated sugar
¼ cup packed light brown sugar
¾ cup sifted flour
¼ teaspoon salt
½ cup butter or margarine
Heavy cream, whipped cream, or ice cream for topping

Recipe continues . . .

Arrange apple slices in greased 2-quart round casserole. Sprinkle cinamon, lemon, and orange rinds and both liqueurs on top of apples. In a separate bowl, mix sugars, flour, salt, and butter with a pastry blender until crumbly. Sprinkle mixture over top of apples. Bake, uncovered, at 350° until apples are tender and top is lightly browned, approximately 1 hour.

Serve warm with cream, whipped cream, or with vanilla or cinnamon ice cream.

YIELD: 8 SERVINGS

Colorado Cache
THE JUNIOR LEAGUE OF DENVER, COLORADO

· · · · · · · · · · · ·

Pear Crumble Pie

5–6 cups sliced pears (about 8)
½ cup sugar
1 teaspoon grated lemon peel
3 tablespoons lemon juice
1 9-inch unbaked pastry shell

TOPPING:
½ cup flour
½ cup sugar
½ teaspoon ground ginger
½ teaspoon ground cinnamon
¼ teaspoon ground mace
⅓ cup butter
½ cup heavy cream, whipped and flavored with
powdered sugar, vanilla, or almond extract

Peel, core, and slice pears. Toss with ½ cup sugar, lemon peel, and lemon juice. Arrange in unbaked pastry shell.

For the topping combine flour, sugar, ginger, cinnamon, and mace. Cut in butter until crumbly. Sprinkle mixture over pears. Bake at 400° for 45 minutes or until fruit is tender.

Serve warm with flavored whipped cream.

YIELD: 6–8 SERVINGS

Colorado Cache
THE JUNIOR LEAGUE OF DENVER, COLORADO

· ·

Pecan Tassies

3 ounces cream cheese
½ cup butter
1 cup flour

FILLING:
1 egg, beaten
¾ cup brown sugar
1 tablespoon soft butter
⅔ cup chopped pecans

Cream cheese and butter. Stir flour into cheese mixture. Shape into 24 1-inch balls. Put into tiny tins and press onto bottom and sides.

Mix egg, sugar, and butter for filling. Put a few nuts in the bottom of each lined tin. Add filling and put a few more nuts on top.

Bake at 325° for 25 minutes.

YIELD: 24 TASSIES

THE JUNIOR LEAGUE OF BILLINGS, MONTANA

· ·

Basic Cookie Mix

9 cups flour
3 cups instant milk
3 tablespoons baking powder
1 tablespoon salt
4 cups shortening
4 cups sugar

Mix flour, instant milk, baking powder, and salt. Sift and set aside. Cream shortening in large bowl. Gradually add sugar and continue mixing until light and fluffy. Gradually blend in flour mixture. Blend thoroughly to a coarse corn meal consistency.

Store in large canister at room temperature. Keeps for several weeks.

CHOCOLATE DROPS:
2 cups basic cookie mix
3 tablespoons cocoa
1 egg
2 tablespoons water
1 teaspoon vanilla
½ cup chopped nuts (optional)

Mix all ingredients and drop by teaspoonfuls on cookie sheet. Bake at 375° for 10–14 minutes.

YIELD: 3 DOZEN COOKIES

PEANUT BUTTER COOKIES:
4 cups basic cookie mix
½ cup firmly packed brown sugar
1 cup peanut butter
1 egg
1½ teaspoons vanilla
1 tablespoon water

Mix all ingredients. Make small balls of dough. Flatten with fork on cookie sheet. Bake at 375° for 10–12 minutes.

YIELD: 3 DOZEN COOKIES

CHOCOLATE CHIP COOKIES:
4 cups basic cookie mix
1 egg
2 tablespoons water
¼ cup firmly packed brown sugar
1½ teaspoons vanilla
1 6-ounce package semisweet chocolate chips
1 cup chopped nuts

Blend all ingredients, adding chocolate chips and nuts last. Drop by tea-spoonfuls on cookie sheet. Bake at 375° for 10–13 minutes.

YIELD: 3 DOZEN COOKIES

OATMEAL COOKIES:
1 cup raisins
2 cups basic cookie mix
1 cup rolled oats
2 tablespoons firmly packed brown sugar
1 egg
1½ teaspoons vanilla
½ teaspoon cinnamon
½ teaspoon allspice
½ cup nuts, chopped

Cover raisins with water. Simmer 5 minutes. Drain raisins, reserving ½ cup of the liquid. Set aside raisins. Combine raisin water, mix, rolled oats, brown sugar, egg, vanilla, cinnamon, and allspice. Stir in chopped nuts and drained raisins. Bake at 375° for 13–15 minutes.

YIELD: 4½ DOZEN COOKIES

Try It, You'll Like It
THE JUNIOR LEAGUE OF OGDEN, UTAH
Heritage Cookbook
THE JUNIOR LEAGUE OF SALT LAKE CITY, UTAH

Lemon Bars

CRUST:
1 cup butter
½ cup confectioners' sugar
½ teaspoon salt
2 cups flour

FILLING:
4 eggs, slightly beaten
2 cups sugar
½ teaspoon baking powder
¼ cup flour
¼ cup lemon juice
rind of 1 lemon, grated

Cream butter and sugar. Add salt and flour and mix well. Pat into a 9 x 13-inch greased baking pan. Bake at 350° for 15–20 minutes.

To make filling, mix all ingredients and pour over hot crust. Bake at 350° for 20–25 minutes. When done, sprinkle with confectioners' sugar. Cut into bars when cool.

YIELD: 16 BARS

Heritage Cookbook
THE JUNIOR LEAGUE OF SALT LAKE CITY, UTAH

Lacy Walnut Cups

3 tablespoons butter
¼ cup firmly packed brown sugar
2 tablespoons light corn syrup
Finely chopped walnuts
⅓ cup sifted flour
¼ teaspoon cinnamon
¼ teaspoon salt
Vanilla or coffee ice cream
Fudge or butterscotch sundae sauce

In saucepan melt butter; stir in sugar and corn syrup. Add ¼ cup very finely chopped walnuts, flour, cinnamon, and salt. Mix well.

Bake one cup at a time. Drop a rounded tablespoon of the batter onto lightly greased baking sheet and flatten with back of spoon to a 3-inch circle. Bake at 375° about 7 minutes, or until evenly browned. Remove from oven and let stand on baking sheet 1–1½ minutes, until edges are firm enough to lift with spatula. Mold over an inverted custard cup and let cool. Repeat with remaining batter.

Fill cooled cups with ice cream, top with sundae sauce, and sprinkle with more nuts.

YIELD: 6 SERVINGS

THE JUNIOR LEAGUE OF LOS ANGELES, CALIFORNIA

· · · · · · · · · · · · · · · · · · ·

Barbecued Banana Split

1 banana per serving
Peanut butter
Chocolate bits or milk chocolate
Miniature marshmallows

Recipe continues . . .

For each person to be served, peel back one section of the skin of a banana. Spread with peanut butter. Add chocolate and marshmallows. Replace the skin and wrap the banana in foil. Place the packages on the grill over the glowing embers. Cook for 10 minutes, turning frequently.

YIELD: 1 SERVING

Colorado Cache
THE JUNIOR LEAGUE OF DENVER, COLORADO

Himalayan Blackberry Cobbler

¾ cup sugar
1 tablespoon cornstarch
¾ cup water
5 cups cleaned, gently washed Himalayan blackberries
1 tablespoon butter
Heavy cream

DOUGH:
1 cup flour
1 tablespoon sugar
1½ teaspoons baking powder
½ teaspoon salt
¼ cup shortening
½ cup plus 1 tablespoon milk

Mix the sugar, cornstarch, and water and stir into the blackberries. Pour into a 1½-quart casserole. Dot with 1 tablespoon butter and bake in a 400° oven for 20 minutes, or until juice of the berries comes to a boil.

Meanwhile, prepare a soft biscuit dough: Sift the dry ingredients together into a mixing bowl and cut in the shortening until it forms fine crumbs. Stir in the milk. Drop the dough in spoonfuls over the hot fruit. Bake for about 30 minutes longer.

Serve in bowls with cream.

YIELD: 6 SERVINGS

THE JUNIOR LEAGUE OF TACOMA, WASHINGTON

Peach Cottage Pudding

1½ cups sliced fresh peaches
½ cup sugar
¼ cup water
Dash nutmeg
1 teaspoon lemon juice
1 egg
½ cup sugar
1 tablespoon oil
1 tablespoon milk
½ cup flour
½ teaspoon baking powder
¼ teaspoon salt

Bring to boil fresh peaches, ½ cup sugar, water, nutmeg, and lemon juice. Set aside.

Beat egg, ½ cup sugar, and oil until light and fluffy. Add milk, flour, baking powder, and salt.

Spread batter in greased 8 x 8-inch dish. Pour *hot* peaches on top. Bake 25 minutes at 375°.

Serve with cream or ice cream.

YIELD: 6 SERVINGS

THE JUNIOR LEAGUE OF TUCSON, ARIZONA

Caramelized Pears

6–8 firm green pears
1 cup sugar
½ cup butter, cut in pieces
1 cup heavy cream

Peel and quarter pears. Sprinkle with sugar and butter. Bake 45 minutes at 450° basting frequently. Add cream; stir, then bake 5 minutes longer. Pears should be caramelized; if not, bake longer.

This is especially good served over ice cream. Make sure it cools some before serving, about 10–15 minutes.

YIELD: 6–8 SERVINGS

THE JUNIOR LEAGUE OF LOS ANGELES, CALIFORNIA

Chocolate Pears

4 pears
1 cup sugar
1 cup water
4 tablespoons butter

Pare, half, and core pears. Cook slowly for 20 minutes in the sugar mixed with the water. Set aside.

When ready to serve, drain pears and cook in the 4 tablespoons butter until lightly brown. Serve warm, topped with Chocolate Sauce.

YIELD: 8 SERVINGS

CHOCOLATE SAUCE:
¼ cup butter
1 square bitter chocolate, grated
¼ cup cocoa
¾ cup sugar
½ cup light cream
1 teaspoon vanilla
Pinch salt

Bring all ingredients slowly to a boil, stirring frequently.

THE JUNIOR LEAGUE OF TUCSON, ARIZONA

. . . .

Poached Pears Zabaglione

8 firm ripe pears, peeled and cored
Lemon juice
3 cups white wine
1–2 cups sugar, (depending on sweetness of wine)
2 inches stick cinnamon
4 whole cloves
Ground nutmeg
Grated lemon rind for garnish

Place peeled whole pears in water acidulated with a little lemon juice to prevent discoloration. Meanwhile make a syrup of wine, sugar, 1 tablespoon lemon juice, and spices. Simmer pears in the syrup for 15 minutes, or until tender. Remove pears; chill until ready to serve. They may be prepared a day or two in advance.

To serve, place a poached pear in a sherbet glass and pour warm Zabaglione Sauce over it. Sprinkle with grated lemon rind.

Recipe continues . . .

ZABAGLIONE SAUCE:
4 egg yolks and 1 whole egg
¾ cup sugar
½ cup Marsala or Amaretto

In a saucepan over simmering water, whisk eggs with sugar for about 10 minutes, until light and creamy. Slowly whisk in the wine as the mixture thickens.

YIELD: 8 SERVINGS

THE JUNIOR LEAGUE OF EDMONTON, ALBERTA

. . . .

Oranges Portuguese Style

4 navel oranges
½ cup snipped dates
1 tablespoon sugar
1 jigger Curaçao
1 jigger cognac
½ cup orange juice

Peel and slice oranges into paper-thin slices. Arrange in an overlapping ring on a glass plate. Sprinkle with dates, sugar, liquors, and orange juice. *Chill* well.

YIELD: 4 SERVINGS

THE JUNIOR LEAGUE OF TUCSON, ARIZONA

. . . .

Raspberry Boccone Dolce

3 cups heavy cream
⅓ cup confectioners' sugar
4 egg whites at room temperature
Pinch salt
¼ teaspoon cream of tartar
1 cup sugar
6 ounces semisweet chocolate chips
3 tablespoons water
2 10-ounce packages frozen raspberries, thawed and well drained
or 1 quart fresh strawberries, sliced, reserving some
whole ones for garnish

The night before serving, whip cream until stiff. Gradually add ⅓ cup confectioners' sugar and beat until quite stiff. Line a strainer or colander with a double layer of damp cheesecloth. Pour whipped cream into strainer placed over a bowl. Cover and refrigerate overnight. This drains liquid which usually accumulates when whipped cream stands.

Beat egg whites until frothy. Add salt and cream of tartar, beating until stiff. Gradually add 1 cup sugar, continuing to beat until the meringue is stiff and glossy. Line cookie sheets with oiled brown paper and trace three circles, each 8 or 9 inches in diameter. Spread the meringue evenly over the circles and bake at 250° for 35–50 minutes, or until the meringues are pale gold and still pliable. Remove from the oven and carefully peel the paper from the bottom. Place on cake racks to dry. The meringues may be made the night before.

Two hours before serving, melt the chocolate bits with water over hot water. To assemble, place a meringue layer on serving plate and spread with a thin coating of melted chocolate. Then spread a layer about ¾-inch thick of the whipped cream and top this with a layer of berries. Put a second layer of meringue on top; spread with chocolate, whipped cream, and berries, then top with third layer of meringue. Frost sides and top smoothly with remaining whipped cream. Decorate top with melted chocolate, whole berries, or rosettes of whipped cream. Refrigerate.

Recipe continues . . .

If whipped cream and meringues are prepared the night before, assemble the day of use. However, the dessert may all be made the same day it will be used—omit the straining of the whipped cream.

YIELD: 8–10 SERVINGS

Colorado Cache
THE JUNIOR LEAGUE OF DENVER, COLORADO

· · · · · · · · · · · · · · · ·

Strawberry Surprise

2 cantalopes
1 envelope unflavored gelatin
5 tablespoons cold water
1 cup heavy cream
2 tablespoons sugar
1 tablespoon vanilla
1 pint strawberries, sliced

Cut 1½ inches off stem end of cantalopes. Scrape out seeds, drain stem end down.

Soften gelatin in cold water and stir over hot water until thoroughly dissolved. Whip cream with the sugar and vanilla. Stir into dissolved gelatin.

Fold strawberries into cream mixture. Spoon into cantalope and chill for at least 3 hours. Slice and serve.

YIELD: 8–12 SERVINGS

THE JUNIOR LEAGUE OF BILLINGS, MONTANA

· · · · · · · · · · · · · · · ·

Grand Marnier Soufflé Glacé

8 egg yolks
1 cup fine granulated sugar
6 tablespoons Grand Marnier
1 quart heavy cream
Flaked chocolate for garnish

Beat the egg yolks until creamy thick; add the sugar very slowly in small amounts, beating constantly. Stir in the Grand Marnier. Whip the cream. Fold into the Grand Marnier mixture.

Make a foil collar extending 2 inches above a 2-quart soufflé dish. Pour in soufflé mixture and freeze until firm. Mixture should be at least 1 inch higher than rim of dish.

Cover top with transparent wrap and freeze for 24 hours before serving.

To serve, remove foil collar and sprinkle powdered or flaked German sweet chocolate over top.

YIELD: 12–16 SERVINGS

THE JUNIOR LEAGUE OF SAN DIEGO, CALIFORNIA

· · · · · · · · · · · · · · ·

Soufflé au Citron Vert

Sweet butter and granulated sugar
Juice and rind of 2 large limes
4 large egg yolks
6 tablespoons superfine sugar
6–8 large egg whites
Confectioners' sugar

Butter sides and bottom of an 8- or 9-cup soufflé dish or individual dishes, and sprinkle lightly with sugar.

Recipe continues . . .

Grate rind of limes, then cut limes in half and squeeze juice into same bowl with the rind. Beat egg yolks with superfine sugar until lemony in color. Beat egg whites until stiff. Add lime juice and rind to yolk mixture and beat to combine. Fold in one-quarter of the whites until well incorporated. Then fold in remaining whites gently. Do not worry about all the lumps of egg white; they are needed to help soufflé rise.

Preheat oven to 400°. Pour mixture into soufflé dish or dishes and bake; for a large soufflé, 12 minutes; for individual soufflés, 6–7 minutes, or until puffed and top is lightly browned. Remove from oven and sprinkle with confectioners' sugar. Serve at once.

Optional: Pass separately a sauce of whipped soft vanilla ice cream.

YIELD: 6 SERVINGS

THE JUNIOR LEAGUE OF LOS ANGELES, CALIFORNIA

· · · · · · · · · · · · · · · · · · · ·

Coffee Mousse

2 tablespoons powdered coffee
⅓ cup boiling water
1 envelope unflavored gelatin
3 eggs, separated
½ cup confectioners' sugar
Pinch salt
1 cup heavy cream
1 meringue or crumb shell
Whipped cream for garnish
Toasted almonds for garnish
Shaved chocolate for garnish

Dissolve coffee in boiling water. Sprinkle with gelatin. Stir until dissolved.

In a bowl beat yolks with sugar until light in color. Stir in coffee mixture. Chill for 2–3 minutes, or until slightly thickened.

Beat egg whites with salt until stiff. Beat heavy cream until stiff. Fold whites and cream into coffee mixture. Spoon mousse into shell and garnish with whipped cream, toasted almonds, and shaved chocolate. Refrigerate.

YIELD: 6 SERVINGS

THE JUNIOR LEAGUE OF BILLINGS, MONTANA

Strawberry Fluff

¼ cup sugar
¼ teaspoon salt
1 tablespoon cornstarch
¼ cup white crème de cacao
1 pint fresh strawberries, hulled and sliced
1 cup heavy cream
Whole fresh strawberries for garnish

In saucepan, blend sugar, salt, cornstarch, and crème de cacao. Add sliced strawberries. Slowly stir to the boil and boil for 1 minute. Chill.

Whip cream until stiff and fold into strawberry mixture. Spoon into six dessert bowls.

Garnish with whole strawberries. Serve with ladyfingers.

YIELD: 6 SERVINGS

THE JUNIOR LEAGUE OF SAN DIEGO, CALIFORNIA

Mexican Rice Pudding

2 cups raw rice
4 cups water
1 cinnamon stick
2 cups sugar
1½ quarts milk
½ stick butter
1½ teaspoons vanilla
Powdered cinnamon

Boil the rice with the water and cinnamon stick for about 30 minutes, or until the water has been absorbed. Stir in sugar and milk. Cook for another 30 minutes, or until about half the milk is absorbed. Remove from heat.

Butter an oblong serving dish with some of the butter. Add remaining butter and vanilla to the rice. Stir to mix, empty into dish and sprinkle surface of pudding with cinnamon.

YIELD: 6–8 SERVINGS

Que Sabroso!
THE JUNIOR LEAGUE OF MEXICO CITY, MEXICO

· · · · · · · · · · · · · · · · · · ·

Old-Fashioned Mexican "Flan"

2 whole eggs
5 egg yolks
2 cups milk
1 13-ounce can sweetened condensed milk
1 teaspoon vanilla
1 cup sugar

Combine whole eggs, egg yolks, milks, and vanilla. Measure sugar into a 6-cup metal pan or mold, set directly over medium heat and stir constantly, with a wooden spoon, until sugar is melted and light caramel in color. Be careful not to overcook or sugar will burn.

Pour custard mixture into prepared mold. Set mold in a large shallow baking dish containing an inch or two of water. Bake at 350° for 45 minutes to an hour. Cool, then chill.

To serve, invert custard onto chilled serving plate. Sugar will be a sauce on top.

YIELD: 6 SERVINGS

> *Que Sabroso!*
> THE JUNIOR LEAGUE OF MEXICO CITY, MEXICO

· ·

Crème Brûlée

1 quart heavy cream
3 tablespoons sugar
8 egg yolks
3 teaspoons vanilla
About ½–¾ pound soft light brown sugar

Heat cream until hot but not boiling. Remove from heat and stir in sugar. In mixing bowl beat egg yolks until well blended. Gradually beat the hot cream into the egg yolks. Stir in vanilla. Pour into 9 x 13-inch baking dish and place in larger pan containing ½ inch hot water. Bake at 325° for 1 hour or until cream is set.

Sprinkle brown sugar evenly on top of custard. Broil 4 inches below heat for 2–3 minutes, or until sugar is glazed and melted (do not burn— watch carefully).

Refrigerate until very cold. This recipe may be made day before or early in the morning.

YIELD: 8–10 SERVINGS

> *Epicure*
> THE JUNIOR LEAGUE OF NEWPORT HARBOR, CALIFORNIA

· ·

Russian Cream

1 envelope unflavored gelatin
1 cup sugar
1 cup boiling water
1 cup heavy cream
½ cup plain yogurt
½ cup sour cream
1½ teaspoons vanilla
Fresh berries

Mix gelatin with sugar; add boiling water. Stir until sugar is dissolved. Stir in heavy cream and chill for 30 minutes. Mixture should become slightly thickened.

Remove from refrigerator. Add sour cream, yogurt, and vanilla. Mix with electric beater at low speed. Pour into glasses or serving bowl. Refrigerate another 2 hours.

Serve with fresh raspberries or strawberries on top.

YIELD: 6–8 SERVINGS

THE JUNIOR LEAGUE OF BILLINGS, MONTANA

. . . .

Bombe à la Lorraine

Chocolate or coffee ice cream
6 tablespoons butter
1⅓ cups sugar
2 eggs
2 egg yolks
Grated rind of 1 orange
¼ cup orange juice or orange-flavored liqueur

Oil an 8–10-cup stainless steel mixing bowl and line it with a 1-inch-thick layer of chocolate or coffee ice cream. Freeze overnight until ice cream is solid.

Prepare frozen orange soufflé as follows: In saucepan combine all remaining ingredients. Beat with wire whisk over moderate heat until foam bubbles appear on surface. Test with finger to see when custard is cooked. When custard is too hot for finger, watch for tiny wisps of steam. At this point, place pan over ice water and beat vigorously. Cool completely. Pour into ice cream-lined bowl. Freeze overnight or longer.

Next day, fill any remaining room left in mixing bowl with more ice cream (chocolate, almond, or vanilla). Cover with foil.

A few hours before serving, unmold on a chilled plate. Decorate with whipped cream rosettes or chocolate curls. Serve with warmed Grand Marnier Sauce:

YIELD: 8–10 SERVINGS

GRAND MARNIER SAUCE:
½ cup butter
½ cup Grand Marnier
½ cup orange juice
1 cup sugar
2 eggs, well beaten

Combine all ingredients and heat to a rolling boil.

THE JUNIOR LEAGUE OF EDMONTON, ALBERTA

·　·　·　·　·　·　·　·　·　·　·　·　·　·　·

Fresh Lemon Ice Cream

1 cup heavy cream
1 egg
1½ cups sugar
2 teaspoons lemon peel
⅓ cup fresh lemon juice
Pinch salt
1⅓ cups milk

Recipe continues . . .

Combine cream and egg. Beat until blended. Add sugar gradually and beat until mixture is almost stiff. Beat in lemon juice, peel, and salt. Stir in milk.

Empty in an 8-inch square dish and freeze for 5 hours. Stir occasionally during the first hour.

Especially good with frozen raspberries—just barely thawed—on top.

YIELD: 8 SERVINGS

THE JUNIOR LEAGUE OF SEATTLE, WASHINGTON

Fresh Peach Ice Cream

8 large ripe peaches
4 lemons
4 cups sugar
1 quart half and half or heavy cream if desired

Peel peaches and purée in electric blender. Pour into large bowl. Squeeze juice from lemons and add to peaches. Add sugar and stir until sugar is dissolved. Refrigerate until ready to make ice cream.

Pour peach mixture into electric freezer, add half and half; let freezer run 2 minutes before adding ice. Then add layers of ice and layers of salt. Let freezer run until motor labors. Drain off all water and pack with ice and salt until ready to serve.

YIELD: 1 GALLON

From an Adobe Oven . . . to a Microwave Range
THE JUNIOR LEAGUE OF PUEBLO, COLORADO

Easy Pineapple Sherbet

1 very ripe fresh pineapple
2 tablespoons brown sugar
2 tablespoons rum or Kirsch
¼ cup heavy cream (optional)

Peel, core, and cut pineapple into chunks. Purée in blender until very smooth. Stir in sugar and rum to taste; stir in cream if desired. Pour into a metal dish and freeze for several hours.

Sherbet should be soft and smooth when served. If it becomes too hard, purée again in blender.

YIELD: 8 SERVINGS

THE JUNIOR LEAGUE OF GREAT FALLS, MONTANA

Bananas Iceberg

Peel ripe bananas and wrap in plastic wrap, twisting ends tightly. Store in freezer 4–5 hours.

When ready to serve cut bananas on diagonal. Sprinkle liberally with a mixture of sugar and cinnamon. Serve immediately with heavy cream.

As soon as the cream is poured on the bananas it freezes almost instantly. Not only does this intrigue children, but adults as well.

Something New Under the Sun
THE JUNIOR LEAGUE OF PHOENIX, ARIZONA

Ice Cream Sherbet

Juice and pulp of 1 lemon
Juice and pulp of 1 orange
1 cup white sugar
1 cup heavy cream
1 cup milk

Mix lemon juice, orange juice, and sugar; let stand 1 hour. Then add cream and milk. Place in 1½-quart loaf pan in freezer. Stir occasionally. Serve when completely frozen.

YIELD: 6 SERVINGS

THE JUNIOR LEAGUE OF BAKERSFIELD, CALIFORNIA

Order Information

Many of the recipes for *The Western Junior League Cookbook* have been selected from the cookbooks published by the individual Junior Leagues. To obtain a particular League's own book of recipes, send a check or money order plus a complete return address to the appropriate address listed below. (Price of all cookbooks subject to change.)

Gourmet Olé
The Junior League of Albuquerque, Inc.
P.O. Box 8858
Albuquerque, New Mexico 87108
Order information available after October, 1980.

The Butte Junior League Cookbook
The Junior League of Butte, Inc.
P.O. Box 3294
Butte, Montana 59701
Price per copy: $3.00
Postage per copy: 50¢
Make checks payable to: The Junior League of Butte, Montana

Colorado Cache
The Junior League of Denver, Inc.
1805 S. Bellaire, #400
Denver, Colorado 80222
Price per copy: $9.95
Postage per copy: $1.25
Make checks payable to: Junior League of Denver, Inc.

A Taste of Oregon
The Junior League of Eugene, Oregon, Inc.
2839 Williamette Street
Eugene, Oregon 97405
A Taste of Oregon is scheduled for publication in the fall of 1980.
Further inquiries may be directed to the above address.

Que Sabroso!
The Junior League of Mexico City, Inc.
Apartado Postal 10–840
Mexico 10, D.F.
Que Sabroso! is in the pre-publication planning stage.
Further inquiries may be directed to the above address.

Epicure
The Junior League of Newport Harbor
Park Newport Apartments
1 Park Newport
Newport Beach, California 92660
Price per copy: $5.50
Postage per copy: 75¢
California residents add 33¢ sales tax per copy.
Make checks payable to: *Epicure*

What's Cooking, published by The Junior League of Ogden, Utah,
is out of print and not available for sale.

Private Collection:
Recipes from The Junior League of Palo Alto
The Junior League of Palo Alto, Inc.
555 Ravenswood Avenue
Menlo Park, California 94025
Purchasing information available after March, 1980

The California Heritage Cookbook
Published by Doubleday & Company, Inc.
Available at book/gift/gourmet shops or from:
The Junior League of Pasadena, Inc.
Huntington-Sheraton Hotel
Pasadena, California 91109
Price per copy: $10.95
Postage per copy: $1.35
California residents add 66¢ sales tax per copy
Make checks payable to: Junior League of Pasadena, Inc.

Pasadena Prefers II
The Junior League of Pasadena, Inc.
Huntington-Sheraton Hotel
Pasadena, California 91109
Price per copy: $5.50
Postage per copy: $1.00
California residents add 33¢ sales tax per copy
Make checks payable to: Junior League of Pasadena, Inc.

Something New Under the Sun
The Junior League of Phoenix, Inc.
1515 East Osborn Road
Phoenix, Arizona 85014
Price per copy: $6.00
Postage per copy: 75¢
Make checks payable to: Junior League of Phoenix, Inc. Cookbook

No Regrets
The Junior League of Portland, Inc.
222 S.W. Harrison
Garden Suite 9
Portland, Oregon 97201
Price per copy (postpaid): $7.50
Make checks payable to: Junior League of Portland, Oregon

From an Adobe Oven . . . to a Microwave Range
The Junior League of Pueblo, Inc.
P.O. Box 3326
Pueblo, Colorado 81005
Price per copy: $5.50
Postage per copy: 75¢
Colorado residents add 33¢ sales tax per copy
Make checks payable to: Junior League of Pueblo

Heritage Cookbook
The Junior League of Salt Lake City, Inc.
P.O. Box 6163

Salt Lake City, Utah 84106
Price per copy: $6.50
Postage per copy: 75¢
Make checks payable to: Heritage Cookbook,
The Junior League of Salt Lake City, Inc.

San Francisco à la Carte
Published by Doubleday & Company, Inc.
Available at bookstores or from:
Cookbook
The Junior League of San Francisco, Inc.
2226 Fillmore Street
San Francisco, California 94115
Price per copy: $14.95
Postage per copy: $1.10
California residents add 97¢ sales tax per copy
Make checks payable to: The Junior League of San Francisco, Inc.

Index

FARM FRESH FRUIT